As America Has Done to Israel

John P. McTernan

PRESS

Dedication

*T*his book is dedicated to the memory of my Grand-father, John Kane Sr. I learned the love of knowledge, reading and studying from him. He passed away long ago, but not too many days go by without my thinking about him, and all the memories are wonderful.

Additional Books
By John McTernan

God's Final Warning to America
Israel: The Blessing or the Curse
Father Forgive Them
Only Jesus of Nazareth Can Be Israel's King Messiah
Only Jesus of Nazareth Can Sit on the Throne of David
Only Jesus of Nazareth Can Be God's Righteous Servant.

John McTernan may be reached by email at:
McT911@aol.com

or visit his website at:
www.defendproclaimthefaith.org

write:
John McTernan
PO Box 444
Liverpool, PA 17045

Table of Contents

Foreword

*O*tarting in 1987, I first noticed the direct correlation between massive natural disasters striking America and national events. These events included Gay Pride Day, Supreme Court decisions protecting abortion and such related events. Starting in 1991, and the Madrid Peace Process, I noticed the correlation between massive disasters and with the United States pressuring Israel to surrender land for peace. The disasters were always occurring within 24 hours of the event.

In 1997, I printed my first book, *God's Final Warning to America*, which documents these correlations of disasters and same day events. The national events and the massive destructive disasters, such as earthquakes, hurricanes, floods and tornado outbreaks began to number in the dozens and dozens. By 2001, the correlation of events was so compelling that I decided to publish the second book focusing just on Israel. This book is the third in my series that deals with Bible prophecy and current events.

In November 2001, I published, *Israel: The Blessing or the Curse*, which exclusively dealt with the United States pressuring Israel to give away sections of its land for peace. The title of that book came from Genesis 12:3:

"And I will bless them that bless thee, and curse him that curseth thee: and in thee shall all families of the earth be blessed."

Genesis 12:3 states that there is a blessing or a curse associated with Abraham and also his descendants, the Jews. The people who bless Abraham will be blessed, while those who curse Abraham will suffer curses. The Bible details that forcing the Jews to divide the covenant land brings a curse. God will judge nations which interfere with the integrity of Israel's borders.

I felt *Israel: The Blessing or the Curse* did an excellent job in detailing how curses or disaster after disaster hit America, as the nation pressured Israel to divide the land; however, there was a blessing also associated with Genesis 12:3. My book did not cover the blessings but only the negative, the curses. Many people questioned me about the blessing part of the verse. I had no examples.

The fact that I had no positive examples of blessings disturbed me. If the negative was true, there should be the blessings for all to see. I pondered this for many years, and finally, I found the answer in the history of the United States. As I correlated the history of the United States with how the country treated and blessed the Jews, an astounding parallel developed. God blessed the United States of America at the very time the nation was blessing the Jews! *As America Has Done to Israel* shows this correlation. I go back to 1654, when the Jews first came to America, and work my way forward to today, the blessings are evident.

From its very founding, America always blessed the children of Abraham. Unlike as it was in Europe, the Jews never suffered organized persecution in America. For most of American history, the Jews were treated as equal citizens; however, the period from 1920 to 1940 proved an exception.

This period was the darkest time in American history for the Jewish people.

This book is also an update to *Israel: The Blessing or the Curse*. In *As America Has Done to Israel*, I fully document the curses or awesome disasters which hit America on the day the nation pressured Israel to divide the land. This book opens in September 1938 and The Great New England Hurricane. It shows how God dealt with America when the nation wronged Jewish people.

I arrived at a balance in this book by showing the blessings and the curses. The facts are not disputable; however my interpretations of these facts are. I interpret all the facts through the Bible.

I chose the name for the book from a Bible verse. The prophet Obadiah wrote of the time we are now living in. He refers to the time of Israel's restoration to the land as the approaching Day of the Lord. The Day of the Lord begins at the Second Coming of Jesus Christ. The prophet states that during this time period God deals with any nation in direct relation to how that nation interacts with Israel. If a nation blesses Israel, God blesses that nation. If a nation curses Israel, He curses that nation. It is that simple.

"For the day of the LORD is near upon all the heathen: **as thou hast done (to Israel)**, it shall be done unto thee: thy reward shall return upon thine own head." Obadiah 1:15.

As America Has Done to Israel also touches on Bible prophecy. The key to prophecy is understanding God's plan for Israel. Israel becomes God's anvil among the nations. Israel's ancient prophets clearly laid out the future. I believe we are now on the verge of what the prophets call the Day of the LORD, when the holy God of Israel judges the nations for rejecting the gospel of His Son. It is also the time when

God once again turns to His people Israel and all Israel will be spiritually saved at the Second Coming of Jesus Christ.

My hope in writing this book is that the reader understands God's prophetic plan and how Israel fits into this plan. I hope the book generates faith in God's word, the Bible, and boldness to stand with Israel. My greatest desire is that the reader will understand that the events involving Israel and Middle East are rushing toward a conclusion. This conclusion will be the greatest event of all time, the Second Coming of Jesus Christ. My prayer is every reader will be ready for this event.

Introduction

hrough the years, I have spoken with many people about God and the Bible. On a number of occasions, the question was posed, What proof is there of God? A similar question asked is, How do you know the Bible is the word of God? There are many ways to answer this question, but I have taken the approach that the authority of the Bible being God's word, can be proven through the history of the Jewish people and the rebirth of the nation of Israel. The rebirth of Israel is the key.

Understanding why God called the nation of Israel, its history, and prophecy related to Israel, all show the awesome authority of the Bible as the word of God. If Israel is understood spiritually and not just politically, an entirely new and exciting reality of the time we live in unravels.

We are now living in the time that the ancient Jewish prophets wrote about, the nation of Israel has been reborn and Jerusalem is once again its capital. The reality of God and the Bible then can be "proved" through the fulfillment of what the Bible states about the nation of Israel. What an awesome concept this is, Bible prophecy is alive before our very eyes!

The rebirth of the nation of Israel is unique among all the nations in history. The entire nation was destroyed, not once, but twice. Amazingly, after each devastation it came back into existence. Not only was the nation destroyed twice, but each time the vast majority of the people were taken captive into foreign countries. Yet, the Jewish people always returned to the land. All this points to the uniqueness of Israel. This nation is not like other nations.

In 586 BC, the great Babylonian king, Nebuchadnezzar totally destroyed the nation, Jerusalem and the temple. This destruction resulted in nearly all the Jews being taken captive to Babylon. When a people were taken captive as the Jews were, they usually were lost to history. The Jewish people were different. They remained in Babylon for 70 years and then returned to rebuild Jerusalem and their temple. This occurred 2540 years ago.

The Romans, some 650 years later in 70 AD, again destroyed the nation, Jerusalem and the temple. In 136 AD, the Jews again revolted against Rome. They were totally defeated and suffered the final dispersion into all the world. Very few Jews remained on the land after this war with Rome. The devastation was awesome. This occurred almost 1900 years ago.

Israel should have ended as a nation and probably as a people in 586 BC, but it survived. Israel, definitely should have ceased to be a nation in 70 AD, but as the ancient Bible prophets wrote, the nation was literally reborn.

After ceasing to be a nation for 1878 years, on May 14, 1948, Israel once again became a nation. In June 1967, Jerusalem once again became the unified capital of Israel. The Hebrew language was almost extinct, yet it was revived and today the Israelis speak Hebrew. They speak the same language as their ancestors. They kept the same religion while in exile. There is simply no other nation like Israel.

Several years ago, I took a tour of the biblical sites in Israel. The tour stopped at the museum of the Dead Sea Scrolls. In the center of the building was a large circular glass cabinet. This cabinet was huge in its circumference, and the complete Isaiah scroll was on display. The scroll was set in the cabinet and lit so it could be read.

I asked the Israeli tour guide if he could read the scroll. He went to the scroll and started to read a 2,000 year old document written in ancient Hebrew. He said it was somewhat hard to read because the letters were shaped slightly different to Modern Hebrew. As he started to read the scroll, I realized it was Isaiah chapter 59. I had him read back in the scroll until he found Isaiah 53 (The Bible was not divided into chapters until the 1500s). This chapter is one of my favorites in the Bible. To my amazement, he read this chapter to me.

A man whose nation was destroyed 1900 years ago read to me a language which was nearly extinct! The English language did not exist 2,000 years ago. It is very difficult to read English from only 200 years ago, never mind 2000 years.

What other nation is like Israel? What is the explanation for the preservation of the Jews and the rebirth of Israel? The explanation is found in the everlasting covenant God made with Abraham 4,000 years ago. The covenant is the reason the Jewish people and the nation of Israel exist today.

Preface

*W*hen I was a youngster growing up on Long Island, NY in the 1950's and 60's, I was raised for the most part by my grandparents, John and Elizabeth Kane. My grandfather was a very big man. He was born in Ireland and came to the United States around 1912. Early in his life, he worked in various mines and developed a powerful build. I can still see his huge hands.

Grandpa had no formal education, but he was highly intelligent. He seemed to know everything about everything. As a youngster, I can remember him building the house with his friends. He built our house with his own hands, block by block! Grandpa was always reading in his spare time. He would read magazines, newspapers, journals and books. He read all the time.

The Irish have a reputation for story telling and my grandfather was no exception. My earliest memories are sitting near him, as he told me about Ireland and his early life in the United States about 100 years ago. I heard about World War I, the roaring 20's, the Great Depression, the rise of Hitler, and about World War II. I vividly remember him telling me of participating in forming unions in the mines of Colorado and the horrors that followed. Many miners died in a conflict that erupted over the unionizing of the mines.

We always seemed to have company. Our door was always open and my grandparent's friends, neighbors and relatives would just drop in to visit. We watched very little TV in those days and soon after the company arrived the story telling started. When the men talked, I just sat and listened. No one ever said I could not ask questions, but it just seemed out of place to ask. I would just sit and listen.

Grandpa with "Johnny Mac" as he called me

They talked about everything and anything. I was getting an education in history, politics, and life, and did not realize it.

It seemed as if the story telling went on for hours late into the night. I sat, almost invisible in the room, just listening and learning. I can still remember my grandfather sitting in his favorite chair talking and telling stories.

Most of the talk was about world and national events. When the talks would get around to local events the two hot topics were, The Great Hurricane of 1938 which devastated Long Island, and the German – American Alliance. The name for this Alliance was the Bund. The Bund (Pronounced Bundt) was the Hitler Nazi organization in the United States. Its headquarters were in New York City and afterwards at Camp Siegfried on Long Island, New York. Camp Siegfried was about 10 miles from where I grew up.

I would hear frightening stories about the hurricane. Everyone had harrowing experiences, and the stories were vivid with such great detail. When I first heard about the hurricane, I was not old enough to fully reason. I can remember being afraid at the beach because a hurricane might come. When at the beach, I was ever watchful of the ocean and ready to flee, should another great hurricane appear. I never told anyone my fears. I just carefully watched the horizon while at the beach.

I heard frightening stories about the Bund. The stories were in great detail about the Nazi activities on Long Island. There were the candle light marches at night.

Nazi youth at Camp Siegfried 1937

The Bundists dressed their children in Nazi uniforms and walked around the towns, "sieg heiling," each other. There were huge gatherings at Camp Siegfried where tens of thousands would congregate.

This was all very confusing to me because I heard the stories of how terrible the Nazis were, and how the United States fought them in World War II. The Bund had been centered near where I lived. I can remember going to the towns where I heard stories about the Bund and being afraid. I thought the Bund was still active in those towns. I would look for the kids dressed like Nazis!

In all my years of college and study, I never heard of the Bund activities other than in my grandfather's house. After World War II, the Nazi activity in the United States was swept under the rug, and it seems never mentioned again. I grew up in the 1950s only 10 miles from the Nazi headquarters and never was one word of it mentioned by others. I only heard about it through Grandpa Kane.

As America Has Done to Israel is the sequel to my book, *Israel: The Blessing or the Curse*. When I first wrote, *Israel; The Blessing or the Curse*, I made no connection between the Bund and the Great Hurricane of 1938. As you read this book, you will see a truly amazing connection.

I had not thought of the Bund for over 45 years, but one day in 2004 I was thinking of all the hurricane disasters recorded in my book *Israel: The Blessing or the Curse*. My mind drifted back to those memories about The Great Hurricane of 1938 and in a flash God quickened my mind to connect it with the Bund. All those stories I heard at Grandpa Kane's came to life 45 years later and now are a part of this book.

Writing this book brought back long forgotten but wonderful memories of my grandparents. One of these memories is worth sharing. My grandparents were good people. I grew up without any prejudice. They seemed to love all people.

My grandmother, Elizabeth Kane, loved Jewish people, and I think she passed this love on to me. My grandfather did not have much to say about Jewish people, but I can remember my grandmother saying, "They're good people, they're good people."

I learned to respect the Jewish people from my grandparents. Before moving to Long Island, New York, we lived in an Irish-Jewish ghetto in the Bronx, New York City. I heard lots of stories about my grandparent's life in the ghetto and with the Jewish people. Actually, I was born in the ghetto, but we moved out when I was very young.

My grandmother told me she was good friends with a Jewish woman who was a seamstress. She made clothes for our family. One day there was a banging on the door and when my grandmother opened it: the woman was lying, hysterical on the floor. My grandfather came and carried her into the apartment. The woman was sobbing that "Hitler got them all." Over and over she was saying, "Hitler got them all!"

She was from Poland and had just learned that the Nazis eliminated her entire family back home. Grandpa stayed with her until her husband came home. He then carried her home. Grandma said the woman lived only a month or so, and died of a broken heart.

I hope this book is a blessing to all who read it. The facts reported in this book are irrefutable, but my interpretations of these facts are open to question. I interpreted these facts based on the Bible. God said of Abraham and the Jewish people in Genesis 12:3 *And I will bless them that bless thee, and curse him that curseth thee: and in thee shall all families of the earth be blessed.* This book proves the promise is to be taken literally.

You will see from this book that Genesis 12:3 has been applied to the United States. The Bible is to be taken literally. The Jewish people and the nation of Israel are living proof to the authority of the Bible that it is God's word.

I always wanted to be like Grandpa Kane. He had such great knowledge and loved to share with those who would listen. He was always reading and reading. I do certainly read a lot and love to talk, so maybe a part of grandpa rubbed off on me. Grandma often said, "You are just like your grandfather." I sure hope she was right.

John McTernan
Millerstown, PA
May 2006

PART ONE

Israel's Past And Present

CHAPTER ONE

September 1938:
Hitler and the Hurricane

"For the day of the LORD is near upon all the heathen: as thou hast done (To the Jews), it shall be done unto thee: thy reward shall return upon thine own head."
Obadiah 1:15.

*S*eptember 1938 was a critical month in world history. The eyes of the entire world, including the United States, were riveted on Europe. Hitler and Nazis were on the move and there was talk of imminent war. For the entire month, the headlines in the nation's newspapers followed the events in Europe. As one reads these newspapers, the feeling of desperation still screams from the headlines. The tension, even 70 years later, is easily felt.

The source of all this tension was Nazi Germany and the Republic of Czechoslovakia. A section of Czechoslovakia called the Sudetenland was mostly ethnic German, and Hitler wanted to annex it as part of Germany. Hitler made the false claim that the Czechs were mistreating the ethnic Germans, and they needed the protection of Germany.

The Nazi propaganda machine began to threaten imminent war unless the Czechs surrendered the Sudetenland to Germany. President Edvard Beneš of Czechoslovakia appealed to Great Britain and France for help, and thus the prospect of war loomed greater and greater each day.

Hitler came to power in January 1933. By September 1938, the Nazi war machine was in high gear. The Nazi army was gaining power and Hitler was now ready to test the will of Great Britain, France and the rest of the world.

Hitler had consolidated his power in Germany and was looking beyond its borders. In early March 1938, he forced Austrian Chancellor, Kurt Schuschnigg to resign. Dr. Arthur Seyss-Inquart, a Nazi puppet, replaced Schuschnigg. On March 12, 1938, the Nazi army crossed into Austria. Hitler achieved his *Anschluss* - the union of Austria and Germany.

No nation objected to what Hitler did to Austria. Now, six months later, he wanted the Sudetenland and tested the will of Europe by threatening war. Little did the nations realize that this would be their last opportunity to stop Hitler before total war broke out.

Czechoslovakia was willing to resist the Nazis but could not do it alone. The nation had a large, well trained 1.5 million man army and with help, could have defeated Hitler. Czechoslovakia's appeal fell on deaf ears and not one Western nation, including the United States, came to its aid, not one. Anyone who stood with Czechoslovakia against Hitler was branded a war monger. Whoever went along with the division of Czechoslovakia and appeasing Hitler was looked upon as favoring peace.

With the hindsight of history, it is chilling to read the newspapers of September 1938. Day after day, the papers were full of headlines about the Nazis, Czechoslovakia and war. One could feel the tension as it mounted to a climax on September 29 at the Munich Conference. At this conference, Britain and France betrayed Czechoslovakia and appeased Hitler by agreeing to all his demands. The Munich Conference resulted in the dismantling of Czechoslovakia.

The following are just a few examples of the September 1938 front-page headlines that gripped the United States:

September 15, New York Times:
> Chamberlain Off By Plane To See Hitler;
> Will Make Personal Plea T o Avert War;
> Prague Firm As Sudetens Battle The Police

September 19, New York Times:
> Britain and France Accept Hitler Demands on Czechs;
> Will Ask Benes Today To Surrender German Areas;
> Prague Incredulous, Regards Action as Betrayal
> Roosevelt Urged to Act in Europe

September 21, New York Times:
> Britain, France Give Prague Hours to Submit
> On The Peril of Immediate German Attack
> Czechs are Declared Determined to Resist

September 24, The Providence RI, Evening Bulletin:
> European Armies Mobilizing
> Hitler Reported Ordering Czechs to Yield in One Week

September 26, New York Times:
> Roosevelt Appeals To Hitler and Benes to Negotiate;
> British and French Premiers Also Plea to Reich;
> Terms Unacceptable; Hitler Talk to Attack Czechs

September 28, New York Herald Tribune:
Roosevelt Appeals Anew to Hitler Against War,
Proposes Conference of All Involved in Europe;
British Mobilize Navy, Chamberlain's Hope Faint

September 30, New York Times:
Four Powers Reach a Peaceable Agreement;
Germans to Enter Sudeten Area Tomorrow
and Will Complete Occupation in Ten Days
Nazi Demands Met

Great Britain, France, Italy and Germany attended the Munich Conference. Czechoslovakia, the subject of this conference, was not represented! The country being divided, by appeasing Hitler, had no say in the matter! Prime Minister Neville Chamberlain represented Great Britain at the Munich Conference.

Without the support of Great Britain and France, the Czechs had no alternative but to agree to Hitler's demands. At the conclusion of the Munich Conference, Jan Syrovy, the Czech Premier, stated, "We have been abandoned." By March 15, 1939, whatever remained of Czechoslovakia fell under Hitler's control. In six short months, Hitler gained the rest of the country. It was clear to Hitler; the European nations had no will to stop him. Hitler's road to European and world conquest was now wide open.

Chamberlain boasted after the Munich Conference that he achieved "Peace in our time," and "Peace with honor." There was even a newsreel of Chamberlain departing a plane having returned from the Conference. In the newsreel, he is waving the treaty with Hitler and saying "Peace in our time." Huge excited crowds met Chamberlain when he returned to Great Britain.

Hulton-Deutsch Collection/Corbis

**Neville Chamberlain with Munich
Agreement in hand saying "Peace in our time."**

These crowds lined the route Chamberlain traveled from the airport to London. He made a speech about "Peace with honor." He told the crowd, "A British Prime Minister has returned from Germany bringing peace with honor." The crowd wildly cheered him all the way back to London.

Looking back to the Munich Conference, it is almost comical from today's standpoint of history. It would be comical except millions soon died. A side issue of the Conference was the "Anti-War Pact" between Hitler and Chamberlain. The Pact called for Germany to demobilize when Hitler was convinced the Czechoslovakian government was carrying out the agreements of the Munich Conference. Chamberlain made a statement about the agreement with Hitler that is truly tragic:

"We regard the agreement signed last night and the Anglo-German naval agreement as symbolic of the desire of our two peoples never to go to war with another again."

The world looked to the United States and President Roosevelt for leadership in this crisis to avert possible war. On September 19, the New York Times in a front page article titled, *Roosevelt Urged to Act in Europe*, reported the desperation of nations to prevent war. This article quoted an editorial from the Canadian newspaper, Toronto Globe, and several French newspapers. The Globe editorial viewed the Czechoslovakian crisis as, "Europe still waits in the shadow of Armageddon." It went on to state that only President Roosevelt had the leadership to end this crisis. A quote from this editorial follows:

"... what is needed is not a plan but fresh leadership ... There is but one man whom the world, if it could speak, would elect for the task. A man universally known for his humanitarianism ... President Franklin D. Roosevelt."

The New York Times article went on to quote former French Premier Leon Blum. Blum wrote in the French newspaper Populaire, and openly requested that President Roosevelt intervene in this crisis. The French wanted Roosevelt to intervene and save France, just as President Woodrow Wilson did during World War I. A quote from the former French Premier follows:

"Is it not time that he address himself to Europe with the prestige of his person and with all the authority of the State whose moral or material support would be finally decisive in any general war?"

Roosevelt did personally intervene and requested the convening of a conference addressing the Czechoslovakian problem. President Roosevelt made two direct appeals to Adolph Hitler. The first was on September 26, and then on September 28 the President made his second personal appeal to Hitler. These requests called for negotiations and a peaceful solution to the crisis. Hitler and the other European leaders responded to the second appeal, and the Munich Conference was set for the following day. A part of the President's appeal to Hitler follows:

"Should you agree to a solution in this peaceful manner I am convinced that hundreds of millions throughout the world would recognize your actions as an outstanding historic service to all humanity."

President Franklin Roosevelt was a party to this appeasement of Hitler as he failed to challenge Hitler and stand with Czechoslovakia. He failed to confront Hitler and instead, twice called for negotiations to end the crisis. Of course, these negotiations meant the dismantling of Czechoslovakia.

The Munich Conference was the idea of President Roosevelt. This conference to appease Hitler originated with him. Afterwards, Roosevelt failed to comment on the results of the Munich Conference. Secretary of State Cordell Hull said there was a "Universal sense of relief" over the peace settlement.

By September 1938, Hitler's attacks on the Jewish people were well known. The very core of the Nazi ideology was the destruction of European Jewry. The Nazis were not secretly carrying out this hatred of the Jews. President Roosevelt was well aware of what the Nazis were doing to the Jews. Surrendering the Sudetenland to Hitler would put thousands of more Jews in grave danger. But, no one seemed to care what the Nazis were doing to Jews. It was as if the

Jews did not exist, and what the Nazis were doing to them did not matter.

The Nazis even tried blaming the Jews for the trouble over the Sudetenland. The Nazis created the tension and then tried to blame the Jews. Hermann Goering the number two Nazi used this tactic in a vicious speech given on September 10, 1938. Goering's speech in part follows:

> "This miserable pygmy race without culture, no one knows where it came from, is oppressing a cultured people [Sudeten Germans] and behind it is Moscow and the eternal mask of the Jew devil..."

The American President, by appeasing Hitler, was in an indirect way condoning Hitler's conduct against the Jews. Roosevelt's failure to confront Hitler about the brutality of his regime, and the appeasement over the Sudetenland, encouraged Hitler to continue his course of destruction.

The nations cared little about the Jews and none came to their aid. They allowed Hitler to attack the Jews with virtually no opposition. On November 8, 1938, just 38 days after the Munich Conference, the Nazis unleashed what became known as Krystal Nacht. Krystal Nacht was the night when the rhetoric against the Jews turned into organized violence and destruction of Jewish businesses throughout Germany. The Munich Conference turned out to be a boost for Hitler's Jew hating agenda. When World War II started, he then attempted to destroy all European Jewry.

The negotiations at the Munich Conference started the dismantling of the Republic of Czechoslovakia. The nations allowed Germany to annex the Sudetenland. Poland obtained the Teschen district while Hungary received the remaining parts of Slovakia. It is truly ironic that Poland was greedy and aided in the dismantling of Czechoslovakia. In a very short time, Hitler dismantled Poland, not by a conference, but with war. Poland greatly suffered for not standing against Hitler.

Thus, to appease Hitler, Great Britain and France dismantled a sovereign nation and divided it into three sections. Now, with the Sudetenland, Hitler solidified greater Germany and gained a powerful industrial base. He was ready to turn east toward Poland and ignite World War II.

The fuse was set on September 29, 1938, for World War II. The Nazi army was becoming more and more powerful day by day. Hitler was fine honing the German war machine. There would be no stopping Hitler. This war resulted in the death of 30-40 million people, including over six million Jews.

The count down from the Munich Conference to the start of World War II was just a mere 335 days. Hitler attacked Poland on September 1, 1939, igniting World War II. There is no doubt that September 1938 was critical in world history.

September 1938: The Long Island Express

"If New York and the rest of the world have been so well informed about the cyclone it is because of an admirably organized meteorological service." New York Times Editorial, Titled, Hurricanes, September 21, 1938.

From reading the September 1938 headlines, it is easy to understand why the United States public focused on Europe. The entire nation was caught up in the specter of another world war. People were glued to the radio trying to get news about a possible war in Europe.

As terrible as Hitler was, an immediate, even greater, danger was heading directly toward the United States. A powerful category 5 hurricane, or as it was called then, a Cape Verde Cyclone, was heading directly toward Florida. Hurricanes were called Cape Verde Cyclones because the storm first developed near the Cape Verde Islands off the West Coast of Africa. These storms then moved on a westward course toward the United States.

In early September, a tropical depression formed off the coast of Africa near Cape Verde. By September 10, it was a tropical depression gaining power by the hour. It was heading west at about 10 miles an hour. On September 18, it was near Puerto Rico and had grown to a monster category 5 storm.

In 1938, the weather bureau did not name hurricanes. If a storm hit land, or fell on a holiday, it was named for the location or date the eye made landfall. An example was The Galveston Hurricane of 1900. It was not until 1951 before the Weather Bureau named hurricanes. This hurricane was named The Great New England Hurricane of 1938 or The Great Hurricane of 1938. Its effect on the Northeast coast is still visible to this day.

Category 5 hurricanes are among the most powerful and destructive forces in nature. This type of hurricane sustains winds of 155 mph or greater with an enormous wave surge as it comes ashore. Very few category 5 hurricanes have struck the United States mainland. Since 1851, only three category 5 have hit the United States' mainland. These three being Andrew in 1992, Camille in 1969, and the Florida Keys Hurricane of 1935.

By 1938 the United States Weather Bureau had developed a hurricane monitoring system. There were hurricane monitoring stations throughout the Caribbean, and ships at sea radioed information about these storms. In 1870, the United States created a national weather monitoring agency called the United States Weather Bureau. During September 1938, the Weather Bureau was closely monitoring all information about this extremely powerful hurricane.

By September 19, the storm was a monster 400 miles in diameter and still heading directly toward Florida. The entire state panicked as the storm grew closer. The storm began weakening to a category 3, then curved away from Florida, and headed north. After the storm turned, the media and the nation had little interest, and focused back on Europe and Hitler. A category 3 is still a very lethal storm. These storms pack winds between 111 and 130 mph, and can do enormous damage.

This curving movement was typical of most Cape Verde Hurricanes. As they approached the United States, the prevailing winds began to curve the hurricane northward. The hurricane then began a looping move, first to the north and then eastward and eventually out into the Atlantic Ocean. A hurricane depends on warm water, at least 80 degrees, to maintain its power. Once over the colder ocean waters, these storms soon lose power and die.

On September 21, as the hurricane turned northward, Charles Pierce, a junior meteorologist with the Weather Bureau in Washington, DC tracked the storm. He carefully reviewed the weather charts, and he immediately recognized the danger this storm posed for Long Island, NY and southern New England.

There were two powerful high-pressure systems which had the hurricane trapped between them. The hurricane could not curve eastward and out to sea because the Bermuda high pressure over the Atlantic Ocean was far to the north. This blocked the hurricane from making the eastward curve and turning harmlessly out into the Atlantic Ocean

The hurricane could not turn west because there was a powerful high pressure system over Ohio. There was a strong low system over New England which would draw the hurricane to it like a magnet. The high pressure systems forced this powerful hurricane on a direct northerly course. Long Island and southern New England were the targets.

Pierce explained all this to his superiors, but they refused to believe his assessment. The last major hurricane to hit New England was 1815 and before that 1635. Category 3 hurricanes hitting New England were extremely rare. Pierce was overruled by his superiors, who believed the hurricane would turn out to sea. In desperation, Pierce held a second meeting and again he was overruled.

On September 21, at 7 AM, The Great Hurricane was off Cape Hatteras, NC. Hurricanes normally weaken north of this location because of the colder water. But this hurricane, accelerating in forward speed, followed the Gulf Stream and thus failed to weaken. The two high pressure systems squeezed the hurricane, and they caused it to tighten and accelerate in speed. Both the tightening and accelerating greatly magnified the power of this storm.

Most hurricanes travel at less than 20 miles per hour. The winds within the hurricane can be swirling at great speed, but the storm itself moves less than 20 mph. If you picture the way a top spins you can understand a hurricane. The top itself spins very fast while it may be moving slowly along the floor. The Great Hurricane of 1938 began to rapidly increase in forward speed and approached 70 mph! This forward speed remains a record to this day.

The Weather Bureau advised the Coast Guard that the hurricane was turning out to sea, and to expect strong winds and high seas along the coast. The Coast Guard then notified the news services, who informed the public that the storm was turning away from the coast and out to sea.

The Great Hurricane of 1938 was bearing down on Long Island at 70 mph and no one knew it was approaching. The only person in the entire nation that knew its true course was Charles Pierce, and no one believed him. The nation was watching Hitler in Europe and not the hurricane in the Atlantic Ocean. Everyone believed it had turned eastward out to sea.

The meteorological equivalent of the surprise attack on Pearl Harbor, which occurred three years later, was bearing down on the East Coast of the United States. No one, but no one, was prepared for this storm. The storm would stretch from New Jersey in the west to Boston in the east. The eye of the storm was 50 miles wide. It was a monster.

The summer of 1938 was extremely wet in New England. The weeks prior to the hurricane, Long Island and New England received record rains. There were torrential rains the week before September 21, and the ground from Long Island to Vermont was soaked. This soaked ground made trees unable to withstand hurricane force winds.

The weather was also abnormally warm. Normally, a hurricane weakens quickly upon landfall; however, the weeks of rain created a situation, that when the hurricane passed over the soaked moist land, it did not weaken, but maintained its strength from the warm moist land. Thus, when the hurricane slammed into the coast, it did not lose power. It actually drew strength from the warm moist ground. This made The Great Hurricane of 1938 incredibly powerful, miles inland. The eye remained intact well into southern Vermont.

This hurricane's force was felt not only along the coast, but far inland. Blue Hill Observatory in Massachusetts, which was miles inland, recorded sustained winds of 121 mph with gusts up to 186 mph. Boston Airport registered winds of 100 mph. This massive hurricane affected the entire New England region. The hurricane maintained its strength well into Canada and finally dissipated near Montreal.

The storm approached at the very worst time. September 21, was the autumnal equinox which created the highest high tide of the year. The storm surge would ride on top of this high tide.

As the winds began to increase, no one paid attention on Long Island or the New England coast. But, by 3:00 pm, something was radically wrong. The wind and waves on the ocean were fierce. To the south of Long Island, there appeared to be a fog or mist on the ocean, but this was no fog. It was a 25 to 30 foot wall of water (called the storm surge) hurtling at 70 mph and heading straight for the Long Island coast. Because this hurricane was moving so fast, a record to this day, it was nicknamed the Long Island Express.

The hurricane hit Long Island with such force that it registered on seismographs from New York to Alaska! More than one powerful wave hit the coast and the seismographs were recording the impacts. So many waves continually hitting the coast caused New England to vibrate and ring like a bell! The coastline was dramatically altered by this collision with the powerful storm surge. Not only was Long Island's coastline altered, but also all of Southern New England's as well.

The storm killed over 700 people. It is a wonder, when reading the accounts of the storm, that the loss of life was not 10 times greater. There were 63,000 people left homeless. The storm destroyed or damaged almost 9,000 buildings and over 26,000 automobiles. The tidal surge wiped out entire marinas together with 3300 boats and ships, and it destroyed most of New England's fishing fleet. Many New England rivers were already at flood stage, and the rains of the hurricane caused record flooding.

The combination of the tremendous velocity of the winds and the soggy ground resulted in the destruction of entire forests throughout New England! Most of the trees that survived the storm died within a few weeks as the salt spray driven into the leaves killed them. The beautiful New England forests were gone. The fierce wind destroyed an estimated 750 million to two billion trees!

The Blue Hill Observatory, located in central Massachusetts, recorded the highest wind gusts of 186 mph. This observatory was 130 miles from the Long Island coast! This was the greatest natural disaster ever to hit the United States. The states of New York, New Jersey, Connecticut, Rhode Island, Massachusetts, Vermont, New Hampshire and Maine all felt the effects of this hurricane. Hundreds and hundreds of miles of the coast line were damaged. Providence, Rhode Island was under 14 feet of water. People drowned as they left work because they had no prior warning the hurricane was upon them. The storm caused a fire which consumed blocks of New London, Connecticut.

The floods cut road and rail lines while bridges washed away. The millions of falling trees took down most of the power and telephone lines. Cities and towns were isolated. The hurricane wiped out electrical power and telephone lines. It traveled so fast it was impossible to warn ahead. Each town was isolated and caught completely without warning. Town by town was devastated without warning.

This was the first time that an entire region of the nation was devastated by a disaster. The Galveston Hurricane of 1900 killed more people but was isolated to that city. The San Francisco Earthquake and Fire of 1906 destroyed more buildings but the massive destruction was limited to that city. This disaster destroyed states. To help these states recover, the Federal government rushed an army of 110,000 workers to assist in the recovery. This was a massive recovery operation the likes of which the United States had never witnessed before this hurricane.

The nation's newspapers before September 21, were fixed on Hitler and events in Europe. Now The Great Hurricane of 1938 shared the front page headlines. Some of these headlines follow:

September 22, New York Times:

Hurricane Sweeps Coast;	Czechoslovakia Decides to Give Up;
11 Dead, 71 Missing, LI Toll;	Crowds Protest, Cabinet in Peril;
80 Die in New England Flood	Chamberlain to Demand Guarantees
And	
Storm Batters All New England;	
Providence Hit by Tidal Wave	

41

September 23, New York Herald Tribune:

Hurricane Deaths Mount to 439;	Berlin Says Czechs Kill 16
Half of Them in Rhode Island;	At Border; Chamberlain
L.I. South Shore Is Devastated	Sees Hitler, Urges Calm

September 24, The Evening Bulletin, Providence, Rhode Island:

Toll of Hurricane Reaches 300	European Armies Mobilizing

September 25, The Providence Sunday Journal:

251 Dead; State Pushes Recovery	Hitler Gives Czechs 7 Days
	to Bow

Reading the newspapers and listening to the radio it was impossible to miss these two awesome events. They were linked together on the front page of every newspaper in the nation. When you read the papers, the two events were literally next to each other on the front page. Encouraged by the United States, Hitler, the Jew hater, was allowed to annex part of Czechoslovakia. All of this happened, at the exact time one of the greatest disasters every to hit the United States occurred.

At first glance, it might appear that these events were not related and that it was all just a coincidence. This was not a coincidence, but rather it was fulfilling a promise of the Bible. God told Abraham and his descendants in Genesis 12:3 that He would bless those that blessed Abraham and curse those who cursed Abraham. This awesome disaster hit at the exact time the United States turned its back on the Jews. It occurred precisely as the President of the United States encouraged Hitler to call for the Munich Conference.

The United States turned its back on the Jewish people and an awesome tragedy occurred. This started a pattern which continues until this day. There are literally dozens of examples just like The Great Hurricane of 1938 where awesome disasters strike America on the very day the United

States meddles with God's covenant land of Israel. This concept is fully developed with numerous examples later in the book.

The hurricane was 400 miles in diameter while the eye was 50 miles wide. The very epicenter of the eye of this massive hurricane was Bellport, Long Island. Bellport is located on Long Island's South Shore about 60 miles east of Manhattan. The lowest barometric pressure for the storm was recorded at Bellport with an incredibly low reading of 27.94. This low pressure shows Bellport was ground zero, where the eye of The Great Hurricane of 1938 made landfall with the greatest force.

The town immediately north of Bellport is Yaphank. This town played a key role in the connection between the disaster and the Nazis. Located in Yaphank, Long Island was Camp Siegfried, the direct link to Hitler and the Nazis. Yaphank, then became ground zero for the Nazi movement in the United States.

Camp Siegfried

Siegfried: a legendary hero in medieval German literature. He killed a dragon and bathed in its blood, which made his body invulnerable.

The 1930s were a very turbulent time in American history. The Great Depression and the tragedy of the Mid-West dust bowl received most of the attention during these years, but the social and political unrest was just as difficult. The very soul of America was being tested in every area. For most people life was hard in every way during the 1930s.

Looking over the span of American history, the 1930s were the worst time for the Jews in America. During this turbulent time, the seemingly ingrained European hatred for the children of Israel tried taking root in the United States.

A certain segment of America singled out Jews as a people, and blamed them as the cause of all the world's problems. Some Americans blamed the Jews for causing The Great Depression and creating Communism. It seems that all the world's problems were focused on them.

There was a concerted effort to exclude Jews from mainstream America and then demonize them. This is exactly what Hitler had done to the Jews in Germany and Europe. Once they were marginalized and demonized, the nation was ready to accept physical attacks against them. This then was the fertile ground for the holocaust to take place.

The holocaust in Europe was the end of a long process of marginalizing, demonizing, dehumanizing and then stripping the Jews of their rights and property. The physical attacks only came after carefully planned character attacks.

During the 1930s, the process of trying to destroy Jews was in high gear in the United States. This was foreign to America, and never in the nation's history had the Jews been singled out and marginalized. It was routinely done in Europe through the ages, but not in the United States. The Jewish people were never fully marginalized and mainstream America rejected the European type hatred of Jews. However, the Jews did suffer in America during the 1930s, although it never rose to the level of European hatred.

The actual foundation for the attack on the Jews began shortly after World War I. It seems the great industrialist Henry Ford of Ford Motor Company was the catalyst for this hatred. Ford was convinced the Jews started World War I and the Russian Revolution. He believed that Communism was a Jewish plot to destabilize nations and take over the world. This is not well known today, but Ford was at the very center of marginalizing and demonizing the Jews in the early 1920s. His legacy was not continued by his son and grandson. They reversed the anti-Semitism of Henry Ford Sr.

In 1920, Ford bought the Dearborn Independent, a small newspaper, to act as his propaganda outlet. On May 22, 1920, Ford began his attack on the Jews. The headline of the paper read, *"The International Jew: The World's Foremost Problem."* This was the greatest and most damaging public attack on the Jewish people in American history. The effect of Ford's anti-Semitism is still felt today.

Starting in May 1920, and continuing for 91 consecutive issues, the Independent attacked the Jews with the headlines: *"The International Jew: The Worlds Foremost Problem."* By 1924 the Independent had 700,000 subscribers, which made it one of the largest papers in the country. Ford was trusted by the majority of Americans, he was looked upon as a great American. This attack greatly poisoned the atmosphere in America against Jewish people. The type of anti-Semitism established in Europe now had a powerful voice in the United States.

Many public figures were alarmed at what Ford was doing and denounced both him and his newspaper. Numerous senators, congressmen, lawyers and clergy denounced Ford. So powerful were Ford's attacks, that the past, present, and future presidents of the United States all denounced this wave of anti-Semitism. These presidents were William Taft, Woodrow Wilson, and Warren Harding. Evangeline Booth, the head of the Salvation Army also denounced the attacks on the Jewish people.

Perhaps the greatest damage done by Ford was publishing a four volume book titled, *The International Jew: The World's Foremost Problem.* This book sold millions of copies and was translated into 16 languages. It was translated into German and had a great effect on Hitler and the Nazis. The book sold millions of copies in Germany. In July 1938, Ford was decorated by the Nazi German government for his service to world industrialism.

Bettmann/Corbis

Henry Ford receives the highest Nazi award given to a foreigner, the Grand Cross of the German Eagle. Karl Kapp, German consul Cleveland, presents the award, while Fritz Heller, German consul Detroit, shakes Ford's hand. July 31, 1938

By 1938/39 the assault on Jews reached its peak. There were dozens of anti-Semitic groups in America verbally attacking the Jews similar to the methods used by Hitler. One leader was Father Coughlin, a radio talk show host from Detroit, who had a huge audience of listeners. It was estimated that one-third of all radio listeners tuned into him. His weekly magazine, *Social Justice* followed the agenda of his radio show.

William Dudly Pelley headed the Silver Shirts a pro-Nazi group. Robert Edonson published the *American Vigilante Bulletin*, while James True published the *Dope Letter*. All were anti Jewish and blamed all problems on the Jews. These are just a few of the groups which had formed to identify the Jews as the cause of all the world's problems.

Of all the anti-Semitic groups in the 1930's one stands out above all the others. It was officially called the German

- American National Alliance, but was known by its German name, the Bund (pronounced Bundt.) The core of the Bund was made up of mostly German immigrants. This was the true Nazi party in the United States.

The Bund identified openly with Hitler. The Bundists marched in Nazi uniforms with swastikas. They called for a boycott of Jewish businesses. They followed Henry Ford by blaming all evil on international Judaism. They promoted an extremely anti-Semitic book titled *The Protocols of the Elders of Zion* which was produced in Russia and proven to be a fraud. They did everything possible to attack the Jews.

The Bund made very clear its beliefs. They published what was titled *The Bund Declaration of Principles* which in part follows:

1. A socially just, white, Gentile-ruled United States.
2. Gentile-controlled labor unions free from Jewish Moscow, directed domination.
3. Gentiles in all positions of importance in government, national defense, and educational institutions.
4. Immediate cessation of the dumping of all political refugees in the shores of the United States. (This meant no more Jews allowed into the country.)

The Bundists were serious Nazis focused on the Jews. The Bund went so far as to begin a petition to amend the Constitution of the United States. They wanted Jews excluded from all governmental functions. This petition in part follows:

"A petition for an amendment .to the constitution of the United States, to elect and appoint none but Arians to Public Office and Supreme, Federal, State, and Municipal Courts. The United States of America is a

White Gentile Nation. The founders of the republic
who gave us our nation, were Aryan men..."
By the end of 1938, the Bund had 65 chapters across
America with 28 camps. The chapters included New York
City, Cleveland, Detroit, Chicago, Milwaukee, St Louis,
Baltimore, Philadelphia, Pittsburgh, Oakland, San Diego
and many more cities. The membership was never known
but estimates ran as high as 250,000.

The Bund bought land near cities and established camps.
They conducted parades, speeches, events and marched just
as in the Nazi camps in Germany. The major camps were
Nordland in New Jersey, Hindenburg near Milwaukee, and
Hindenburg Park near Los Angeles. But, the largest and most
infamous was Camp Siegfried in Yaphank, New York. This
camp in the United States was similar to Nuremburg which
was the very heart of the Nazi movement in Germany.

Camp Siegfried was a 45 acre compound located about
60 miles east of New York City on Long Island. The Bundist
held their largest meetings at this camp. The Bundists rented
entire trains running from Manhattan, called the Camp
Siegfried Special, to the Yaphank station. From there, thousands marched about two miles from the station to Camp
Siegfried. They held torch light marches at night just as the
Nazis did in Germany. At Camp Siegfried, the Nazis initiated thousands of youth into the Bund.

The largest Nazi rallies outside of Germany took place
at Camp Siegfried. This camp became ground zero for the
Nazis in the United States. Of all the fascists groups in
America, the Bund was the worst, and Camp Siegfried was
the heart of the Bund.

The Bund liked Camp Siegfried so much, they decided
to build a little Nazi village. In January 1937, the local township approved a tract of land for development. It was named
German Gardens. The township approved names for the
streets which included: Hindenburg Street, German Street,

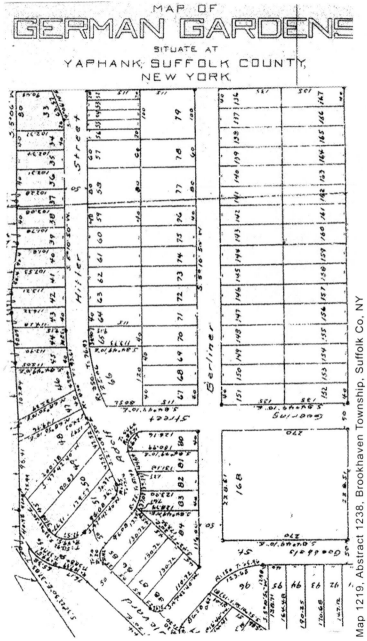

Map showing Adolph Hitler Street, Camp Siegfried

Map 1219, Abstract 1238, Brookhaven Township, Suffolk Co, NY

49

Goering and Goebbels Streets and worst of all Adolph Hitler Street. To this day, Adolph Hitler is still the official name for this street! Now, it is named Park Boulevard, but the deed map and town tax records for the homes still reflect Adolph Hitler Street! Amazingly, there is a street named after Adolph Hitler in the United States.

The newspapers reported the first large crowd at Camp Siegfried on September 25, 1935, with over 5,000, and it ended with a torch light procession. On July 21, 1936, there were 5,000, and the rally centered on attacking the Jews. Italian fascists joined the Bund for a rally on September 1, 1936 and over 12,000 attended this rally. Some of the speakers were Bernhard G. Lippert of the German consul-general and the Reverend Kropp of the Evangelical Lutheran Church, New York City.

Two huge Nazi rallies were later held at Camp Siegfried. The first was on August 29, 1937, when up to 30,000 attended. Various fascist groups joined the Bund for this meeting. On August 14, 1938, the largest Nazi rally outside of Germany took place. The New York Times reported that 40,000 attended this rally! It is amazing, but the largest Nazi rally outside of Germany took place on American soil. It was held at Camp Siegfried, Yaphank, NY.

The very epicenter of Nazism in the United States was Yaphank, NY. This is not to say the people of Yaphank were Nazis, but this was where the Nazis met and held their huge Jew hating rallies. This also was the location of Adolph Hitler Street.

The Lord's Tempest

"But the LORD sent out a great wind into the sea, and there was a mighty tempest in the sea..."

Jonah 1:4.

On September 4, 1938, just three weeks after the largest Nazi rally in America, a weather depression moved off the coast of West Africa to the Cape Verde Islands and then headed westward. The Great Hurricane of 1938 was born and started its long journey across the Atlantic Ocean toward America.

By September 18, the storm was a massive category 5 heading directly toward the United States. By September 20, it turned north as a category 3 storm and headed toward Long Island. At 7:00 AM on September 21, it greatly increased in speed. The closer it approached Long Island, the faster it moved until it reached an incredible 70 miles per hour. Because of this speed, it was nicknamed the Long Island Express. At approximately 3:00 PM, the hurricane smashed into Long Island with a 25-30 foot wall of water with such fury that it registered on seismographs as far away as Alaska.

The very epicenter of the storm was Bellport, NY with the lowest barometric reading of 27.94. Within minutes, the eye moved inland with the small town of Yaphank next in line. The epicenter of the eye of The Great Hurricane of 1938 then passed directly over Camp Siegfried and Adolph Hitler Street!

This happened a mere 38 days after Camp Siegfried was the center of the largest Nazi rally outside of Germany. Since 1635, close to 400 years, this was just the third hurricane of this magnitude to hit Long Island and New England. The Great Hurricane of 1938, perhaps the most powerful of the three, went directly over Adolph Hitler Street.

It happened during the time the President of the United States turned his back on Czechoslovakia and the Jews. He, with the rest of the world, was feeding into Hitler's plan of world domination and annihilating world Jewry. In September 1938, the national headlines were The Great Hurricane of 1938 and Hitler. This correlation was front page headlines on every newspaper and radio news show in America!

This timing was breathtaking because, just a mere five days before the United States helped appease Hitler, the eye of The Great Hurricane of 1938 went directly over Adolph Hitler Street. It seems this hurricane was a stern warning.

These events were not a coincidence, but an example of a fulfilled promise in the Bible. There are special promises recorded in the Bible regarding the Jewish people and the land of Israel. For most of the history of the United States, the Jews lived quietly without persecution. The 1930's were an exception.

You will see later in this book starting in 1991 with the Madrid Peace Conference and the attempt to divide the land of Israel, incredible disasters like Hurricane Andrew, the Northridge Earthquake and Hurricane Katrina occurred. These events fell on the very day the United States was involved in pressuring Israel to divide its land. The parallel that began on September 21, 1938, continues to this day.

"For the day of the LORD is near upon all the heathen: as thou hast done, it shall be done unto thee: thy reward shall return upon thine own head."

Obadiah 1:15.

CHAPTER TWO

The Apple of God's Eye

"For thus saith the LORD of hosts; After the glory hath
he sent me unto the nations which spoiled you: for he
that toucheth you toucheth the apple of his eye."
                                        Zechariah 2:8.

A direct connection between The Great Hurricane of
1938 and Nazism in the United States is not wild
speculation. The Bible is the anchor for this connection. The
key to understanding the Jewish people is not political, soci-
ological, economic or any other method. The Bible reveals
this key is spiritual.

The prophet Zechariah stated that whoever touches the
Jewish people to harm them touches "the apple," pupil, of
God's eye. The pupil is one of the most sensitive parts of the
body. If an object such as a finger gets close to the pupil, a
person immediately reacts to this. A finger poked in the eye
inflicts tremendous pain. This is the picture of what happens
when the Jewish people suffer persecution. This suffering
gets God's attention and not as a mere annoyance, but as a
painful situation that requires immediate attention. The Bund

building a Nazi enclave, complete with Adolph Hitler Street, had God's attention on September 21, 1938.

The everlasting covenant God made with Abraham 4000 years ago is a direct relationship between God and the Jewish people. God created this covenant for several reasons and one was to bless all the families of the earth. Through Abraham, God blessed not only the Jews, but all the families of the earth. Abraham's descendants are the vehicle for this blessing. The complete fulfillment of this blessing associated with Abraham comes through the Lord Jesus Christ. Through Him all the families of the earth will be blessed.

God then issued a universal warning. The people who blessed Abraham and his descendants God would bless, but those who cursed, they would receive a curse. The Bible very clearly issued a warning which continues to this day.

"And I will bless them that bless thee, and curse him that curseth thee: and in thee shall all families of the earth be blessed."

Genesis 12:3

The Everlasting Covenant With Abraham

"Which covenant he made with Abraham, and his oath unto Isaac; And confirmed the same unto Jacob for a law, and to Israel for an everlasting covenant."

Psalm 105:9, 10.

God established an everlasting covenant with Abraham and his descendants as a blessing to all people. This covenant focused on the land now called the nation of Israel. God deals with nations according to this covenant. God is in a covenant relationship with the descendants of Abraham that is still in effect. God never abrogated the everlasting covenant concerning the land of Israel.

"And I will establish my covenant between me and thee and thy seed after thee in their generations for an **everlasting covenant**, to be a God unto thee, and to thy seed after thee. (8). And I will give unto thee, and to thy seed after thee, the land wherein thou art a stranger, all the land of Canaan, for an **everlasting possession**; and I will be their God."

Genesis 17:7, 8.

The Bible shows God passed this covenant on to Abraham's son Isaac and his grandson Jacob. God made the same covenant with them over the land of Israel that He instituted with Abraham. Each time the covenant was renewed, it also included their descendants which are the Jewish people. God established this covenant to follow a definite genealogy.

The covenant passed to Isaac:

"...I will be with thee, and will bless thee; for unto thee, and unto thy seed, I will give all these countries, and I will perform the oath which I swore unto Abraham thy father; (4)...and will give **unto thy seed** all these countries; and in thy seed shall all the nations of the earth be blessed..."

Genesis 26:3, 4.

The covenant passed to Jacob and his descendants:

"And the land which I gave Abraham and Isaac, to thee I will give it, and **to thy seed after thee** will I give the land."

Genesis 35:12.

Each time God reinforced the everlasting covenant He included the descendants, "thy seed," of Abraham, Isaac and Jacob. This means Jewish people are still under the everlasting covenant God made with Abraham, and whoever blesses them will be blessed or curses them will be cursed.

God's Chosen People

"For thou art an holy people unto the LORD thy God: the LORD thy God hath chosen thee to be a special people unto himself, above all people that are upon the face of the earth."

Deuteronomy 7:6.

Sometimes people use the expression that Jews are "God's chosen people." When questioning a person, very few know the reason for this expression. The reason is God wanted to reveal Himself and He chose Abraham and his descendants as the vehicle.

Actually, God has several reasons for making the covenant. He wanted a people to bring forth the prophets and give the world the Bible. Jewish prophets wrote the entire Bible both the Old and New Testaments. The Bible is part of God's blessing through Abraham to all the families of the earth. Israel, both the land and people, became the central location for the prophets to write the Bible.

In a central location, the Jewish people could maintain the unfolding revelation of the prophets. Think of the impossibility of having a cohesive Bible if one prophet was from Europe, one from India, one from Africa etc. The prophets' central location in Israel, allowed for their message to be codified in the Bible and then disseminated throughout the world. God did this through the everlasting covenant.

"What advantage then hath the Jew? or what profit is there of circumcision? (2) Much every way:

56

chiefly, because that unto them were committed the oracles of God."

Romans 3:1.

God called the nation of Israel as a light and witness to the surrounding pagans. The pagans committed unspeakable acts including sacrificing their children to idols. Israel was a source of God's truth to these pagans.

"I have declared, and have saved, and I have showed, when there was no strange god among you: therefore ye are my witnesses, saith the LORD, that I am God."

Isaiah 43:12.

God made the covenant which included a people, culture and genealogy in order to bring the Messiah, the Savior of mankind, into the world. The Messiah had to be the son of David, the son of Abraham. Genealogy proved this link to David and Abraham. The nation of Israel provided both the location and genealogy for God's Messiah. In Him, God blesses all the families of the earth.

The location:
"But thou, Bethlehem Ephratah, though thou be little among the thousands of Judah, yet out of thee shall he come forth unto me that is to be ruler in Israel; whose goings forth have been from of old, from everlasting."

Micah 5:2.

The genealogy:
"The book of the generation of Jesus Christ, the son of David, the son of Abraham. (2) Abraham begat Isaac; and Isaac begat Jacob; and Jacob begat Judas and his brethren."

Matthew 1:1, 2.

This everlasting covenant is a way of testing the Bible's authority as God's word. The fulfillment of the everlasting covenant is a way of witnessing God's mighty power and the authority of His word. The prophet Ezekiel writes about a day, way in the future from his time, when a huge confederation of nations tries to destroy the regathered nation of Israel. God supernaturally destroys these nations to defend His covenant land.

The prophet then states what happens after this awesome judgment. God uses the tiny nation of Israel so the entire world can see His faithfulness to His covenant people. The authority of God's word is directly linked to the Jewish people and the nation of Israel.

"Thus will I magnify myself, and sanctify myself; and I will be known in the eyes of many nations, and they shall know that I am the LORD."

Ezekiel 38:23.

The Bible emphatically reveals in many places that God will deal in judgment with nations that attempt to destroy the covenant people. Tyrants and despots through the centuries have tried in every way possible to destroy Jews or prevent the rebirth of Israel. All these attempts have failed. The tyrants are gone but Jews are still here and Israel is once again a nation. A few verses to show God judges nations for attempting to break His covenant with Abraham, Isaac, Jacob and their descendants, follow:

"For it is the day of the Lord's vengeance, and the year of recompenses for the controversy of Zion."

Isaiah 34:8.

"For the day of the LORD is near upon all the heathen: as thou hast done, it shall be done unto thee: thy reward shall return upon thine own head."

Obadiah 1:15.

"For thus saith the LORD of hosts; After the glory hath he sent me unto the nations which spoiled you: for he that toucheth you toucheth the apple of his eye."

Zechariah 2:8.

Notice in Isaiah 34:8 the Bible uses the word Zion. Zion in the Bible is a good word. Zion can have five different applications depending on the context. In the Old Testament the word can mean the people or nation of Israel. It can also mean the city of Jerusalem, or the location of the temple within Jerusalem. This location is Mt Zion. The New Testament makes reference to Zion as heaven. There is no doubt when studying the Bible that God is a Zionist. He is the one creating the events restoring the nation of Israel or Zion.

God had clearly linked His name with Abraham and his descendants.

"And they shall put my name upon the children of Israel; and I will bless them."

Numbers 6:27

CHAPTER THREE

The People Whose God Is Jehovah

"May the Children of the Stock of Abraham, who dwell in this land, continue to merit and enjoy the good will of the other Inhabitants; while every one shall sit under his own vine and fig tree, and there shall be none to make him afraid."

President George Washington, 1790.

*I*n 2004, the Jewish people celebrated their 350 year anniversary in America. Most people are astonished to find out that Jewish colonists first arrived in America in 1654. They arrived 30 years before the Germans and 50 years before the Scot-Irish! The Jewish people experienced a very long and successful history in pre-United States. This success continued after the creation of the United States and right up to today.

Jews never suffered in America as they did in European nations. The United States has been a great blessing to the Israelites, as Americans called them 300 years ago. In American history, there is no record of even one organized government attack on them, nor have there been any attacks sanctioned by religious organizations.

The Israelites fought in large numbers, percentage-wise, in the American Revolution. Many were heroes and gave all they had for America, including their lives. They won the respect of the American people. They fought in great numbers during the Civil War and at least six won the Medal of Honor and one, from the Stock of Abraham as the non-Jews also called them, became a major general.

The Jewish people first came to America in 1654 from Brazil of all places. To escape persecution, many Portuguese Jews fled to Brazil which was then a Dutch colony. Holland lost the colony to Portugal and the Jews fled. One ship with 23 Jews arrived in New Amsterdam, now New York City, late in September 1654. This was the beginning of Jewish migration to the United States.

The governor, Peter Stuyvesant, objected to the Jews and contacted Holland about their presence in New Amsterdam. His orders allowing the Jews to stay are a hallmark of America to this day. When 350 years ago the Dutch gave Jews religious freedom, they first sowed the seeds of religious freedom in this nation. This freedom has endured to the present day. Stuyvesant's superiors ordered him to:

"Shut your eyes, at least do not force people's consciences, but allow every one his own belief, as long as he behaves quietly and legally, gives no offense to his neighbor and does not oppose the government."

Great Britain defeated Holland and renamed the city New York and in 1667 also guaranteed Jews full rights to worship, trade and own property. Most Jews became merchants and were involved in trade.

By the Revolutionary War, Jews were full citizens, and there was virtually no institutionalized prejudice against them. There were no laws specifically enacted against the Jewish people and no forced conversions from Judaism. History does not report any Jewish business or home destroyed because of their religion. The Jewish community was small, about 3,000, but they fully blended into America.

When the Revolution started, almost the entire Jewish community joined the American cause. This was the time the Hebrews began to shine in American history. Jewish merchants rallied to the American Revolution. They supplied the army with clothing, guns, powder and food. Jewish merchants used their ships as blockade runners bringing supplies from Europe. Aaron Lopez of Newport, RI used his 130 ships to supply the American army. Most Jewish merchants lost all by the end of the war.

The Hebrews fought in the war and some attained high military ranks. For example, the British seriously wounded Solomon Bush in battle and captured him. They soon freed him, and he then rose to the rank of lieutenant colonel in the Continental army. Francis Salvador was the first Jewish person elected to a state legislature. South Carolina elected him to the General Assembly. Later the people elected him as a delegate to the state's revolutionary Congress. In 1776, he was killed in battle.

George Washington's personal physician, Dr. Philip Moses Russell was a Jew. He was with the General at Valley Forge and suffered through the terrible winter ordeal. But, the most famous Jewish person of the Revolution was Haym Salomon.

The "Little Jew Broker"

Robert Morris, the first Treasurer of the United States, affectionately called Haym Salomon the "little Jew broker." Salomon was born in Poland in 1740 and traveled throughout Europe. He became fluent in seven languages and international finances. He came to America in 1772 and immediately joined the Sons of Liberty in New York City. The Sons of Liberty were among the most radical revolutionary groups in America. He also became a very successful businessman in New York City.

When the war broke out he stayed in New York and worked behind the British lines. The British captured him as a spy, and imprisoned him; however, he was freed. He was captured a second time as a spy and sentenced to death. Salomon was able to escape and settled in Philadelphia, but in the process lost all his wealth. In Philadelphia, he started over again and established a very successful brokerage firm. He became the top broker in America. His fluency in languages, plus being extremely honest and having the knowledge of international finances, enabled him to become a top broker.

By 1781 the American currency collapsed and the treasury was empty. The nation was bankrupt. America had no funds for continuing the war and paying its debts. Robert Morris, Secretary of the Treasury, turned to Salomon for help, and it was the skill, knowledge, honesty and generosity of Salomon that kept America financially solvent. America at this time had no banking system, but Salomon's own credit backed the finances of the United States! Later, when Morris established a bank, Haym was its first and largest depositor.

He personally made large loans with no interest to many of the leading Americans of the Revolution; people such as future Presidents James Madison, Thomas Jefferson, James Monroe, and also Generals von Steuben and St Clair. Salomon personally supported the Spanish ambassador which created Spanish good will toward America.

Robert Morris made 75 entries in his diary about turning to the "Jewish broker" for financial help. Salomon was maybe the one person most responsible for establishing the credit of the United States in Europe. He was backing the loans! The Continental Congress appointed him as, "The Official Broker to the Office of Finance of the United States."

American Jewish Archives

Portrait of Haym Salomon (1740-1785)

Salomon died in 1785 of sickness he contracted while in prison in 1776. He was only 45 years old and died penniless. The exact amount of money the United States owed Salomon was never determined. There was a Congressional investigation which produced evidence that the United States owed Salomon $656,000; however, the investigation never conclusively proved this. In 1814 when the British burned Washington, DC, the fire destroyed all of Salomon's records; thus, the exact amount remains unknown.

Haym Salomon was a true American patriot. He gave his all to America. He helped financially stabilize America during a critical time when the nation was at its economic worst. During Salomon's lifetime, he never received the recognition due him. In 1975 the United States issued a commemorative stamp in his honor. On the back of the stamp was printed:

"Financial hero-businessman and broker Haym Salomon was responsible for raising most of the money needed to finance the American Revolution and later saved the new nation from collapse."

George Washington's Letters

When George Washington was elected President in 1789, the Jewish centers around the nation sent him letters of congratulation. His response to these letters set the future tone for Jews in America. At the very beginning of the United States, President Washington manifested the attitude of Americans toward Jewish people.

Washington had the highest esteem for the "Children of the Stock of Abraham." With affection for the Jewish people seldom, if ever, seen by the leader of a nation, Washington thought of Jews as equals and even stated the God of the

Jews was his God. This is truly amazing in the light of the world-wide history of the Jewish people. In 1790, Jews in America were the freest on earth.

In his letter addressed to the Hebrews in Savannah, GA, the President connects the God of Israel, who delivered the Jews from Egypt, as the same God who established the United States. He asked the God of Israel to bless the Hebrews with the "dews of heaven," and he requested the material and spiritual blessings on the people whose God is Jehovah! This letter in part follows:

> "May the same wonder-working Deity, who long since delivered the Hebrews from their Egyptian oppressors, planted them in a promised land, whose providential agency has lately been conspicuous in establishing these United States as an independent nation, still continue to water them with the dews of heaven and make the inhabitants of every denomination participate in the temporal and spiritual blessings of that people whose God is Jehovah." (See Addendum A for the complete letter)

President Washington also wrote to the Hebrews in Newport, RI. His letter to the "Children of the Stock of Abraham" contained the same type of blessings. He wanted Jews to have the good will of the nation, and he desired that America might be as the time of the Messiah's future reigning for the Jews! He actually made a direct reference from the Bible to show the peace he wanted Jews to live under!

The President wanted the United States to be as the time of the Messiah's reign for them. Micah 4:4 was the verse he referred to. This was a far cry from the tyrants of Europe throughout the ages and the horrors they inflicted on Jewish people. What nation ever exhibited such favor to the Jewish people as America! What other nation started with such a favorable attitude toward the Jewish people? America is unique among the nations. The letter in part follows:

> "May the Children of the Stock of Abraham, who dwell in this land, continue to merit and enjoy the good will of the other Inhabitants; while every one shall sit under his own vine and fig tree, and there shall be none to make him afraid.
>
> May the father of all mercies scatter light and not darkness in our paths, and make us all in our several vocations useful here, and in his own due time and way everlastingly happy." (See Addendum B for the complete letter)

The President clearly referred to Micah 4:4 when he wanted the children of Abraham to sit under his own vine and fig tree and none to make him afraid. The context is verse three when the Messiah is the Judge of all the nations. He will end war and bring universal peace. The President chose these tremendous verses to pronounce a blessing on the Children of Abraham. These verses follow:

> "And he shall judge among many people, and rebuke strong nations afar off; and they shall beat their swords into plowshares, and their spears into pruninghooks: nation shall not lift up a sword against nation, neither shall they learn war any more.
>
> (4) But they shall sit every man under his vine and under his fig tree; and none shall make them afraid: for the mouth of the LORD of hosts hath spoken it." Micah 4:3 4.

Stand By the Flag

The attitude of President Washington persisted into the future of America. After the Revolution, Jewish immigration from Europe picked up, especially in the 1820's. The immigrants came mostly from Germany and central Europe. By the time of the Civil War, there were approximately 200,000 Jews in America. They excelled as merchants, bankers, lawyers, doctors and educators.

The American acceptance of Jews even reached into foreign policy. In 1840, Arabs were killing and torturing Jews in Damascus. The American Jewish community brought this to the attention of President Martin Van Buren. The Ottoman Empire ruled over Syria at this time. The President directed the American ambassador to ask the Ottoman ruler to stop the killing and torturing of Jews. The President stated that all of America was against this suffering.

President Van Buren then made statements in his letter to the Ottomans which were very revealing about America's attitude toward Jewish people. By 1840, Americans viewed Jewish people as equals and considered them patriotic citizens. In the letter, the President cited America's institutions and said, "They place upon the same footing, the worshipers of God, of every faith and form." He followed by stating this intervention was "in behalf of an oppressed and persecuted race, among whose kindred are found some of the most worthy and patriotic of [American] citizens." The Ottoman Empire responded and the killing stopped.

The Civil War once again showed how Jewish people acted as patriots and American citizens. At this time, the *Jewish Messenger* was one of the most influential Jewish newspapers in America. This was a national paper published weekly.

In December 28, 1860 as the war neared, Samuel Mayer Isaacs, the editor, wrote an astonishing editorial titled *A*

Day of Prayer. Isaacs wrote a very moving account of how blessed Jews had been in America. He recounted the freedoms and equality the Jews had enjoyed as Americans under the Constitution as equal citizens. Isaacs wrote how Judaism was not an impediment to advancement in the United States, and that America was the first republic to recognize Jews as absolute equals.

He then makes a direct quote from President George Washington's 1790 letter to the Hebrews in Newport. The quote is the one taken from Micah 4:4 stating Jews can sit "each under his vine and fig-tree and none to make him afraid." This amazing editorial by Samuel Mayer Isaacs in part follows:

> "The Union for whose prosperity we ask Divine aid, has been the source of happiness for our ancestors and ourselves. Under the protection of the freedom guaranteed us by the Constitution, we have lived in the enjoyment of full and perfect equality with our fellow citizens.
>
> We are enabled to worship the Supreme Being according to the dictates of conscience, we can maintain the position to which our abilities entitle us, without our religious opinions being an impediment to advancement.
>
> This Republic was the first to recognize our claims to absolute equality, with men of whatever religious denomination. Here we can sit each under his vine and fig tree, with none to make him afraid."

This war started on April 12, 1861, and for a second time The Jewish Messenger ran an amazing editorial written by Samuel Mayer Isaacs. This one, dated April 28, 1861, and titled, *Stand By the Flag*, called for Jewish people to defend the United States and the Constitution. In the editorial, Isaacs also urged the readers to defend the Constitution which guaranteed free exercise of religion and lends to liberty, justice and equality. He calls the Constitution the admiration of the world.

He made a stirring call to stand by the flag and asked Jews to defend it with their lives if needed! Jews were totally accepted and had all the benefits of Americans. Isaacs's editorial in part follows:

"And the Constitution, guaranteeing to all, the free exercise of their religious opinions, extending to all, liberty, justice, and equality, the pride of Americans, the admiration of the world, shall that Constitution be subverted, and anarchy usurp the place of a sound, safe and stable government, deriving its authority from the consent of the American People?

The voice of millions yet unborn, cried out, 'Forbid it, Heaven!' The voice of the American people declares in tones not to be misunderstood: `It shall not be!'

Then stand by the Flag! What death can be as glorious as that of the patriot, surrendering his life in defense of his country, pouring forth his blood on the battlefield, to live forever in the hearts of a grateful people..." (See Addendum C for the complete editorial)

During the Civil War, about 9,000 Jews fought for the North and eight rose to the level of general. Major General Frederick Knefler became the highest ranking Jewish general. By the end of the war the army recognized Brigadier General Alfred Mordecai as the leading expert in explosives and gunnery.

Edward S. Salomon was a Colonel of the 82nd Illinois Volunteer Infantry at the battle of Gettysburg. He led his men to withstand the final assault by the Confederates against Cemetery Ridge. His regiment took 50 percent casualties. He ended the war as a Brigadier General. The Union's Surgeon general was Phineas Horowitz, a Hebrew. There were six Jewish Medal of Honor winners. These Medal of Honor winners, along with their unit and the battle for which they were honored, follow:

Sergeant-Major Abraham Cohn, 6th New Hampshire Volunteers, Battle of the Wilderness and Battle of Petersburg, VA.

Corporal Isaac Gause, 2nd Ohio Cavalry, Berryville, Virginia.

Sergeant Henry Heller, 66th Ohio Infantry, Chancellorsville, Virginia.

Sergeant Leopold Karpeles, Company E, Massachusetts Infantry, Battle of the Wilderness, Virginia.

Sergeant Benjamin B. Levy, 40th New York Regiment, Battle of the Wilderness, Virginia.

Private David Orbansky, 58th Ohio Infantry, Vicksburg, Mississippi

Jews fought in the Civil War with great honor just as they did in the American Revolution. They were patriots in every sense of the word. Americans accepted Jewish people. There was always individual prejudice, but the hatred and organized prejudice they experienced in Europe was unknown in America.

During the Revolution, Haym Salomon played a tremendous part in getting the nation through a difficult financial period. Joseph Seligman, a Jewish American, accomplished the same during the Civil War. Seligman was an American international clothier. He had vast contacts with European banks. The United States needed large amounts of cash to fund the war. He bought United States bonds and then used his banking contacts in Europe to cash them. He cashed over

$200 million worth of bonds through Germany. At the beginning of the war, Seligman lent the American government one million dollars to purchase uniforms.

After the Civil War, President Grant offered Seligman the position of Secretary of the Treasury which he turned down. Amazingly, Jews were instrumental in getting the United States through two very difficult economic times with their own credit. These difficult times happened to be the Revolution and Civil War!

President Lincoln became a good friend of the Jewish people just as did President Washington. There were no Jewish chaplains allowed in the military. He personally had a law passed allowing Jewish chaplains. This was the first time in United States' history a federal law was enacted specifically to benefit Jewish people.

On December 17, 1862, General Ulysses S. Grant issued the infamous General Order 11. This order expelled all Jews from Kentucky, Tennessee and Mississippi. It gave Jewish people 24 hours to leave the area. There was a serious problem with unscrupulous merchants trading with the South and some were Jewish. General Grant issued this Order against the Jews as a class. A Congressman brought this matter directly to the President's attention and immediately he had General Order 11 rescinded. The President rescinded the Order just a mere three days after General Grant issued it.

Cesar J. Kaskel, a Jew from Paducah, Kentucky, with the aid of a Congressman, first brought this order to the President's attention. Kaskel immediately went to Washington and met with President Lincoln. Kaskel afterwards wrote of the meeting where Lincoln said, "And so the Children of Israel were driven from the land of Canaan." Kaskel responded, "Yes, and this is why we have come to Father Abraham, to ask his protection." Lincoln followed, "And this protection they shall have at once."

President Lincoln immediately contacted the Union's Commanding General Henry W. Halleck and had General Grant's General Order 11 revoked. The President issued a short note that General Halleck telegraphed, and General Grant immediately revoked the order. This note from the President follows:

> "A paper purporting to be General Orders, No 11, issued by you December 17, has been presented here. By its terms, it expels all Jews from your department. If such an order has been issued, it will be immediately revoked."

Rabbi Isaac M. Wise of Cincinnati led a delegation to visit President Lincoln. They wanted to thank the President for revoking General Order 11. The rabbi reported many statements by President Lincoln. Rabbi Wise said the President drew no distinction between Jew and Gentile; and he would allow no wrong to any American because of his religious affiliation. The President stated General Grant was wrong.

This incident with General Grant failed to cause long term damage with the Jewish community. There were no lasting effects against the General. In 1868 when Grant ran for president, the Jewish vote went heavily for Grant.

On April 15, 1865, President Lincoln died from an assassin's bullet. The entire country went into deep mourning. Jewish people were in mourning like the rest of the country. All across America, Jews held special services in honor of the President. The one given in, of all places, the Southern city of New Orleans, best summed up the attitude of the Jews toward the President. P. J. Joachimsen spoke on behalf of the congregation. This Southern Hebrew congregation held President Lincoln in high esteem for defending Jews over General Order 11. The newspapers throughout

America reported this very touching eulogy. This speech in part follows:

> "And we, as Jews, had a distinct ground to love, respect and esteem him... When an order was made to banish Jews as a class from a particular Department, and their immediate and indiscriminate departure was being carried out, our deceased President at once revoked the unauthorized command.
>
> We can carry the memory of Abraham Lincoln with us as that of a triumphant martyr to humanity, and we can also carry into practice the lessons taught us by the short but eventful life of the great departed: To be true and honest to ourselves and to our neighbors and to stand bravely and fearlessly to the performance of our duties as citizens of this great Republic."

Unquestionably, two of the greatest presidents in the history of the United States were also great friends of the Jewish people. They set the example for the rest of the nation to follow.

The Land of Freedom
Beyond the Ocean

At the time of the Civil War, America was the envy of world Jewry. American Jews had complete freedom and equality and this caught the attention of world Jewry. The European Jews attributed this freedom to the American Constitution which established religious liberty. European Jewry was amazed how quickly their brothers in America prospered and they were able to reach all levels of society.

In 1862 the London Jewish Chronicle reported this observation:

"We now have a few words of the Jews of the United States in general...The constitution having established perfect religious liberty, Jews were free in America...They, therefore in a comparatively short time, prospered, and throve there in a degree unexampled in Europe. Jews were found in all positions of life filling offices from the highest to the lowest."

By 1862 there were about 200,000 Jews in America which was only a fraction of the number in Europe. Although there was such freedom in America, the report went on to explain why so few Jews had left Europe for the United States. The explanation made was that Jews had grown accustomed to persecution, and traveling to America was so difficult. The report follows:

"But although their happy condition was known in Europe, and although oppression weighed heavily upon them in the Old World, yet, so few were the facilities for traveling, and so accustomed had the grown up generations been to persecution, that but few sought asylum in the land of freedom beyond the ocean."

This reluctance of European Jewry to seek asylum in the land of freedom, beyond the ocean, soon came to an end. In 1881, just 16 years after the close of the Civil War, events in Russia would send millions of desperate Jews to the land of freedom. The center of world Jewry was about to shift from Europe to the land beyond the ocean.

American Jewish Archives

**Statue in Chicago with
Robert Morris, George Washington, Haym Salomon**

CHAPTER FOUR

The Modern Day Moses

"But lift thou up thy rod, and stretch out thine hand over the sea, and divide it: and the children of Israel shall go on dry ground through the midst of the sea."

Exodus 14:16.

The European-Jewish resistance to American emigration changed abruptly, virtually overnight. A census in 1877 listed the Jewish population in America as 250,000. Just 30 years later this population reached two million. A tidal wave of Jews mostly from Russia flooded into America. Events in Russia changed the course of world history in a dramatic way. This change affected history down to this day.

On March 1, 1881, Tsar Alexander II of Russia was assassinated. This incident set off a series of events that cascaded down through history to this day. The Russian government blamed the assassination on Jews, and violence immediately broke out. The terrible pogrom of 1881 resulted in the murder of hundreds of Jews, with thousands injured, and their homes and property destroyed. A pogrom is an organized massacre of helpless people.

The Russian government did nothing to stop the pogroms, but blamed the destruction of Jews on the Jews! Jewish life was terrible in Russia before the pogrom, but it was about to significantly worsen. On May 3, 1882, the Russian government enacted what became known as the May Laws. The assassination of the Tsar followed by the May Laws were turning points in world history. These laws directed at the Jews made life intolerable. The May Laws included the following:

Jews were forbidden to settle outside of towns or shetls (small towns)
Jews were not allowed to purchase land or a home.
They were not allowed to relocate.
Deeds of sale or lease of real estate of Jews who lived outside the towns were canceled.
Jews were prohibited from business on Sunday or Christian holidays
Jewish education was strictly limited.

The May Laws now forced Jews into ghettos. They could not travel throughout Russia without permits. The police brutally enforced the May Laws. The authorities systematically expelled Jews from their houses and forced them to relocate. Jewish people lived in terror.

Jewish reaction to the pogrom and May Laws was a mass exodus from Russia to America. Starting in 1881 and accelerating well into the Twentieth Century, Jews fled Russia to America, and America took them in. No country in the world wanted the Russian Jews except America.

Tens of thousands of poverty stricken Jews literally walked out of Russia into Western Europe trying to get to America. Western Europe refused to accept them. The Jews were terrified and desperate. They heard about the freedoms of America. They heard that the people of the United States accepted Jews. They referred to America as "The famous land."

Mary Antin was a Russian Jew who escaped to America. She wrote about leaving Russia, and the charged emotional atmosphere as Jews were readying for the mass exodus. Mary wrote:

> "America was in everybody's mouth. Businessmen talked of it over their accounts; the market women made up their quarrels that they might discuss it from stall to stall; people who had relatives in the famous land went around reading their letters for the enlightenment of less fortunate folks...Children played at emigrating; old folks shook their sage heads over the evening fires and prophesied no good for those who braved the terrors of the sea and the goal beyond it. All talked about it..."

In total desperation, the fleeing refugees literally walked west without any idea of how to reach America. They flooded into Germany by the tens of thousands. Some local people in Germany helped them. European Jews helped by providing the finances for passage to America. Nothing could stop the Russian Jews from getting to America. This turned out to be one of the greater migrations in history. When the great Russian emigration was over 35 years later, more than two million had come to America. It equaled the previous Irish immigration of the 1840's and 1850's.

The vast majority of Jews entered America through New York City. As they entered the harbor, the Statue of Liberty was staring at them. The Statue of Liberty came to represent the hope which America offered to the desperate peoples of the world. In 1883 at the base of the Statue, a poem was inscribed which almost everyone today has knowledge. Emma Lazarus, a Jew, wrote the poem!

How ironic that Jews fleeing Russian first saw the Statue of Liberty as they approached New York harbor, and on it a Jewish woman wrote a poem that described them. Lazarus' poem perfectly described the Russian Jews fleeing to America. This inscription follows:

Give me your tired, your poor,
Your huddled masses yearning to breathe free,
The wretched refuse of your teeming shore,
Send these, the homeless, tempest-tost to me,
I lift my lamp beside the golden door!

Although the vast majority of the Russian Jews left for America, a small number headed south to what is now Israel. The May Laws also triggered the first modern move of Jews back to Israel. Those considered to be the first zionists in the modern Zionists movement, were Russian Jews fleeing the pogroms. The events occurring in Russia directly influenced the creation of modern Israel.

The world looked upon America as the New Jerusalem for the Russian Jews. In 1881, a political cartoon published by a weekly American/German newspaper called *Puck* captured this idea. The cartoon showed the Atlantic Ocean splitting and Jews coming through to America. Uncle Sam in the cartoon became the "Modern Moses." The Jews, leaving the horrors of Russia, and coming to America was similar to them leaving Egypt for the promised land.

Coinciding with this cartoon, *Puck* ran an amazing article about the Jewish people flooding into America. The article was written as if Uncle Sam, the Modern Moses, was speaking. It is difficult to imagine an article like this written in any country at any time; only in America. Remember, this article is "Uncle Sam" speaking at the very beginning of the great Russian Jewish immigration to the United States:

All he (Uncle Sam) says to the persecuted races of Europe, whether Jew or Christian, believer or unbeliever, is: "You are welcome to America."

"Practice any religion you please...If you wish, cover the land with churches or synagogues ...

As my ancient servant predecessor, Moses, did with the Red Sea, I do with the Atlantic Ocean. The waters are divided, and you can safely pass through them to the land of liberty, and leave oppression, persecution and brutality behind you."

President Washington wanted the United States to resemble the future reign of the Messiah for Jews living in America. Now, the nation became just that for the Russian Jews as they fled the oppression of Tsarist Russia. What a contrast between President George Washington and the Tsar of Russia with his May Laws! The President's letter to the Hebrews of Newport is worth repeating:

"May the Children of the Stock of Abraham, who dwell in this land, continue to merit and enjoy the good will of the other Inhabitants; while every one shall sit under his own vine and fig tree, and there shall be none to make him afraid."

God used the horrors of Russia to begin the migration of Jews back to Israel. Jews flooding into America had a profound impact on the Church and ignited the modern Zionist movement. God also used the Church in America to spearhead the modern return of the Jews to their Biblical homeland.

Thus the assassination of Tsar Alexander II on March 1, 1881 was the catalyst for the modern rebirth of the nation of Israel. The pogroms and May Laws which followed started a tiny movement of Jews back to Israel. But, more significantly it awakened the Evangelical Church in America to the

Jewish plight and the need for a Jewish state in Palestine. The world is still reverberating from March 1, 1881 and the May Laws of 1882 that followed.

Christian Zionism

After the Civil War, and building toward the end of the century, huge segments of American Christianity began focusing on the Second Coming of the Lord Jesus, and the rebirth of the nation of Israel. This was a powerful movement that reached to the highest levels of society.

America, prior to the Civil War, had several powerful spiritual revivals. These revivals were not just local but touched the entire nation. The Great Awakening of the 1740s, started by the preaching of Jonathan Edwards, spread throughout the nation and changed the course of society. In the year 1800, a great revival started in Kentucky and spread eastward until it affected the entire nation. The Second Awakening began in 1820 under the preaching of Charles Finney and shook the nation.

Just before the Civil War, in 1857, a revival started on Fulton Street in New York City that spread throughout the nation. But, the revival that took place in the 1880s and 1890s was different. The focus of this revival was the Second Coming of the Lord Jesus and the restoration of Jewish people back to Israel. This belief became known as premillenialism.

The premillenialist doctrine is a belief that God would restore the nation of Israel before the Second Coming of the Lord Jesus Christ. The nation's restoration would be in unbelief. The Lord Jesus summons the born-again believing Church to be with Him in heaven before He returns to Israel. When Jesus Christ returns to Israel, He comes with His Church. After this, He will rule and reign from Jerusalem for a 1000 years (millennium), thus the term premillenial.

Powerful evangelists like D.L. Moody and William E. Blackstone were proclaiming this message together with hundreds of lesser known preachers. Blackstone's book, *Jesus Is Coming*, first printed in 1878 sold huge numbers and affected millions of people. A network of new Bible colleges spread across the country as well as dozens of publications, all promoting the premillenialist doctrine.

In the midst of this revival, the Russian Jews began pouring into America. The horrors of what happened to them in Russia touched the hearts of the Christians. They began to help these Jewish refugees with food, clothes and medical attention. The crisis awakened the Church to the need for a Jewish homeland. Blackstone became the leader of this movement and extensively traveled throughout America promoting a Jewish homeland in Palestine.

His efforts reached the highest levels of American society from Church leaders, to influential Jews, to the halls of Congress. Blackstone chaired a conference in 1890 titled the Past, Present and Future of Israel. Some of the most influential leaders, both in the Jewish and Christian communities, attended. One result of the conference was that the leaders sent resolutions to the Tsar for the plight of the Russian Jews.

Blackstone felt the resolutions were not strong enough and the following year on March 5, 1891, he met with Benjamin Harrison, President of the United States and Secretary of State James Blaine. During this meeting, he presented the President with, what is now known as, The Blackstone Memorial.

The Blackstone Memorial

The Blackstone Memorial, with the actual title, "What Shall Be Done For the Russian Jews," was an amazing document that actually became the forerunner of the modern

Zionist movement. Modern Zionism actually sprang from the Church in the United States. The Church witnessed the terrible conditions of the Russian Jews and believed it was time for Jews to go back to their Biblical homeland.

Blackstone presented the Memorial to President Harrison six years before world Jewry initiated the first Zionist Congress for the purpose of creating a Jewish state. The Memorial addressed the plight of the Russian Jews and then suggested that Palestine become the Jewish homeland. The idea was that poverty stricken Turkey owned the land of Palestine, and the combined wealth of world Jewry could purchase from Turkey the vast tracts of uninhabited land in Palestine. World Jewry could then relocate in Israel.

Blackstone stated that, "According to God's distribution of nations it is their home, an inalienable possession from which they were expelled by force." The idea of the land being an "inalienable possession" is anchored in the everlasting covenant God made with Abraham, Isaac, Jacob and their descendants. Blackstone used the covenant to show that the land of Israel belonged to the Jewish people! He claimed that Palestine rightfully belonged to Jews.

The Memorial stated it was time for the Christian nations to show kindness to Jews and help restore them to the land. He requested the President call an international conference of all nations to consider a Jewish state and alleviate the suffering of the Russian Jews. Remember, this was years before the initiation of the Jewish Zionist movement. This Memorial in part follows:

> "Why not give Palestine back to them again? According to God's distribution of nations it is their home, an inalienable possession from which they were expelled by force...
>
> We believe this is an appropriate time for all nations and especially the Christian nations of Europe

to show kindness to Israel. A million of exiles, by their terrible suffering, are piteously appealing to our sympathy, justice, and humanity. Let us now restore to them the land of which they were so cruelly despoiled by our Roman ancestors...

To secure the holding at an early date, of an international conference to consider the condition of the Israelites and their claims to Palestine as their ancient home, and to promote, in all other just and proper ways, the alleviation of their suffering condition." (See Addendum D for the complete Memorial)

Over 400 leading Americans from all walks of life signed the Memorial. Many religious leaders from various denominations signed. The greatest evangelist of the era, D.L. Moody signed it along with the outstanding pastor T. De Witt Talmage. Some of the leading members of Congress and mayors of cities signed. The powerful industrialists and bank presidents signed it, such as, John D. Rockefeller, J. P. Morgan, Cyrus McCormick, and Charles Scribner. Editors and publishers from the leading 93 national newspapers and religious periodicals signed it.

Most of America was behind protecting Jews and the creation of a Jewish nation! A brief list of the signatories follows:

Dewitt C. Cregier, Mayor of Chicago
Robert C. Davidson, Mayor of Baltimore
Edwin H. Fitler, Mayor of Philadelphia
Hugh J. Grant, Mayor of New York
N. Matthews Jr., Mayor of Boston
Wm. E. Russell, Governor of Massachusetts
George. Jones, New York Times
Melville W. Fuller, Chief Justice of the United States Supreme Court

T. B. Reed, Speaker House of Representatives
Robert R. Hitt, Chairman House Committee on Foreign Affairs
William. McKinley, Congressman, future President
Several other Congressmen
B.F. Jacobs, President of the Security and Stock Exchange Commission
Cyrus H. McCormick. President McCormick Harvester Company

Blackstone included a cover letter with the Memorial. The cover letter revealed the depth of his literal belief in the Bible as the word of God. Blackstone's faith, with millions of others, was the driving force behind this Memorial. In the letter, he refers to God as the ever living God of Abraham, Isaac and Jacob. Amazingly, like a prophet, he stated this is the time in history for the Gentiles to help bring Jews back to their land. He even refers to Isaiah 49:22 and Ezekiel 34! This section follows:

> "That there seem to be many evidences to show that we have reached the period in the great roll of the centuries, when the ever living God of Abraham, Isaac and Jacob, is lifting up His hand to the Gentiles, (Isa 49:22) to bring His sons and Hs daughters from far, that he may plant them again in their own land, Ezk34, &c. Not for twenty-four centuries, since the days of Cyrus, King of Persia, has there been offered to any mortal such a privileged opportunity to further the purposes of God concerning His ancient people..."

He then closes the letter with an amazing statement. Blackstone requested that the President and Secretary of State take a personal interest in this matter about the Jews. By pursuing this issue, they might receive the promise of God who said to Abraham, "I will bless them that bless thee," Genesis 12:3. This section follows:

> "May it be the high privilege of your Excellency, and the Honorable Secretary to take a personal interest in this great matter, and secure through the Conference, a home for these wandering millions of Israel, and thereby receive to yourselves the promise of Him, who said to Abraham, "I will bless them that bless thee,"
>
> Genesis 12:3.

President Harrison failed to call an international conference or put diplomatic pressure on Russia to end the persecution of Jews. In Harrison's State of the Union message, he mentioned the plight of the Russian Jews, but he failed to act any further.

For the first time in world history, a powerful Gentile nation supported the creation of a Jewish state. Jews found favor at all levels of American society. The Blackstone Memorial showed that America was concerned for the welfare of Jews. But, this concern went beyond welfare; it went all the way to the creation of a Jewish homeland.

Millions of Americans were now praying for the restoration of the Jewish people to their ancient homeland. The Church in the United States, and also to some extent in Great Britain, awakened to the Jewish plight and their need for a homeland. The spiritual force of the Church was now engaged in a real way for God's restoration of Israel.

This awakening never died in America, and remains alive to this day. The support for Israel by Americans is not a recent phenomenon, but its roots go back to 1891 and beyond. It goes back to the founding of America. The Church in America has a special relationship with Jewish people.

Actually, the Blackstone Memorial was just a continuation of the respect Americans had for the Bible and the Jewish people. The long held American benevolent attitude toward Jews flowed right into the Memorial.

Blackstone continued with his efforts for the establishment of a Jewish state. In May 1916, he once again petitioned the United States government to help in the creation of a Jewish state. He presented the Memorial to President Woodrow Wilson who supported the British with the Balfour Declaration. This declaration became the foundation for the modern Jewish state. Blackstone once again called for an international conference to convene for the creation of a Jewish state.

On June 30, 1922, the United States Congress passed a joint resolution supporting the establishment of a Jewish State in Palestine. This resolution put the American government firmly behind the creation of this state. This resolution titled: Favouring the establishment in Palestine of a national home for the Jewish people, follows:

> Resolved by the Senate and the House of Representatives of the United States of America in Congress assembled. That the United States of America favours the establishment in Palestine of a national home for the Jewish people, it being clearly understood that nothing shall be done which should prejudice the civil and religious rights of Christians and all other non-Jewish communities in Palestine, and that the holy places and religious buildings and sites in Palestine shall be adequately protected.

Blackstone's effort in 1891 proved successful as, 31 years later, the United States government officially supported a Jewish state. In 1916, Blackstone was not far off in calling for an international conference. Just six years later, in 1922, the League of Nations convened such a conference. Great Britain assumed the responsibility of overseeing this Jewish state in Palestine. This oversight by Great Britain was called the British Mandate of 1922.

William E. Blackstone (1841-1935)
American evangelist and father of modern Zionism

CHAPTER FIVE

The Tale of Two Countries:
America Blessed, Russia Cursed

"And I will bless them that bless thee, and curse him that curseth thee…"

Genesis 12:3.

*A*merica and Russia provide a good test to the accuracy of the Bible regarding the treatment of Jews. Russia has a long and well established history of hating Jews. America has a long and well established history of accepting and blessing Jewish people. The comparison of these two nations is astonishing. It will show the authority of God's word regarding the blessing or cursing of the Jews: "*And I will bless them that bless thee, and curse him that curseth thee…*" Genesis 12:3.

America and Russia are very similar nations. They both are huge countries in area with large populations. They have great areas of farm land. They have abundant natural resources such as coal, iron, lumber, oil and other minerals. They both have tremendous rivers. They both claim Christianity as the major religion with Russian Orthodox as the state religion of Russia. America did not have a state religion. Bible based Evangelical Christianity greatly influenced America from the very beginning.

In 1727, Queen Catherine of Russia banned all Jews from the country. Russia partitioned Poland in 1772 and huge numbers of Jews came under the authority of the Tsar. The Tsar forced them to live within the Pale of Settlement. This meant the Russians allotted a section of western Russia for Jews called the Pale of Settlement. The Russians prohibited the Jews from traveling beyond "the Pale." Life in the Pale created terrible hardships; however, the pogroms of 1881 became a turning point in the history of the Jews.

With 1881 as the starting point, the blessings and the curses between these two nations becomes very clear. Starting in 1881, Russian Jews experienced a number of pogroms up to the Russian Revolution of 1917. The May Laws of 1882 were the catalyst to begin the massive Jewish exodus from Russia.

After the Civil War, the United States military shrank to almost nothing. By 1880, the American ocean going navy was nonexistent. In 1881 Congress began debating the need for a modern navy. After two years of debate, Congress then passed the Navy Act of 1883. This act called for the building of four modern cruisers. This modest act was the beginning of the United States movement toward becoming a world naval power.

Congress started this debate the very year the great Jewish exodus began from Russia! The Naval Act of 1883 was enacted while tens of thousands of desperate Jews were pouring into America from Russia. The great Jewish exodus from Russia and the American thrust into a world naval power, started the very same year!

America's major thrust toward a world naval power occurred seven years later. In 1890, the Navy Act called for the building of four battleships. This Act propelled America toward becoming a world naval power, as these battleships were able to challenge any navy. In 1890, Christian Zionists and Jews met in Chicago and passed resolutions calling on the Tsar to stop the persecution of the Jews. The following year, this Christian Zionist meeting resulted in the Blackstone Memorial. America's rise to becoming a world power parallels this blessing of the Jews!

On February 15, 1898, the battleship Maine exploded in the harbor of Havana, Cuba. Congress declared war on Spain in April 1898. The war resulted in the complete defeat of Spain. The United States became a major power on the world scene. On July 3, 1898, the American Navy completely destroyed the Spanish Navy at the sea battle of Santiago de Cuba. America went from no navy in 1883 to a world power in just 15 years.

The first Zionist Congress met in Basil, Switzerland in 1897 and called for a Jewish state in Palestine. America was thrust forward just one year after the Zionist Congress called for a Jewish homeland. The ascent of America as a world power and the official birth of modern Zionism coincided. This was not an accident. America was part of God's plan to restore the nation of Israel.

Russia continued its brutal treatment of Jews up to the close of the nineteenth century. Early in the twentieth century, additional vicious pogroms broke out. The pogroms started in the spring of 1903 and continued through 1906. In the middle of the pogroms the Russo-Japanese War of 1904 started. On May 27, 1905, the Japanese totally destroyed the Russian navy at the battle of Tsushima Strait. The Japanese also defeated the Russian army in a series of land battles. During the battle of Mukden, the Russians suffered 90,000 casualties.

By August 1905 Russia wanted to end the war. President Theodore Roosevelt acted as a mediator and the two sides agreed on September 5, 1905, to the Treaty of Portsmouth.

Japan got what it wanted from this treaty and Russia was humiliated. This humiliation of Russia was at the very time a vicious pogrom was taking place!

There is irony to all this. Anti-Jewish Russia had to agree to a treaty mediated by an American President who greatly favored Jews. Russia was driving Jews out and America was taking them in! The Russian emissary came to America to sign the treaty! What irony as Russia, the greatest Jew-hating nation of this time, came to the greatest Jew-favoring nation to sign a humiliating treaty!

President Roosevelt and Portsmouth Treaty delegation.
Notice expression of the Russians

President Roosevelt won the Nobel Peace Prize for his effort in ending the war. He refused to accept the cash award for the Nobel Peace Prize while in office. In 1910, he received $45,482.83 as his cash award. He gave the entire amount to charity including such organizations as the Red Cross and Salvation Army. Then with more irony, he gave $4,000 to the Jewish Welfare Fund! There was no prejudice in the President toward Jews.

In 1898, the United States defeated Spain and became a world sea power while just seven years later in 1905 Russia was humiliated as a world power. America was blessing the Jewish people. Russia was conducting a pogrom.

In 1914, World War I started. Like the Russo-Japanese war nine years before, this conflict resulted in the defeat of Russia and the complete destruction of the Russian army. Before losing the war, the Germans totally annihilated the Russian army. The Russian army literally threw their weapons down, left the battlefield and walked back to Russia. This directly led to the Russian Revolution of 1917 and the Communist control of the country. Following the revolution, pogroms again broke out in Russia until 1921. It is estimated that 100,000 Jews or more were killed at this time.

From 1917 until today, Russia has been a "living hell." Communist tyrants such as Lenin and Stalin rose to power which resulted in tens of millions dying. Millions starved to death and millions died in prison camps. The people lived in terror. When looking at Russia from 1917 forward, it appears that God applied the May Laws of 1882 in the form of Communism to the entire country.

Jews lived in terror. Under Communism, the entire Russian population lived in terror. Jews could not own property. The entire Russian population could not own property. The Tsar forced Jews to relocate. The Communists uprooted huge numbers of Russians and forced them to relocate. The Jewish people starved, while huge numbers of Russians also starved to death. The Tsar hindered Jewish worship, and the entire Soviet Union was forbidden worship under Communism.

The Russian Orthodox Church played a big part in the persecution of Jews. This "church" displayed a vicious hateful spirit toward Jews. In fact, it added to the pogroms and encouraged the attacks. Rather than show the love of Jesus Christ they manifested hatred. V. Pobedonostsev the head of the governing body of this "church" best summed up their position on the May Laws. He expressed hope that "one-third of Jews will convert, one-third will die, and one-third will flee the country."

The Russian Orthodox Church soon suffered as the Jewish people did. The Communists applied their own form of May Laws to the Russian Church. They closed the churches and turned them into museums. The Communists killed huge numbers of ministers and herded the rest into concentration camps. The church was without freedom and actively persecuted by the Communists. The Russian Church suffered under the Communists exactly as Jews suffered under the Tsars, maybe worse!

Communism became the May Laws on a grander scale. It took 36 years for God to apply the principals of the May Laws to the entire country of Russia. Russia remained a living hell until Communism fell in 1989. Even after the fall, Russians are still suffering from poverty and disease. Russians have the lowest life expectancy in the Western World. This country paid a fearful price for violating God's word about blessing the Jews. The prophet Obadiah gave a verse which fits this situation:

"For the day of the LORD is near upon all the heathen: as thou hast done (to Israel), it shall be done unto thee: thy reward shall return upon thine own head."
Obadiah 1:15

In April 1917, the United States entered World War I. The power of the American army helped drive the Germans out of France and affect Germany's surrender. In November 1917, Britain issued the Balfour Declaration which granted Jews the right to return to Palestine and create a nation. The British drove the Turks from Palestine and gained control of Jerusalem in December 1917.

During World War I, Turkey and Germany were allies. A German victory in Europe would have changed the military situation in Palestine. The Germans, teamed with the Turks, would have assured a victory and kept Jerusalem under Turkish control.

The American involvement in the war assured an allied victory and set the stage for the restoration of Israel. The same happened in World War II. God used America to help defeat the Nazis and prevent them from totally destroying European Jewry and the Jewish enclave in Palestine. When David Ben Gurion declared Israel a nation on May 14, 1948, the United States was the first country to recognize the new nation of Israel.

From 1948 onward, the United States became the new nation's best friend in the world. America continues to vote with Israel in the United Nations. The United States supplies Israel with its latest military equipment. Russia continues to curse Israel. The Russians always vote against Israel in the United Nations. Russia continues to supply Israel's enemies with the weapons to attack the Jewish state. These nations included Iraq, Syria, Egypt, and now Iran.

The United States became the leader of the free world. The nation became the greatest military power and the greatest economic power. The nation had the finest universities and medical centers. God blessed America as no other nation.

The contrast between America and Russia is so clear. Russia was cursed in every area while America was blessed.

Freedom abounded in America while the entire nation of Russia came under the "May Laws" of Communism. What a vivid example of blessings or curses. While tens of millions wanted to come to America because of the blessings, who wanted to immigrate to Russia at any time!

It is no accident the United States became a world power in a few years after opening the country to the Russian Jews. God prepared America as protection for the fledgling nation of Israel, and America did its job well. Remember, the evangelical church was the driving force behind America standing with Israel.

CHAPTER SIX

The Valley of Dry Bones Shall Live

"The hand of the LORD was upon me, and carried me out in the spirit of the LORD, and set me down in the midst of the valley which was full of bones...there were very many in the open valley; and, lo, they were very dry...Son of man, can these bones live? And I answered, O Lord GOD, thou knowest."

Ezekiel 37:1.

*A*bout 500 years after Abraham, God created a second covenant. God gave the law of Moses to the children of Israel. The law was a covenant and reflected God's holiness. This time the covenant was conditional and based upon the Jewish people keeping the requirements of the law. The law did not replace the everlasting covenant with Abraham; however, the law was conditional as the following verse shows:

"Now therefore, **if ye** will obey my voice indeed, and
keep my covenant, then ye shall be a peculiar treasure
unto me above all people: for all the earth is mine."

Exodus 19:5.

If the Jewish people obeyed the laws, God would bless them
above all people; however, if they disobeyed He would
punish them. One of the punishments was the destruction of
the nation and the dispersion of the people into all the world.
Either way, the authority of God's word was witnessed
through Israel being blessed above all nations or cursed, and
dispersed into the world.

Israel now reflected God's holy name. The entire world
could witness God's awesome power working through
His people Israel. God linked His plan for the redemption
of mankind directly to the descendants of Abraham. King
Messiah, the Lord Jesus was a son of Abraham.

In the second covenant, the blessings or the curses
depended on the actions of the nation of Israel. God warned
that if the people disobeyed His covenant, He would drive
them off the land and into the nations. He would destroy
Israel because of sin and rebellion against His word. Israel
did break the covenant, and exactly as God had warned, the
nation was destroyed and the people were driven into the all
the countries of the world.

God sent prophet after prophet to warn Israel of the
coming judgment. Ancient Israel rejected the prophets'
warnings and based on the second covenant, the nation
was destroyed. God kept His word. Actually the nation was
destroyed twice. The first destruction, by the Babylonians,
began in 586 BC and lasted 70 years. The second began in
70 AD and lasted until 1967 when Jerusalem was once again
the unified capital of Israel.

The following are some of the Scriptures which warned
Israel of the dispersion into the nations:

"And I will bring the land into desolation: and your enemies which dwell therein shall be astonished at it. (33) And I will scatter you among the heathen, and will draw out a sword after you: and your land shall be desolate, and your cities waste."

Leviticus 26:32, 33.

"And the LORD shall scatter thee among all people, from the one end of the earth even unto the other; and there thou shalt serve other gods, which neither thou nor thy fathers have known, even wood and stone."

Deuteronomy 28:64.

"And it shall come to pass, when all these things are come upon thee, the blessing and the curse, which I have set before thee, and thou shalt call them to mind among all the nations, whither the LORD thy God hath driven thee..."

Deuteronomy 30:1.

In 70 AD, the Roman army destroyed Israel, Jerusalem and the temple. This began the second dispersion; however, this time it was into all the world. God fulfilled His covenant, under the law of Moses with Israel, to the very letter. Remember, the dispersion was not according to the everlasting covenant with Abraham, but it was based on the covenant with Moses. The covenant with Abraham never changed. The dispersion of the Jews was an awesome witness to the authority of God's word, the Bible.

The dispersion was only half the equation. The second part involves God's promise to restore the people back to the land and literally have the nation of Israel reborn. The history of the nation of Israel shows the awesome power of God ruling over the affairs of the nations.

When studying the Bible about the history of Israel, one must understand that Jews are no different to any other people, when it comes to sin. Without understanding the human heart, it could be very easy to condemn Israel for failing God and rebelling against Him. If God had chosen any other people to work through, the result would have been the same.

The sin nature is the same in the Jew as in others and any other people would have also failed. The prophet Jeremiah speaks about the sin nature and states, *"The heart is deceitful above all things, and desperately wicked: who can know it?"*

Although Israel broke the second covenant of the law, God said that He would never completely reject the nation. He would always honor the everlasting covenant with Abraham, Isaac and Jacob and their descendants. Because of this everlasting covenant, He would one day restore the nation of Israel and bring the people back into the land.

Modern Israel exists because of the everlasting covenant. The destruction of Israel and the restoration of the nation, 1900 years later, is an awesome witness to the authority of the Bible as the word of God.

The Bible, with great clarity, states that Israel would one day be reborn, and this would happen because of the everlasting covenant with Abraham. Let us look at some of these verses:

"Then will I remember my covenant with Jacob, and also my covenant with Isaac, and also my covenant with Abraham will I remember; and I will remember the land.

(43) The land also shall be left of them, and shall enjoy her sabbaths, while she lieth desolate without them: and they shall accept of the punishment of their iniquity: because, even because they despised

my judgments, and because their soul abhorred my statutes.

(44) And yet for all that, when they be in the land of their enemies, I will not cast them away, neither will I abhor them, to destroy them utterly, and to break my covenant with them: for I am the LORD their God.

(45) But I will for their sakes remember the covenant of their ancestors, whom I brought forth out of the land of Egypt in the sight of the heathen, that I might be their God: I am the LORD."

Leviticus 26:42-45.

The Ancient Prophets Speak to Us Today

Prophet after prophet in the Bible tells of the restoration of Israel after the dispersion into all the world. God sent prophets to Israel to warn them of the coming judgment on the nation. But, these same prophets also comforted the Jewish people by telling them of the restoration. The prophets also spoke of the coming of the Messiah and the golden age of His rule on earth; however, before the rule of the Messiah, God had to restore the nation.

The theme of the dispersion and restoration of Israel is one of the major focuses in the Bible. There is verse after verse in the Bible about the rebirth of Israel. The prophets Ezekiel and Zechariah devote entire chapters to this theme. The prophecy about the rebirth of Israel from a world-wide dispersion is not a footnote in the Bible. It is written on page after page by prophet after prophet for all to clearly see.

When the prophets spoke about the rebirth of Israel, the everlasting covenant with Abraham was their foundation. This was the foundation of the promise. This covenant was everlasting and not based on performance of the Jewish people. Let us look at what some of these ancient prophets wrote that has such a clear message for today.

Isaiah

About 750 BC, the prophet Isaiah wrote about the rebirth of Israel after a second world-wide dispersion. The first dispersion occurred when King Nebuchadnezzar of Babylon took Israel captive around 600 BC. This captivity was limited to Babylon and the Jews returned to their land 70 years later.

Isaiah prophesied that their return from a world-wide dispersion would be far greater than the one from Babylon. This restoration would bring Jews back from the ends of the earth and this has happened in our lifetime. The Jewish people have now come back to Israel literally from the east, west, north, and south. They have returned from the ends of the earth or as Isaiah calls it the "islands of the sea."

"And it shall come to pass in that day, that the Lord shall set his hand again the second time to recover the remnant of his people, which shall be left, from Assyria, and from Egypt, and from Pathros, and from Cush, and from Elam, and from Shinar, and from Hamath, and from the islands of the sea."

Isaiah 11:11.

"Fear not: for I am with thee: I will bring thy seed from the east, and gather thee from the west;(6) I will say to the north, Give up; and to the south, Keep not back: bring my sons from far, and my daughters from the ends of the earth."

Isaiah 43:5, 6.

Jeremiah

Jeremiah also prophesied at the time of this first dispersion about 600 BC. He warned the people not only of the coming Babylonian captivity but of a greater dispersion into all the world. He prophesied that the people would return from both captivities. Jeremiah, like all the prophets, told of the rebirth of the nation. Jeremiah states that God, by His sovereign will, caused the Jews to return. God scattered the Jews and one day He would restore them to the land. He would be directly involved in leading Jews back to Israel. This regathering of the people was a warning to the nations. Remember, the prophet wrote these verses 2600 years ago.

"Behold, I will bring them from the north country, and gather them from the coasts of the earth, and with them the blind and the lame, the woman with child and her that travaileth with child together: a great company shall return thither.

(9) They shall come with weeping, and with supplications will I lead them: I will cause them to walk by the rivers of waters in a straight way, wherein they shall not stumble: for I am a father to Israel, and Ephraim is my firstborn.

(10) Hear the word of the LORD, O ye nations, and declare it in the isles afar off, and say, He that scattered Israel will gather him, and keep him, as a shepherd doth his flock."

Jeremiah 31:8-10.

Ezekiel

The prophet Ezekiel lived and wrote during the first exile about 570 BC. King Nebuchadnezzar took him captive to Babylon. While in Babylon, Ezekiel wrote incredibly detailed prophecies about the worldwide dispersion and rebirth of the nation of Israel. In beautifully written language with awesome imagery, the prophet gives a detailed look at God's plan for Israel and the nations. Entire chapters of Ezekiel are devoted to the dispersion, restoration, and events that happen after the restoration.

Chapter 36 gives a panoramic view of what was going to happen to Israel. The prophet first mentions the destruction of the nation and the wasting of the land. He then follows with the promise that the land will once again be fruitful and inhabited. Ezekiel promises the Jewish people would again dwell in the land that God promised to their fathers. The fathers are Abraham, Isaac, and Jacob with whom God made the everlasting covenant. Ezekiel links the regathering of Jews from all the nations with the everlasting covenant. Let us look at some of these Scriptures from Ezekiel:

> "And I scattered them among the heathen, and they were dispersed through the countries: according to their way and according to their doings I judged them.
>
> (24) For I will take you from among the heathen, and gather you out of all countries, and will bring you into your own land. (28) And ye shall dwell in the land that I gave to your fathers; and ye shall be my people, and I will be your God."
>
> Ezekiel 36:19, 24.

Ezekiel follows the general statements in chapter 36 about the regathering of the nation by a vivid picture in chapter 37. With some of the most graphic imagery in the entire Bible, Ezekiel describes the rebirth of the nation of Israel. He describes the nation as being a huge pile of dead dried bones lying in a valley.

When reading this chapter, the picture comes to mind of the prophet standing on a mountain ledge overlooking a large valley full of dead men's dry bones. These bones represent the nation of Israel. God gives this picture to show the utter hopelessness of the nation. The nation was completely dead with no hope of ever living. What hope can dead men's bones have for ever living again, none!

To the natural eye, Israel had no hope. The nation was destroyed and the people dispersed into all the world. The Romans destroyed the temple, their center of worship. The Hebrew language was gone. The nations persecuted and rejected them from country to country. The vision of the valley of the dead bones was a perfect picture of the nation of Israel after its destruction in 70 AD. There was no hope.

Ezekiel does not end with the hopelessness. He shows that by a sovereign act of God, the nation was to be reborn. The prophet watched as the nation came together in a piece-meal method. The first step is the bones coming together. The sinew holding the bones follows this. And, finally the flesh covers the bones. At the very end of this process, God put life in the body, and that life will happen at the second coming of the Lord Jesus.

God is working in the affairs of men and governments to resurrect the valley of dried bones into an exceedingly great army. This will happen according to the will of God in order to fulfill His covenant with Abraham, Isaac and Jacob.

Let us look at the picture Ezekiel gives of the hopelessness of the nation of Israel ever being reborn.

"The hand of the LORD was upon me, and carried me out in the spirit of the LORD, and set me down in the midst of the valley which was full of bones, (2) And caused me to pass by them round about: and, behold, there were very many in the open valley; and, lo, they were very dry.

(3) And he said unto me, Son of man, can these bones live? And I answered, O Lord GOD, thou knowest. (4) Again he said unto me, Prophesy upon these bones, and say unto them, O ye dry bones, hear the word of the LORD.

(5) Thus saith the Lord GOD unto these bones; Behold, I will cause breath to enter into you, and ye shall live: (6) And I will lay sinews upon you, and will bring up flesh upon you, and cover you with skin, and put breath in you, and ye shall live; and ye shall know that I am the LORD.

(7)...there was a noise, and behold a shaking, and the bones came together, bone to his bone. (8) And when I beheld, lo, the sinews and the flesh came up upon them, and the skin covered them above: but there was no breath in them.

(9) Then said he unto me, Prophesy unto the wind, prophesy, son of man, and say to the wind, Thus saith the Lord GOD; Come from the four winds, O breath, and breathe upon these slain, that they may live. (10) So I prophesied as he commanded me, and the breath came into them, and they lived, and stood up upon their feet, an exceeding great army."

Ezekiel 37:1-9.

Immediately, after this powerful imagery of the nation, Ezekiel then goes on to explain the vision. There can be no doubt whatsoever as to the theme of this vision. The bones are the people of Israel without hope, and they are dead in the nations. The prophet calls the nations of the world Israel's graves. The coming together of the bones into a body is the nation being reborn:

"Then he said unto me, Son of man, these bones are the whole house of Israel: behold, they say, Our bones are dried, and our hope is lost: we are cut off for our parts. (12) Therefore prophesy and say unto them, Thus saith the Lord GOD; Behold, O my people, I will open your graves, and cause you to come up out of your graves, and bring you into the land of Israel.

(21) And say unto them, Thus saith the Lord GOD; Behold, I will take the children of Israel from among the heathen, whither they be gone, and will gather them on every side, and bring them into their own land:

(25) **And they shall dwell in the land that I have given unto Jacob my servant**, wherein your fathers have dwelt; and they shall dwell therein, even they, and their children, and their children's children for ever:"

Ezekiel 37:11, 12, 21, 25.

Ezekiel connects the resurrection of the dead nation with God granting the land to Jacob. This is again a reference to the everlasting covenant. Time after time, over and over again, the Bible connects the dispersion and then rebirth of Israel to the everlasting covenant. The Bible is crystal clear that when the nation is reborn, it is because God honored His covenant. God is working in the affairs of men and nations to fulfill His ancient promise. God cannot lie, and His word cannot fail.

Zechariah

After the Jews returned to Israel from the Babylonian captivity, Zechariah was one of the prophets. He wrote about 520 BC. Zechariah is unique in that so much of his focus is on the city of Jerusalem. The other prophets talk about the land and some touch upon Jerusalem, but Zechariah gives many details about the city.

The prophet says that God chose Jerusalem for His purpose. Of all the cities of the world, God chose this city to work out His redemption plan for man, "And the LORD shall inherit Judah his portion in the holy land, *and shall choose Jerusalem again.* Zechariah 2:12.

The prophet Zechariah shows that Jerusalem, just as Israel, would be inhabited and restored. The people would come back to Jerusalem from all over the world.

"Thus saith the LORD of hosts; Behold, I will save my people from the east country, and from the west country; (8) And I will bring them, and they shall dwell in the midst of Jerusalem: and they shall be my people, and I will be their God, in truth and in righteousness."

Zechariah 8:7, 8.

The city will be the center for the worship of God. All the peoples from the nations of the world come to Jerusalem. The city will be the center of world attention. Jerusalem is unlike any city in the world because it is the city God chose. This city will be once again the capital of a reborn nation of Israel.

"Yea, many people and strong nations shall come to seek the LORD of hosts in Jerusalem, and to pray before the LORD."

Zechariah 8:22.

"…and Jerusalem shall be inhabited again in her own place, even in Jerusalem."

Zechariah 12:6.

When Jews return from their world-wide dispersion and the nation is reborn, this is the final return. There will be no subsequent third or fourth dispersions into all the world.

For this reason, the events that are unfolding before our very eyes are so significant. God is working in the affairs of the nations bringing Bible prophecy to a conclusion. Remember, when the Jews return from the worldwide dispersion, it is the final one.

The world is now entering into the end play of God's prophetic plan for our age. The prophetic plan centers on the Day of the Lord. The Day of the Lord will be examined later in the book. The prophets have already written the entire script. It is there for everyone to read, understand and believe. Remember, this is the final restoration of the Jews.

"And I will plant them upon their land, and they shall no more be pulled up out of their land which I have given them, saith the LORD thy God."

Amos 9:15.

CHAPTER SEVEN

The Modern
Building of Zion

"When the LORD shall build up Zion, he shall appear in his glory."

Psalm 102:16

*T*he foundation of the Zionist movement began in the 1880's when the Church in America started crying out to God for the persecuted Jews. In 1891, Blackstone petitioned the world governments to create a Jewish homeland in Palestine. With amazing speed, God responded. Just six years later, in 1897, the first Zionist Congress met and launched the modern Zionist movement. The existence of modern Israel can be traced back to 1897 and this congress. It took just 51 more years to the rebirth of Israel in 1948.

During 1894, a sensational trial in France was the catalyst that triggered the Zionist Congress. This incident shook Jewry and sparked the return of Jews in an organized manner back to Israel. The trial revolved around Captain Alfred Dreyfus, an intelligence officer on the French general staff.

The French government charged and convicted him of spying for Germany.

Dreyfus was the only Jew on the general staff, and it became apparent that because he was Jewish, they framed him. The trial had world attention and the media followed it very closely. The trial brought a tremendous wave of anti-Semitism in France.

Theodor Herzl, a Jewish journalist from Switzerland covered this trial. He observed the irrational hatred of Jews in France that this trial caused, because Dreyfus was Jewish. He realized it was only a matter of time before all of Europe exploded with a hatred of Jews. The pogroms were raging in Russia against Jews, and now this hatred in France. This prompted Herzl to take action.

In 1896, Herzl published his book, *The Jewish State: A Modern Solution to the Jewish Question.* The book was almost identical to the ideas found in the Blackstone Memorial. The book called for the creation of a Jewish state and had an enormous impact. It led directly to the founding of the Zionist Organization which spearheaded the return of Jews back to Palestine. The first Zionist Congress then met in August 1897. This meeting set the economic foundation for the modern state of Israel.

Thus, the hatred for Jews in France and Russia set the stage for the rebirth of Israel. The pogroms in Russia started a small trickle of Jews heading to Israel, while the hatred in France, set the ideological framework. God was using this hatred to put in the hearts of Jewish people a desire for Israel. It was the Roman sword which drove them into all the nations, and then European hatred started the drive back.

At one point Herzl had severe doubts about the restoration of Israel in Palestine. Blackstone heard of this and sent Herzl a Bible with all the verses underlined about the Jews returning to Israel. The Herzl Museum in Jerusalem displays this Bible.

The early Zionists recognized the importance of William Blackstone toward the creation of Israel. Louis Brandeis, an Associate Justice of the United States Supreme Court, and also one of the leading Jewish Zionists, stated that Blackstone was the "father of modern Zionism." This is an amazing statement which one can easily overlook. Justice Brandeis, perhaps the leading Zionist of his era, credited Blackstone not Herzl, as the "father of modern Zionism." This shows the powerful connection between the American evangelical church and the formation of modern Israel.

Blackstone addressed the Convention of the Federation of American Zionists in 1916. Justice Brandeis attended this meeting and heard Blackstone speak. He was extremely impressed and realized the significance of the Blackstone Memorial. Justice Brandeis reaction to Blackstone follows:

"Those of you who have read with care the petition presented twenty-five years ago by the Rev. Wm. Blackstone and others, asking that the President of the United States use his influence in the calling together of a Congress of the Nations of the world to consider the Jewish problem with a view to the giving of Palestine to the Jews, must have been struck with the extraordinary coincidence that the arguments which Rev. Blackstone used in that petition were, in large part, the arguments which the great Herzl presented five years later, in setting forth to the world the needs and the hopes of the Jewish people. That coincidence alone, the sameness of the arguments presented in America and later by Herzl, shows how clearly and strongly founded they are."

Zionism and
The End of The Times of the Gentiles

"And they shall fall by the edge of the sword, and shall be led away captive into all nations: and Jerusalem shall be trodden down of the Gentiles, until the times of the Gentiles be fulfilled."

Luke 21:24.

The expression "The times of the Gentiles be fulfilled" by the Lord Jesus means that at some point in history non-Jewish control of Israel, and especially Jerusalem, will cease. The non-Jewish control of Jerusalem had a time period set by God. With the completion of this time period, God would once again restore the nation of Israel.

The times of the Gentiles began in 606 BC when King Nebuchadnezzar first conquered Jerusalem. In 586 BC, he destroyed Jerusalem and led the Jews captive to Babylon. He ended the rule of the Kings of Israel. From 586 BC onward, Israel never had another earthly king. The nation was at the mercy of one empire after another. The Babylonian, Persian, Greek and Roman empires all ruled over Jerusalem. During this entire time, the Jews remained under the everlasting covenant with God. This covenant never ceased.

In 66 AD, the Jews revolted against Rome. In 70 AD, the Roman general Titus destroyed Israel including Jerusalem. The temple was destroyed and never rebuilt. This ended the priesthood and sacrificial system. This resulted in the total destruction of Jerusalem with the Romans killing over one million Jews. The Roman army captured many of the survivors of this war and sold them as slaves.

In 136, the Romans crushed a second Jewish revolt. They then literally plowed up Jerusalem and then salted the soil to poison it. The Roman Emperor Hadrian renamed Jerusalem calling it, Aelia Capitolina. Very few Jews remained on the covenant land. From this time until 1948, the nation of Israel was literally dead. For almost 1900 years, there was no nation of Israel. On May 14, 1948, through United Nations action, Israel once again became a nation. On this day, David Ben-Gurion, the first Prime Minster of the modern state of Israel, proclaimed the State back into existence.

God fulfilled His covenant with Israel by using the Babylonians and Romans. These pagan nations only had authority over God's covenant people because the Jews failed to keep the law. The Babylonians took away the kingdom, and the Romans, the priesthood. They were God's instruments of judgment. The everlasting covenant with Abraham still stood through these judgments.

Even though the Romans completely destroyed the nation, the covenant was still in effect to bring Jews back into the land. The Bible did not mention the duration of the dispersion, but the promise of the restoration remained.

The prophet Hosea, writing about 750 BC, said that Israel would suffer a long time without a king and priesthood. In the latter days they would return to the land. At the end of the age, Jews would return to the land and the coming of the Messiah would follow. They have returned in our lifetime.

"For the children of Israel shall abide many days without a king, and without a prince, and without a sacrifice... (4) Afterward shall the children of Israel return, and seek the LORD their God, and David their king; and shall fear the LORD and his goodness in the latter days."

Hosea 3:3, 4.

The expression seeking David their king, means seeking the Messiah. David had been dead for 200 years when Hosea wrote this. The Messiah was to be a direct descendant of David. He was the son of David, and King over all the earth.

The prophet Jeremiah told of a captivity into Babylon that was to last for 70 years. This captivity did not destroy the priesthood.

When the Jews returned after 70 years, they immediately restored the sacrificial system and rebuilt the temple. The captivity Hosea wrote about was for a very long time during which there would be no sacrificial system. This destruction of the priesthood began in the year 70 AD, and continues to this day.

The Roman destruction of the Jewish temple in Jerusalem has a remarkable similarity with the Babylonian destruction of the temple. This connection is amazing. Both temples were destroyed on the very same day 655 years apart. In 586 BC, King Nebuchadnezzar's Babylonian army broke through the defenses of Jerusalem and stopped the sacrifices in the temple on the 9th of Av.

The Jewish calendar is lunar, and the month of Av would correspond with the months of July and August. Over 600 years later, the Roman army under General Titus broke through the defenses of Jerusalem, destroyed the temple and ended the sacrifices on the same day, the 9th of Av! Both destructions marked the beginning of the Jewish captivity into the nations. They occurred on the same day! To this day, the 9th of Av is a day of mourning to the Jewish people.

With the nation of Israel reborn, the times of the Gentile's rule over Jerusalem is drawing to a close. The events now transpiring are all leading to the final climax between the God of Israel and the nations of the world which have rejected His word. The final world battle recorded in the Bible will take place over Jerusalem and the land of Israel. All the nations of the world will be involved in this final conflict.

This Land That Was Desolate

"And they shall say, This land that was desolate is become like the garden of Eden; and the waste and desolate and ruined cities are become fenced, and are inhabited."

Ezekiel 36:35

The Prophet Ezekiel said Jews would go into all the nations and the land would be desolate. The destruction of the temple in 70 AD began the world-wide dispersion. The Bible does not indicate how long the dispersion would last.

In 136 AD, the Roman army crushed the second revolt. This time they also destroyed a rebuilt Jerusalem with over 500,000 Jewish deaths in Israel. The rest were sold into slavery throughout the Roman Empire. The Romans even changed the name of the area to Philistine. This is where the modern name Palestine originated. God fulfilled His covenant under the law as the Jews were then scattered into all the world and the nation of Israel destroyed.

The death of the physical nation continued for century after century with no end in sight. Empire after empire ruled the area. There was always a small remnant of Jews living on the land and especially in Jerusalem. From 70 AD onward, a remnant of Jews always lived on the land. Jerusalem was never the capital of another nation. The nations that ruled over Jerusalem from the year 70 follow:

1. Romans and Byzantines ruled until 638. Romans first called the land Palestine.
2. Moslems capture Israel and Jerusalem in 638. This began the rule over the area by the Moslem Caliphs and the religion of Islam. They ruled until 1072.
3. Seljukes ruled from 1072 until 1096.
4. Crusaders ruled from 1096 until 1291.

5. Mamelukes ruled from 1291 until 1516.
6. Ottoman Turks ruled from 1516 until 1918. This ended the rule of Islam over the area of Israel.
7. British were given mandate to rule after WWI from 1918 until May 14, 1948.
8. From May 14, 1948, to the present, the nation was once again under Jewish control.

In June 1967, all of Jerusalem came under the authority of the nation of Israel. In July 1980, Jerusalem officially became the capital of Israel. Jerusalem was again the capital, as it was nearly 3,000 years ago under King David.

The Romans, Byzantines, Persians, Arabs, Kurds, Mamelukes, Mongols, Tartars, Crusaders, Turks, French and British invaded the land. Through all of this war and conquest, there was a continual Jewish presence on the land. There never was an independent sovereign nation ruling over the land of Israel; or even a province, with its capital as Jerusalem. Even under the rule of the Ottoman Turks, Jerusalem was a desolate city with Damascus as the provincial capital over it.

God seems to have preserved the land for His covenant people with Jerusalem as the capital. All of those empires came and went, but the Jews re-established their homeland as an independent nation. Nothing in history seems to have prevented the rebirth of the nation.

Jews trickled back to Israel through the early part of the Twentieth Century. The Turks owned the land and Jews bought whatever land they could. In 1914, World War I started. By November 1917, it was apparent that the British were going to defeat the Turks in the Middle East. The Ottoman Empire was coming to an end. In anticipation of this defeat, and with the Turks losing control over the covenant land, British Foreign Secretary Arthur James Balfour issued what is now the famous Balfour Declaration.

This rather short document recognized the right of the Jewish people to return to Israel as a homeland. It seems that World War I prepared *the land* for the return of the Jewish people. The Balfour Declaration follows:

November 2nd, 1917
Dear Lord Rothschild,
I have much pleasure in conveying to you, on behalf of His Majesty's Government, the following declaration of sympathy with Jewish Zionist aspirations which has been submitted to, and approved by, the Cabinet.
"His Majesty's Government view with favour the establishment in Palestine of a national home for the Jewish people, and will use their best endeavors to facilitate the achievement of this object, it being clearly understood that nothing shall be done which may prejudice the civil and religious rights of existing non-Jewish communities in Palestine, or the rights and political status enjoyed by Jews in any other country."
I should be grateful if you would bring this declaration to the knowledge of the Zionist Federation.
Yours sincerely,
Arthur James Balfour

On December 9, 1917, British General Edmund Allenby captured Jerusalem. General Allenby understood the significance of capturing this city. He gave orders that Jerusalem was not to be taken by force. His army was not to shell or fight in Jerusalem. The Turks retreated without firing a shot. Jerusalem and the covenant land fell to the British. For the first time in over 600 years the land was no longer under the control of an Islamic nation. In 1922, the League of Nations placed Britain in charge of a future Jewish state.

The Palestinians refused to recognize the right of Jews to a homeland and rioted. The Arabs put pressure on the British government to restrict Jewish emigration. There were Arab riots throughout the 1920's and 1930's. In 1929 for example, they massacred all the Jews in the city of Hebron. The riots pressured the British to reduce the original land grant planned for the nation of Israel. The rebirth of the nation was not going to be easy. The Moslem resistance that started in the 1920's has continued to this day. There has been continual fighting over the covenant land to this very day.

Throughout history, Moslems fail to recognize the covenant with Abraham, Isaac and Jacob over the land. The establishment of the nation of Israel was extremely difficult, but God's word clearly stated it was going to happen. No force on earth could stop the rebirth of Israel. God had to fulfill the promise in order to bring about His physical redemption of mankind. Israel and Jerusalem both play a key role in this plan. God laid the foundation for modern Israel in 1917.

World War II was the next big step in the rebirth of Israel. Following the horrors of the Nazis and the defeat of Germany, the United Nations was created. In 1947, the UN voted to partition Palestine into two sections. One partition designated a small section of land for Jews. The rebirth of Israel took place on May 14, 1948. The Nazi holocaust of Jews drove many of the survivors out of Europe. They wanted to go to Israel. By 1948, there were approximately 600,000 Jews in Israel. It seems that World War II prepared *the Jewish people* for the land.

The two world wars of the Twentieth Century had an enormous impact on the rebirth of Israel. World War I broke the hold of Islam over the area and prepared the land for the rebirth. World War II prepared the heart of the people to want to go back to the land. Remember, God works in the affairs of the nations to fulfill His covenant with Abraham, Isaac and Jacob. The horrors of the Nazis failed to stop the rebirth of Israel. In fact, the atrocities seemed to accelerate the establishment of the nation.

These wars aided directly in the creation of Israel. Hitler tried to destroy world Jewry. Yet, in just three years after the defeat of the Nazis, Israel was reborn! The Nazi empire was in ashes, while Israel became a nation. What the Nazis did to Jews directly caused the creation of Israel.

God told Ezekiel that He would cause the Jewish people to leave the nations and come back to Israel. The horror of World War II was among one of the main forces that drove Jews back to Israel. The sword drove the Jews from the land, and in many respects it was the sword that drove them back home.

On May 14, 1948, five Arab nations attacked Israel in an attempt to destroy the newly formed nation. Israel took no aggressive action against the Arabs, but the mere existence of the Jewish state was enough for the Arabs to attack. The Arab nations of Egypt, Syria, Iraq, Jordan and Saudi Arabia all attacked. These combined armies were defeated and the nation survived its very difficult rebirth.

When the war ended, Israel was a land area of about 8,000 square miles or the size of New Jersey. The war ended with Jews in control of about two-thirds of Jerusalem. Jordan controlled the rest of the city including the Temple Mount.

The majority of the land for the new nation of Israel came from two sources. Jews bought some of the land from the Turks, and when Turkey was defeated, it turned over to the British tracts of state owned land. Britain then, turned this land over to the newly formed state of Israel.

In 1967, war again broke out. This war became known as the Six Day War. In May 1967, Egypt and Syria mobilized their armies and threatened to attack Israel. The Egyptian army crossed the Suez Canal and headed toward Israel. Egypt demanded that the United Nations peace keepers in the Sinai leave, and Egypt closed the Gulf of Aqaba to Israeli shipping. This action by Egypt was an act of war.

On June 5, the Israeli army attacked Egypt and Syria. This attack crushed the Egyptian and Syrian armies. On the last day of the war, Jordan attacked Israel. In one day, Jordan lost Jerusalem and all the land west of the Jordan River. The tiny nation of Israel became a world military power in only 20 years of existence.

As the ancient prophets stated, Israel was reborn with Jerusalem as the capital. For the first time since 606 BC, Jerusalem was once again the capital of an independent Israel. Jesus Christ said that Jerusalem was God's prophetic timepiece. Just as the Lord Jesus had said in Luke 21:24, all of Jerusalem was again under complete Jewish control. God's unseen hand was working in the affairs of men to fulfill the everlasting covenant.

The fighting over the land continued. In 1973, Syria and Egypt once again attacked Israel. This resulted in the Yom Kippur War. The attack was a complete surprise. This attack came on Yom Kippur, one of Israel's holiest days. The nation was nearly defeated but survived the initial surprise attack and began a powerful counterattack. When a truce was declared, the Israeli army was advancing on both Cairo and Damascus.

The land continues to be a source of turmoil. Fighting continues to rage over the land. The attacks on Israel from Lebanon caused war in the 1980's and 2006. There were riots and terrorist attacks by the Palestinians in the 1980's and 1990's. On September 28, 2000, fighting broke out in Jerusalem over the Temple Mount. This conflict expanded into a low grade war between Israel and the Palestinians. This fighting has the possibility to escalate into a regional war using weapons of mass destruction that could destroy entire nations. The covenant land of Israel has become the source of world attention just as the Bible said it would. God's prophetic word is right on target.

The Latter Day is Today

"Afterward shall the children of Israel return, and seek the LORD their God, and David their king; and shall fear the LORD and his goodness in the latter days."

Hosea 3:5.

The prophet Hosea said in the latter day the Jews would return. Ezekiel also said they would return to Israel in the latter years. Ezekiel described the latter day as the time when Jews would return to Israel from a world-wide dispersion, and the nation was reborn. For centuries upon centuries the land was wasted and the Jews scattered throughout the world.

Ezekiel puts the latter day in the context of Jews returning after a world-wide dispersion. Ezekiel describes a huge army that is going to attack Israel. He then identifies the time when this tremendous confederation of nations is going to attack. This event occurs in the latter years, when the Jewish people return from the dispersion.

"After many days thou (invading army) shalt be visited (mustered): in the **latter years** thou shalt come into the land that is brought back from the sword, and is gathered out of many people, against the mountains of Israel, which have been always waste: but it is brought forth out of the nations, and they shall dwell safely all of them."

Ezekiel 38:8.

The Jews are back and the nation of Israel is a reality. The land for centuries was a true waste land, defoliated of trees and full of malaria swamps. The area was poor with little agriculture. When Jews left, a curse seemed to have settled on the land. Now, with the Jewish people back on the land, it is again flourishing. They planted millions of trees and drained the swamps. Israel has developed a wonderful agricultural industry that supplies Europe with much of its fruit.

In 50 years, Israel has become a world military power with nuclear weapons. The rebirth of Israel is no fluke of history. Israel is the fulfillment of the everlasting covenant God made with Abraham 4,000 years ago.

Viewing Israel as just another nation is a huge mistake. Prior to 100 years ago, if one was to predict that Jews would return to Israel from all over the world; Jerusalem would again be the capital; the land would produce incredible agriculture; and the nation would be a world military power, few if any, would believe. Such a prophecy would have seemed incredible. This is exactly what has happened! If you look at history through the Bible, the modern nation of Israel is supernatural.

No nation in history was destroyed twice similar to Israel. The capital and religious center was twice destroyed. The people en masse were twice taken captive off the land. The second captivity lasted 1900 years. The language was all but extinct. For this nation then to be reborn and have the same capital has a supernatural element! The people even speak the same language and have the same religion.

What force has kept this people as a nation even though they were scattered into all the world for 1900 years? What force kept the language and religion intact? What force has kept the Jews from complete destruction through pogroms, crusades, holocausts, intifadas and all the other attempts to destroy them? Jewish people and the nation of Israel are an enigma unless you understand the Bible.

The rebirth of the nation shows the authority of the Bible as the word of God. It shows the invisible hand of God working to fulfill His word. The everlasting covenant is in effect. The covenant that God made with Abraham, Isaac and Jacob cannot fail. God's covenant is that force which has kept Israel through the centuries. According to the Bible, the return of the Jews makes this time the "latter day."

The nation of Israel was reborn just as the Bible said would happen. We are now living in the times the ancient Jewish prophets wrote about. The prophecy about Israel does not stop with the rebirth of the nation. The Bible has laid out the future. As time goes on, God's prophetic plan as outlined in the Bible has become clearer and clearer.

The nation of Israel, and Jerusalem in particular, are God's timepieces. By watching events involving Israel and Jerusalem the prophetic time can be determined. Jesus Christ said that Jerusalem was God's prophetic timepiece. He said that non-Jews (Gentiles) would tread down Jerusalem until a certain fixed period of time. This fixed period of time had to do with the end of the age and His second coming.

> "And they shall fall by the edge of the sword, and shall be led away captive into all nations: and Jerusalem shall be trodden down of the Gentiles, until the times of the Gentiles be fulfilled."
>
> Luke 21:24

CHAPTER EIGHT

Jerusalem, God's Anvil

Anvil: *An iron or steel block on which objects are hammered into shape.*

"And in that day will I make Jerusalem a burdensome stone for all people: all that burden themselves with it shall be cut in pieces, though all the people of the earth be gathered together against it."

Zechariah 12:3.

The rebirth of the nation of Israel has been a very slow process. The process started in the 1880's and has continued right up to the present time. At times, this process seems to stop and then suddenly a world shaking event takes place that accelerates it.

Jews leaving Russia, and trickling back to Israel, did not seem significant at first. There was just a small steady stream of them from Russia. Then came 1914 World War I and in 1917 the Balfour Declaration. Like an explosion, World War I prepared the land for the return.

The period between world wars was one of tension and terrorism. There was no apparent move of God toward fulfilling the covenant, but then came World War II and the Nazi holocaust. These events set the stage for hundreds of thousands of Jews to flee back to Israel. Almost like an explosion, there were huge numbers of Jews back in Israel. World War II certainly had prepared the people for the land.

Then came the rebirth of the nation on May 14, 1948, and the immediate war that followed. The war ended with Israeli independence, but Jerusalem a divided city. Once again there was a period of tension and terrorism. For 20 years, there seemed no end to the shelling and terrorists attacks. Next came the Six Day War in 1967, and like a bolt of lightning, Jerusalem was the united capital. Since 1967, there has been a major war, plus fighting in Lebanon, continuing terrorist attacks, and several intifadas against Israel.

Starting in September 2000, a low grade war started over Jerusalem. This war was a continuation of the fighting that started in the 1920s. Although the fighting and terrorism appears endless, there will be an end. There seems to be tension, terrorism and fighting between all the major moves of God to restore Israel. The terrorism and fighting against Israel will continue up to the next major event which may be the rebuilding of the temple in Jerusalem.

Jerusalem was united nearly 40 years ago. Now, the focus of tension is over Jerusalem and the Temple Mount area. The Bible states the possession of Jerusalem will be the cause of the last great world war. The issues involving Jerusalem will draw all the nations of the world into this battle. God is going to use Jerusalem as an anvil against the nations of the world. In September 2000, the Temple Mount became the scene of bloody combat. This could be the fuse that ignites the last world war.

God is moving to fulfill the promises of His everlasting covenant, but one needs patience. God moved very slowly with Israel in fulfilling the promise. Looking back since 1917, the Israelis have made tremendous progress as a people and nation. Millions of Jews have returned home. Israel is a nation with Jerusalem as the capital. Israel is a mighty military power with a powerful economy. Hebrew is the national language. In God's time, He will fulfill the rest of the covenant promises. Israel will rebuild a temple in Jerusalem in the near future. It is just a matter of time.

No matter what the British, Moslems, United Nations, European Union or any other group tried, their attempts have not been able to stop the rebirth and development of the nation. Israel is truly like an anvil, and nations are broken that try to destroy God's everlasting covenant. In watching God at work, great patience is required.

The restoration has taken over a century to get this far. God has His own agenda and timetable. Watching Jerusalem, and the intifada that started in September 2000 over the Temple Mount, shows that God's timetable may be accelerating. Remember, Jesus Christ said that Jerusalem was the key to the timetable.

> "And they shall fall by the edge of the sword, and shall be led away captive into all nations: and Jerusalem shall be trodden down of the Gentiles, until the times of the Gentiles be fulfilled."
>
> Luke 21:24.

With the rebirth of Israel and Jerusalem as the capital, this nation becomes an anvil for false views of God and Bible doctrine. Most religions of the world do not recognize God's everlasting covenant with Israel. Some believe Jews had a covenant, but they believe this covenant is no longer in effect.

God is using the restoration of Israel to show the literalness of His word. The rebirth of Israel confronts false teaching, false doctrine and false prophets. Israel becomes an anvil breaking many false doctrines and misunderstandings about the Bible.

Islam

The Islamic religion does not recognize the covenant with Isaac and Jacob, but instead believes God made the covenant with Abraham and Ishmael. The Bible actually states that the everlasting covenant was not with Ishmael but with Isaac. Islam refuses to accept the authority of the Bible and insists the covenant was with Ishmael. It is ironic that Israel was reborn right in the very midst of Islam! The Bible verses to show this follow:

"And God said, Sarah thy wife shall bear thee a son indeed; and thou shalt call his name Isaac: and I will establish my covenant with him for an **everlasting covenant**, and with his seed after him.
(20) And as for Ishmael, I have heard thee: Behold, I have blessed him, and will make him fruitful, and will multiply him exceedingly; twelve princes shall he beget, and I will make him a great nation.
(21) But **my covenant** will I establish with Isaac, which Sarah shall bear unto thee at this set time in the next year."

Genesis 17:19-21.

Islam could not prevent the rebirth of Israel, although they claim the authority of the Koran over the Bible. Islam controlled Palestine for most of the time since 638, yet could not prevent the restoration of Israel. Muslims fought Israel in 1948, 1967, 1973 followed with continuous terrorist acts right up to our present day. With all these wars and attacks, the Muslim nations failed to destroy Israel. Yasser Arafat made his life's goal the destruction of Israel. He is now dead and buried and Israel lives on.

The Koran fails to mention Jerusalem even once, and it does not mention the rebirth of the nation of Israel. The Bible mentions Jerusalem 811 times. The rebirth of Israel is on page after page in the Bible, while the Koran is silent. The rebirth of Israel shows the authority of the Bible as the word of God.

God's everlasting covenant with the rebirth of Israel, are like an anvil against the Koran. The rebirth of Israel is proof that the Koran and Mohammed are incorrect. For this reason, there will always be tension between Israel and Islam. This tension will not last forever.

This tension between Israel and the Koran can never be peacefully resolved. For Islam to recognize the nation of Israel this would be an admission that the Koran and Islam are wrong. Moslem fundamentalists refer to Israel as the "Zionist entity." They refuse to even recognize the existence of the nation of Israel.

There is a huge confrontation on the horizon between the holy God of the Bible and Islam. The heart of the confrontation is Jewish control of Jerusalem. God is using Israel as an anvil against Islam. When the Islamic nations come against Israel and Jerusalem, God will judge them. This destruction will lead them to realize the Bible is the word of God, and the holy God of Israel is the true God.

Thus will I magnify myself, and sanctify myself; and I will be known in the eyes of many nations, and they shall know that I am the LORD."

Ezekiel 38:23.

Christian Replacement Theology

God is using Israel as an anvil against false teachings within the Christian Church. There are false doctrines that are called dominion theology, covenant theology and preterism. These doctrines are fluid and there are many branches to them; however, there is one basic tenet to which they all agree: the christian church has now replaced Israel in the everlasting covenant with Abraham.

These doctrines hold that God has no future plan with national Israel, and when the Roman armies destroyed Jerusalem and the temple in 70 AD, it ended the everlasting covenant. Israel then fell under the curse of the Law, and all the blessings in the Bible now belong to the Church. The Church now is the seed of Abraham. These doctrines falsely state that God has no future with the nation of Israel.

These doctrines are in stark contrast to what prophet after prophet states. Jeremiah, for example, states the LORD will never cast off all Israel for sin. Jeremiah claims that the nation of Israel will remain forever, and God will never cast them all away.

> "Thus saith the LORD, which giveth the sun for a light by day, and the ordinances of the moon and of the stars for a light by night, which divideth the sea when the waves thereof roar; The LORD of hosts is his name:
>
> (36) If those ordinances depart from before me, saith the LORD, then the seed of Israel also shall cease from being a nation before me for ever.
>
> (37) Thus saith the LORD; If heaven above can be measured, and the foundations of the earth searched out beneath, I will also cast off all the seed of Israel for all that they have done, saith the LORD."
>
> Jeremiah 31:35-37

Ezekiel records that God dispersed Israel into all nations because of sin, but God would one day bring them back because of His holy name. God tied His name to the everlasting covenant and for this reason He will restore Israel. God will not restore Israel because of their righteousness but because of His holy name. The nation of Israel exists today only because of the holy name of the God of Israel.

"And I scattered them among the heathen, and they were dispersed through the countries: according to their way and according to their doings I judged them.

(21) But I had pity for mine holy name, which the house of Israel had profaned among the heathen, whither they went. (22) ...Thus saith the Lord GOD; I do not this for your sakes, O house of Israel, but for mine holy name's sake, which ye have profaned among the heathen, whither ye went. (23) And I will sanctify my great name, which was profaned among the heathen...

(24) For I will take you from among the heathen, and gather you out of all countries, and will bring you into your own land.

(28) And ye shall dwell in the land that I gave to your fathers; and ye shall be my people, and I will be your God."

Ezekiel 36:19, 21-24, 28

Zechariah prophesied the restoration of Israel; however, when they return it is in unbelief toward God and the Messiah, the Lord Jesus Christ. The prophet shows God will restore Jerusalem, and He will judge the nations for trying to destroy Jerusalem. At the time of this judgment, then Israel turns to belief in the Lord Jesus, *"...and they shall look upon me whom they have pierced, and they shall mourn for him..."*

Israel is in unbelief today, just as Zechariah stated would happen. The day of their restoration to the Lord God of Israel remains yet in the future:

> "And it shall come to pass in that day, that I will seek to destroy all the nations that come against Jerusalem. (10) And I will pour upon the house of David, and upon the inhabitants of Jerusalem, the spirit of grace and of supplications: and they shall look upon me whom they have pierced, and they shall mourn for him, as one mourneth for his only son, and shall be in bitterness for him, as one that is in bitterness for his firstborn."
>
> Zechariah 12:9, 10.

God is using the rebirth of Israel to prove these replacement doctrines are incorrect. Just as Moses and the prophets wrote, the physical descendants of Abraham have returned and restored the nation. In the Bible, Jerusalem literally means the city of Jerusalem. Israel means Israel, and one cannot spiritualize it to mean the Church. Islam and replacement theology both refuse to believe the Bible about the restoration of Israel and Jerusalem. These combined false beliefs fail to prevent the restoration of Israel.

If this restoration of Israel is not of God, then what is it? Could it be a Divine trick of some sort? Page after page in the Bible prophesied the restoration. The restoration of modern Israel matches these prophecies of the Bible. So, it comes down to the final authority. Is a manmade doctrine like replacement theology or Islam the final authority, or the Bible with its clear verses that establish the restoration of Israel?

The restoration of Israel smashes replacement theology. This restoration proves the error of this belief system. The foundation of replacement theology is very simple. It rests upon unbelief in God's word. This is a very serious error that leads to consequences with God, including spiritual blindness.

To try and get around the error of the replacement and covenant theology, some believers in these doctrines have gone so far as to say that the Jews in Israel are not real Jews. When the Tsar was killing "Jews" in the Russian pogroms, no one said to the Tsar "stop they are not real Jews." When the Nazis were killing these "Jews", no one said to Adolph "stop they are not real Jews." Now, when these same "Jews" go back to Israel, all of a sudden they are no longer Jews!

God is using the rebirth of Israel to cut right through false and incorrect views of His word. The promise of God in the Bible is crystal clear on page after page. Manmade doctrines and false prophets have tried to alter this covenant, but in the latter day, God has made the truth clear for all to see. God is very serious about His word. *Then said the LORD unto me, Thou hast well seen: for I will hasten my word to perform it.* Jeremiah 1:12.

Belief in false doctrines concerning the literalness of the rebirth of Israel blinds people to the work of God that is occurring right before their eyes. God is moving to fulfill His word, and millions cannot see it because they are following false prophets or wrong doctrine about Israel and Jerusalem. The very sad part is that believers in Jesus Christ, because of false doctrine, are actually against the work of God. Many fail to support God's covenant nation and oppose it, because of a false understanding of Israel, and the everlasting covenant.

Replacement theology and Islam are in 100 percent agreement against Israel. They both refuse to recognize that Israel exists because of the everlasting covenant. It is a scary thought that someone who names Jesus as their Savior, can be in such rebellion against God that they are in agreement with Islam. As time goes on, the faithful Church will grow closer and closer with Israel while the church in great error may grow closer to Islam.

It is very serious, to be on the wrong side of God when He is defending His everlasting covenant. The wrong doctrine can cause apathy toward Israel and the Jews. This can lead to failure to pray for and support Israel in a time of crisis. This incorrect doctrine blinds a person's ability to recognize God's judgment falling on America for forcing Israel to divide the covenant land. Therefore, this person is spiritually unable to intercede for America as it faces judgment.

God is very serious about the land and covenant. The Lord God of Israel will literally use Jerusalem as an anvil to destroy the nations that come against it. Jerusalem will draw the nations like a moth to a light. Multitudes of people have rejected God and the Bible or just do not believe His word. This rebellion will cause the nations to come against God's anvil. God has warned beforehand what happens, when armies try to destroy Israel and take Jerusalem. The entire world will see the mighty power of God, as He uses Israel as His anvil.

Thus God is using the rebirth of Israel to expose false prophets, false doctrines, and to have a literal witness on the earth to the authority of His word. It is important that one's faith be in accord with the truth of the Bible. God's word has been tested in the furnace of the earth. The Bible has proven itself to be like pure gold and silver. The everlasting covenant has been tested now for 4,000 years of history. It is in effect for all to see. God's is faithful to His word and promises.

Application to join the American Nazi Party

The application reads: I hereby apply for admission to the membership in the "German American Bund." The purpose and aims of the Bund are known to me, and I obligate myself to support them to the best of my ability. I recognize the leadership principle, in accordance to which the Bund is being directed. I am of Aryan descent, free from Jewish or colored blood.

Anschriften der Ortsgruppen von Gross New York

ASTORIA
Amerikadeutscher Volksbund, c o Turnhalle, 44-01 Broadway, Astoria, L. I.

BERGEN COUNTY
Amerikadeutscher Volksbund. P. O. Box 128, Hackensack, N. J.

BROOKLYN
Amerikadeutscher Volksbund, 267 St. Nicholas Avenue, Brooklyn, N. Y.

BROOKLYN SOUTH
Amerikadeutscher Volksbund, Prospect Hall, Prospect Ave., Brooklyn, N. Y.

BRONX
Amerikadeutscher Volksbund, New Hofbrau, 222½ St. Anns Ave., Bronx, N. Y.

HUDSON COUNTY
Amerikadeutscher Volksbund, 754 Palisade Avenue, Union City, N. J.

JAMAICA
Amerikadeutscher Volksbund. 168-15 91. Avenue, Jamaica, L. I.

LINDENHURST
Amerikadeutscher Volksbund, P. O. Box 555, Lindenhurst, L. I.

NASSAU COUNTY
Amerikadeutscher Volksbund, Brauhof, 3rd Street and Jericho Turnpike, New Hyde Park, L. I.

NEWARK
Amerikadeutscher Volksbund, P. O. Box 65, Irvington, N. J.

NEW ROCHELLE
Amerikadeutscher Volksbund, P. O. Box 724, New Rochelle, N. Y.

NEW YORK
Amerikadeutscher Volksbund, P. O. Box 75, Station K, New York, N. Y.

PASSAIC COUNTY
Amerikadeutscher Volksbund, 269 Passaic Street, Passaic, N. J.

STATEN ISLAND
Amerikadeutscher Volksbund, Atlantic Rotisserie, 191 Canal Street, Stapleton, St. Isl.

WHITE PLAINS
Amerikadeutscher Volksbund, Odd Fellows Home, Main Street, White Plains, N. Y.

YONKERS
Amerikadeutscher Volksbund, Polish Community Center, 92 Waverley Street, Yonkers, N. Y.

National Archives

Bund chapter locations in NYC area

DEUTSCHER TAG

von

LONG ISLAND

AUF

Camp Siegfried

AM SONNTAG, 14. AUGUST 1938

UNTER DER PAROLE

„Allen Gewalten zum Trotz sich erhalten"

Für Ehre, Recht und Freiheit,

Für ein starkes, nationalbewusstes und sozialgerechtes Amerika

◆◆◆◆◆◆

═══════════PROGRAMM═══════════

Feldgottesdienst: Pastor Kropp

Fahnenaufmarsch - Der grosse Festakt - Militär-Konzert - Sportliche Wettkämpfe

Volksbelustigungen aller Art - Luna Park-Betrieb - Abends Tanz

RIESEN-FEUERWERK

Kommt in Scharen und beweist, dass wir DOCH zusammenhalten können!

Kinder frei!	EINTRITT 25 CENTS		Parken 25 Cents

3 special trains leave Penn. Station New York and Flatbush Station Brooklyn

first train		second train		third train	
Lv. New York	8.51 AM	Lv. New York	10.38 AM	Lv. New York	11.45 AM
Lv. Woodside	8.59 AM	Lv. Woodside	10.39 AM	Lv. Woodside	11.54 AM
Lv. Flatbush	8.48 AM	Lv. Flatbush	10.21 AM	Lv. Flatbush	11.35 AM
Lv. Jamaica	9.11 AM	Lv. Jamaica	10.52 AM	Lv. Jamaica	12.07 PM
Ar. Yaphank	10.30 AM	Ar. Yaphank	11.55 AM	Ar. Yaphank	1.10 PM

Trains leave Yaphank 9.58 PM; 10.58 PM and 11.58 PM.   Roundtrip $1.25; Children 6-12 years 65 cents; under 6 years free.

UNTER DEN AUSPIZIEN DES

Amerikadeutscher Volksbund

Ad for largest Nazi meeting outside Germany
(Notice train schedules—This was the Siegfried Special to Yaphank, 8/14/38

143

Corbis

Main entrance to Camp Siegfried

National Archives

Youth Parade Camp Siegfried 1937

Das Wirtschaftsgebäude auf „Camp Siegfried"

American Jewish Archives

**Nazi headquarters at Camp Siegfried,
ground zero for the Bund.**

Bettmann/Corbis

**Fritz Kuhn, Bund Fuehrer,
leading Nazi salute, Camp Siegfried 8/29/37.**

Bettmann/Corbis

Meeting at Camp Siegfried German Day 1937

Bettmann/Corbis

Large groups of Bundists with Nazi salute at Camp Siegfried

Bundist marching in NYC 10/30/37

Corbis

Corbis

Then, Adolph Hitler Street, Camp Siegfried 1938

Jesse McTernan

**Now, John McTernan at corner of Hitler St (Park Blvd)
and Goering St (Oak St.) Yaphank, NY.**

President Bush Library

President George H. W. Bush speaking at Madrid 10/30/91.
The speech that altered the course of America.

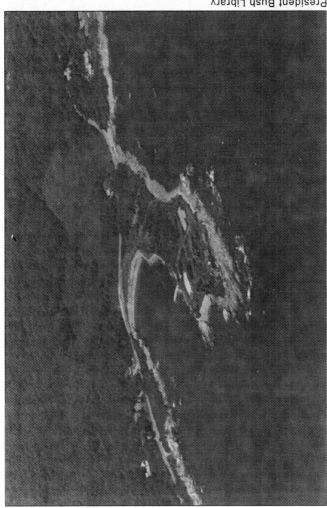

President Bush Library

Aerial view of President Bush's home Kennebunkport, Maine

Bettmann/Corbis

**Destructive power of the Great Hurricane,
Westhampton Beach, Long Island**

Bettmann/Corbis

Awesome destruction of New London, Conn. 9/21/38

National Archives

Power of Great Hurricane's storm surge, Rhode Island

National Archives

Some of the 110,000 WPA workers sent to New England

National Archives

Millions of trees fell like this all over New England.

Thousands of homes destroyed by storm surge.

National Archives

Hurricane takes train off tracks in Mass!

National Archives

The Great Hurricane destroyed entire forests.

CHAPTER NINE

America On a
Collision Course With God

"For, behold, in those days, and in that time, when I
shall bring again the captivity of Judah and Jerusalem,
I will also gather all nations, and will bring them
down into the valley of Jehoshaphat, and will plead
(punish, judge) with them there for my people and for
my heritage Israel, whom they have scattered among
the nations, and parted (divided) my land."

Joel 3:1, 2.

God greatly used America in His plan for the Jewish
people and the nation of Israel. From its very beginning, the United States was a source of protection and blessings to them. Millions of Jews escaped the tyrants of Europe
and found safety in America. God used the Church in the
United States during the late 1880s as the spiritual catalyst
for Jews to return to Israel. America cooperated with God's
agenda for Israel. This assistance continued until 1991. That

year, was the turning point as the United States began to directly interfere with God's prophetic plan.

The first phase in God's plan was restoring Israel to the covenant area of land. The second phase involved judging the nations for unbelief and rejecting God's covenant. The third phase will usher in the Second Coming of the Lord Jesus. And, connected with the third phase, is the nation of Israel turning to the Lord Jesus for salvation. Jerusalem is the central location of His Second Coming, as the Bible shows He will stand on the Mount of Olives. The second and third phases are examined in subsequent chapters.

"For I will gather all nations against Jerusalem to battle… (3) Then shall the LORD go forth, and fight against those nations, as when he fought in the day of battle. (4) And his feet shall stand in that day upon the mount of Olives, which is before Jerusalem on the east…"

Zechariah 14:2-4.

The restoration of the nation under the first phase includes Jerusalem, Gaza, Judea, Samaria, the Mountains of Israel, the Golan Heights and other areas. The prophets are very clear in their writings, that when the nation of Israel is reborn it contains specific land areas. Let us look at a few of the prophets and what they state Israel's boundaries will resemble when restored.

The prophet Obadiah writes about the time period just prior to the Day of the Lord. This is the time period immediately prior to the Second Coming of Jesus Christ. Obadiah says that fierce fighting erupts between Jews and Arabs over the land but that the Jewish people prevail. The fighting reaches the point where the Israelis drive all the Arabs from the land. In the following verse, Jews are the houses of Jacob and Joseph, while the Palestinians are the house of Esau.

"And the house of Jacob shall be a fire, and the house of Joseph a flame, and the house of Esau for stubble, and they shall kindle in them, and devour them; and there shall not be any remaining of the house of Esau; for the LORD hath spoken it."

Obadiah 1:18.

The prophet then writes that Jews will possess the Plain of the Philistines, (modern Gaza); and Ephraim and Samaria, this is most of the West Bank. The land of Israel also comprises Gilead which is the western section of Jordan. The land of the Canaanites and Jerusalem includes the rest of modern Israel.

"And they of the south shall possess the mount of Esau; and they of the plain the Philistines: and they shall possess the fields of Ephraim, and the fields of Samaria: and Benjamin shall possess Gilead.

(20) And the captivity of this host of the children of Israel shall possess that of the Canaanites, even unto Zarephath; and the captivity of Jerusalem, which is in Sepharad, shall possess the cities of the south."

Obadiah 1:19, 20.

The prophet Ezekiel wrote a very detailed description of a geographic location he identified as the Mountains of Israel. This mountain chain runs north – south, straight down the center of Israel. These mountains start about 50 miles north of Jerusalem and then run south until Hebron. Jerusalem is located in this mountain range.

The prophet writes that when the Jewish people return, they will inhabit these mountains and God blesses them. The control of this mountain chain by the Israelis is extremely important in Bible prophecy. Today, the Mountains of Israel are located in the West Bank and control is in dispute between the Arabs and Israelis. According to the Bible there is no dispute, they belong to Israel.

> "And I will bring them out from the people, and gather them from the countries, and will bring them to their own land, and feed them upon the mountains of Israel by the rivers, and in all the inhabited places of the country." Ezekiel 34:13.
>
> "For I will take you from among the heathen, and gather you out of all countries, and will bring you into your own land."
>
> Ezekiel 36:24.

The prophet Zechariah states that God brings the Jewish people from all over the world back to Jerusalem. The city is restored as Israel's capital. This restoration is very important in both phase one and two of God's prophetic plan.

> "Thus saith the LORD of hosts; Behold, I will save my people from the east country, and from the west country; (8) And I will bring them, and they shall dwell in the midst of Jerusalem..." Zechariah 8:7.
>
> "And it shall come to pass in that day, that I will seek to destroy all the nations that come against Jerusalem."
>
> Zechariah 12:9.

In 1991, President George H.W. Bush led America to victory over Iraq in the Desert Storm War. Following the war, President Bush took upon himself the creation of a comprehensive peace plan for the Middle East. In October 1991, he convened the Madrid Peace Process. The heart of this peace plan involved Israel and the covenant land. The President used the power of the United States to pressure

Israel into this peace process with the Palestinians, Syrians and Egyptians. The focus of the peace process was Israel giving away land for peace. The term "peace plan" was a code word that meant Israel must surrender covenant land. The "negotiable" area was a part of the land grant God gave Abraham, Isaac and Jacob and their descendants. It was the land that Obadiah, Ezekiel and Zechariah so clearly wrote about, that God restores to the reborn nation of Israel.

President Bush brought the United States into a direct head-on confrontation with God. The prophets wrote that this land was not negotiable, as it was part of restored Israel. President Bush said it was negotiable, and for the sake of peace, must be surrendered. The President placed the United States in a position diametrically opposed to God's word.

In 1993 the Madrid Peace Plan evolved into the Oslo Accords. The Oslo Accords set a timetable for Israel's withdrawal from parts of the covenant land. The Oslo Accords also focused on the issue of Jerusalem. By 1998, seven years after the peace process started, the heart of the land issue centered on Jerusalem. The United States became the prime force in this peace process.

The prophet Joel states that God judges nations which are involved in parting the land of Israel. Jerusalem is God's anvil for any nation that tries to divide this city. This includes the United States of America. The United States challenged God's word regarding Jerusalem. In November 1991, President Bush Sr. started the peace process. President Clinton continued it, and President George W. Bush followed through.

President Clinton pressured Israel to give away large sections of the land, and he made Jerusalem negotiable. He condemned Israel for building apartments in East Jerusalem. Presidents Bush Sr. and Clinton brought America into a confrontation with God over Jerusalem and Israel; however, President George W. Bush went even further.

President George W. Bush committed the United States to recognizing a Palestinian State. He first announced this during his speech to the United Nations on November 10, 2001. This was the first time a United States President used the words "Palestinian State." This speech was an historic event. The two-state idea was later reinforced, when after the President's speech, Secretary of State, Colin Powell met with Yasser Arafat. A section of the President's speech follows:

> "The American government also stands by its commitment to a just peace in the Middle East. We are working toward a day when two states, Israel and Palestine, live peacefully together within secure and recognized borders as called for by the Security Council resolutions. We will do all in our power to bring both parties back into negotiations..."

President Bush then made a major policy speech on June 24, 2002. During this speech, he expanded upon his United Nations' speech. He called for two states, Israel and Palestine, living side by side. He totally committed the United States to the creation of a Palestinian state.

He directed Secretary of State Powell to work with international leaders to fulfill his vision of a Palestinian state. The President continued by stating the Israeli occupation of Palestinian land since 1967 needed to end, and United Nations Resolutions 242 and 338 are the documents for settling Israel's borders. This meant Israel was required to withdraw from huge sections of the covenant land including East Jerusalem. He referred to his plan as the "Road Map to Peace."

Part of the President's speech of June 24, follows:

"This means that the Israeli occupation that began in 1967 will be ended through a settlement negotiated between the parties, based on U.N. Resolutions 242 and 338, with Israeli withdrawal to secure and recognized borders."

The President remained focused on his "Road Map to Peace," and the two-state position. Time and again, since June 24, 2002, he reaffirmed his agenda. Thus this was a fixed American policy, which started in October 1991 by President George Bush Sr.

Since November 1991, God warned America that the nation was on a collision course with Him over Jerusalem and the covenant land. As America pressured Israel to surrender land, warning-judgments hit the nation.

These warning-judgments occurred through all three presidencies, whether democrat or republican. These judgments resulted in some of the greatest natural disasters in the nation's history. They include three of the most expensive natural disasters in history, Hurricane Andrew, the Northridge earthquake, and Hurricane Katrina. These disasters occurred on the very days the United States government pressured Israel to divide the land.

America is no longer cooperating with God's agenda, but is actually hindering it. This appears to be happening by ignorance of the everlasting covenant. Presidents Bush Sr., Clinton and Bush Jr. did not purposely try to thwart God's word. It appears they are doing this for political expedience. The word of God is clear that their actions against Israel bring judgment.

A president acting in ignorance of God's word is no excuse. The Prophet Hosea warns that lacking knowledge of the Bible leads to destruction, *"My people are destroyed for lack of knowledge..."* The Presidents' personal ignorance of the Bible, plus the church leaders' failure to warn the Presidents, placed the United States in grave danger. Most likely the religious leaders believe replacement theology; therefore, their doctrine blinds them to the warning-judgments.

America is trying to divide the covenant land and God judges any nation for this. God is trying to warn America of the awful consequences of interfering with His prophetic plan. God always warns before judgment, and He uses people as His instrument of warning.

For example, Noah warned the people for 120 years prior to the great flood. Before God judged the ancient Canaanites, He warned them for 400 years. He warned Israel, with prophet after prophet, for close to two hundred years before the Babylonian captivity. He warned Israel through the New Testament apostles and prophets for 40 years before the second dispersion. God is now warning America.

The Bible lists all of God's warnings. God is verifying these warnings with awesome disasters which have hit America on the very day the nation pressured Israel to divide the covenant land. For example, every time Yasser Arafat came to America there was an awesome disaster. At some point, the warning-judgments cross over to destruction-judgments. The destruction-judgments will break the nation and stop the interference with God's plan for Israel. There is no recovery from destruction-judgments. It appears Hurricane Katrina was the first destruction-judgment.

God takes His covenant with Abraham, Isaac and Jacob very seriously. The judgments begin after a nation hardens it heart and is adamant against His word. It appears that the rebellion and unbelief in God's word has now taken America to the brink of wrath-judgments.

God has warned and warned, but most people seem asleep. Maybe, unbelief toward the Bible and also replacement theology has taken its toll on the spiritual discernment of the people. God has warned but are people making the connection?

The following is a partial list of the warning-judgments that have hit America. These events all happened on the very day the nation pressured Israel to divide the land. God loves America. He is trying to warn the nation of this collision course with Him. God is very serious about not dividing Israel and Jerusalem. He will not allow any nation to thwart His prophetic plan. The following examples bring to reality the authority of God's word.

"I will also gather all nations, and will bring them down into the valley of Jehoshaphat, and will plead with them there for my people and for my heritage Israel, whom they have scattered among the nations, **and parted my land.**"

Joel 3:2.

October 1991

After the Gulf War ended in 1991, President George H. W. Bush began the initiative to start a Middle East Peace plan involving Israel, the Palestinians, and countries surrounding Israel. The talks began on October 30, 1991, in Madrid, Spain. On October 30, 1991, President Bush opened the talks with a speech. In this speech, the President said, "territorial compromise is essential for peace."

From the very start of the Madrid Peace Process, the President made it very clear that Israel was required to surrender parts of the covenant land for peace. This surrender was the foundation of this peace process. The following excerpt of the President's speech shows this:

"Throughout the Middle East, we seek a stable and enduring settlement. We've not defined what this means. Indeed, I make these points with no map showing where the final borders are to be drawn.

167

Nevertheless we believe territorial compromise is essential for peace." (See centerfold for a picture of President Bush speaking at the Madrid Peace Conference.)

In their opening speeches, the Egyptian, Syrian and Palestinian delegations said that for peace Israel must surrender land. At the very beginning of these talks, the land of Israel was the key issue. The Egyptian Foreign Minister, Amr Moussa summarized the Arab position regarding the land of Israel. He listed and addressed four points and three dealt with the land of Israel. Jerusalem became the very heart of this conference. An excerpt of Mr. Moussa's speech follows:

"Secondly, the West Bank, Gaza and the Golan Heights are occupied territories.

Thirdly, settlements established in territories occupied since 67, including Jerusalem are illegal, and more settlements will foreclose potential progress toward real peace and cast doubts on the credibility of the process itself.

Fourthly, the holy city of Jerusalem has its special status...The occupying power should not exercise monopoly or illegal sovereignty over the holy city. It should not persist in unilateral decisions declared to annex the holy city as this lacks validity or legitimacy."

On October 30, a powerful storm developed off Nova Scotia. The storm caught the National Weather Bureau completely by surprise. It just suddenly developed from unusual weather patterns and unleashed tremendous power. These weather patterns occur once every 100 years. The National Weather Service never officially named this storm although it did reach hurricane strength.

This storm was extremely rare, because it traveled for 1,000 miles in an eastward to westward direction. This was the wrong direction because the weather pattern for the United States is westward to eastward! Meteorologists called this storm extra - tropical because it did not originate in the tropics, as do most hurricanes.

On October 31, this ferocious storm smashed into New England. It was a monster hundreds of miles wide. The National Weather Service later nicknamed this hurricane, "The Perfect Storm." Sebastian Junger wrote a best selling book about this storm, and even a motion picture was made capturing the drama of ships caught in it. The *Perfect Storm* was the title of both the book and movie.

Meteorologists described The Perfect Storm as one of the most powerful to ever occur! It created ocean waves over 100 feet high which were among the highest ever recorded. The Perfect Storm traveled down the East Coast into the Carolinas doing millions of dollars in damage. The storm damaged the entire East Coast from Maine to Florida. Remember, this storm was going the wrong way! The Perfect Storm caused damage which classified it among powerful hurricanes.

President Bush owns a home along the East Coast in Kennebunkport, Maine. The Perfect Storm heavily damaged President Bush's home. Eyewitnesses said that waves as high as 30 feet rose from the ocean and smashed into the President's sea front home. When the President returned from Madrid, he canceled speaking engagements to inspect the damage done to his home. (See centerfold for a picture of President Bush's home in Kennebunkport.)

This storm hit the President's home the same day he initiated the Madrid Peace Conference. What awesome timing for this to happen! An extremely rare and powerful storm developed in the North Atlantic Ocean and went 1000 miles the wrong way. The storm then struck the President's own home, the very day he was opening the Madrid Peace

Conference. The President's land was touched the very day he attempted to touch the covenant land of Israel!

The front page headlines of the USA Today newspaper on November 1, even had the Madrid conference and The Perfect Storm next to each other! The newspaper titled one article, "One-on-one peace talks next." The article touching it was titled, "East Coast hit hard by rare storm."

At the very beginning of a peace plan involving Israel, a rare and powerful storm, smashed into the entire East Coast of the United States. On October 30, 1991, the Lord God of Israel put America on notice.

August 1992

On August 24, 1992, the Madrid Peace Conference moved to Washington, DC. The nations involved felt the United States was a better location for continuing the negotiations. The key issue remained for Israel to surrender land for peace. The United States representative was the Acting Secretary of State, Lawrence Eagleburger. The New York Times interviewed Eagleburger about the opening of the Madrid Peace talks in Washington and part of the interview follows:

> The peace talks were resuming "in the context of an Israeli Government that is prepared to be far more forth coming." He predicted that the issue of Palestinian self-rule in the Israeli-occupied territories would be the focus of discussion.

On August 24, 1992, Hurricane Andrew smashed into Southern Florida. Hurricane Andrew was the worst natural disaster, up to this time, ever to hit America. This storm left 180,000 homeless in Florida and another 25,000 in Louisiana. The hurricane caused an estimated $30 billion in damage.

This was an awesome category 5 hurricane with top winds recorded at over 175 mph. The winds were even stronger, but the hurricane destroyed the anemometer, the wind speed device, before the eye hit. The winds may have reached 200 mph or higher! The National Hurricane Center described this storm as a 25 to 30 mile-wide tornado! Hurricane Andrew struck just a few hours before the Madrid peace conference met in Washington, DC. It was one of the greatest natural disasters ever in American history. There was no mistaking that the purpose of this conference was to divide the land of Israel.

On August 24, the front-page headlines of the USA Today newspaper contained several articles so that one could visually make a link between the hurricane and the Madrid Peace Process. These headlines follow:

"1 Million flee Andrew,"   **"Mideast peace talks**
"This will make Hugo look weak,"   **to resume on positive**
                                        note."
"Monster storm targets Fla."

A few days after the hurricane on August 26, the front page of the New York Times contained three articles where one could visually link the Madrid Peace Process with the disaster. The articles and the order in which they appeared follow:

"Bush's Gains   **"Israel Offers Plan For**   **"Thousands**
From Convention   **Arabs to Rule in**   **Homeless in**
Nearly Evaporate   **Occupied Lands"**   **Florida"**
in the Latest Poll"

The Madrid meeting article was at the top in the very center of the front page while the hurricane story was directly to the right. Directly to the left of the Madrid Peace Plan article, was a story about President Bush's ratings collapsing in the polls. At this time, Bill Clinton, Bush's presidential challenger, was leading in the polls by a substantial margin.

It was just a year before, following his victory in the Iraq War, President Bush's approval rating was a tremendous 92 percent. In October 1991, he personally initiated the Madrid Peace Process and pressured Israel into these negotiations. By August 1992, less than one year later, he crashed in the polls and was heading for a re-election defeat. The irony was that President Bush's crashing in the polls coincided with the Madrid Peace Process meeting in Washington, DC. He initiated the peace process in 1991, and when the first meeting took place on American soil in 1992, his popularity was crashing.

Thus three major events converged on the same day. The Madrid Peace Process meeting for the first time on American soil; the destruction caused by Hurricane Andrew; and the collapse of the Presidency of George H.W. Bush.

The man, who initiated the plan forcing Israel to give away land, was removed from office almost exactly one year after the beginning of the meetings. His political collapse was apparent, for all to see, at the exact time the Peace Process moved to America! The timing of all this was breath taking. The front page of the nation's largest national newspapers once again, plastered this link between dividing the land of Israel and judgment. God hid nothing.

September 1993

On September 1, 1993, the front-page headline of the New York Times newspaper read: "Israel and PLO Ready to Declare Joint Recognition." and the subtitle: "Met Secretly in Europe." The article went on to say that diplomatic action was going on secretly in Europe. They reached an agreement known as the Oslo Peace Accords.

This agreement involved Israel surrendering Gaza and Jericho, followed quickly by the rest of the West Bank, to the Palestinians. In return, the Palestinians agreed to recognize the state of Israel and live in peace. This peace plan was to conclude within seven years ending in September 2000. Israeli Prime Minister Yitzhak Rabin and Yasser Arafat agreed to sign this document in Washington on September 13, 1993. At this time, the agreement failed to address the issue of Jerusalem as the negotiators put it off for two years.

Also, the New York Times had a second front page headline article which was titled, "Hurricane Hits Outer Banks as Thousands Seek Safety Inland." Hurricane Emily had meandered across the Atlantic Ocean for five days, but finally hit North Carolina the very day of this peace accord agreement! This Hurricane had 115 mph winds. It brushed the coast of North Carolina, and it then turned and headed out to sea. The damage caused by this hurricane was light.

Hurricane Emily was the third hurricane to hit the United States on the very day Israel was planning to surrender covenant land. The pattern was firmly established. The United States interfered with God's prophetic plan, and on the first three occasions, three hurricanes hit! The judgment-warnings were crystal clear.

January 1994

On January 16, 1994, President Clinton met with Syria's dictator, President Hafez Assad in Geneva. They met to discuss peace between Israel and Syria. President Clinton said Syria was ready for a peace agreement with Israel. He said this peace agreement included Israel giving the Golan Heights to Syria. (The Golan is the border between Syria and Israel. In 1967 during war with Syria, Israel gained this territory. The Golan is part of the land covenant given to Abraham.) The newspapers quoted President Clinton as saying, "Israel must make concessions that will be politically unpopular with many Israelis."

On January 17, 1994, a powerful 6.8 magnitude earthquake rocked the Los Angeles area. Northridge was the center of this quake, about 25 miles from downtown Los Angeles. This powerful quake caused an estimated $25 billion in damage with widespread destruction. The quake was so powerful that it caused the Santa Susanna Mountains to rise one foot and the Los Angeles basin area to shrink. This was a massive movement of a huge land area.

What is extremely interesting about this earthquake was that scientists failed to identify the fault which triggered this quake. The location of the fault that caused the earthquake was a mystery to scientists. This powerful earthquake just seemed to happen. The scientists also found this earthquake appeared as two separate quakes. The first earthquake movement was a powerful upward thrust followed by a violent shaking of the earth. The upward thrust was so powerful that it lifted buildings off their foundations. Scientists described this earthquake as having a "one-two punch."

Less than 24 hours after President Clinton pressured Israel to give away Israel's covenant land, a unique, powerful and damaging earthquake rocked America. What an awesome warning-judgment to America!

March - April 1997

On March 1, Yasser Arafat left Israel and arrived in Washington, DC. for a meeting with President Clinton. They discussed the building of a Jewish housing project in an East Jerusalem section called Har Homa. The Palestinians claimed this section of Jerusalem. The Israeli government began building 6,500 housing units in Har Homa. Arafat was upset and met with President Clinton to discuss this issue.

President Clinton gave Arafat a warm welcome. The New York Times reported the meeting with this headline article: "Welcoming Arafat, Clinton Rebukes Israel." The President rebuked Israel for building the homes in East Jerusalem, and he condemned Israel for creating mistrust.

Arafat went on a speaking tour of the United States and many warmly received him. He also spoke in the United Nations about the situation in Jerusalem. In one speech he used the example of the Vatican in Rome as an example of what should happen in Jerusalem, a proposed Palestinian city within Jerusalem.

The issue of Israel building homes in Jerusalem upset the entire world. On five separate occasions between March 6 and July 15, the United Nations Security Council and the General Assembly voted to condemn Israel for building homes in East Jerusalem. The entire world was upset because the Israelis were building houses in Jerusalem! A percentage of these homes were for Arabs.

On March 6, the Security Council voted and strongly criticized Israel. The resolution said that the housing was a violation of international law and a threat to peace in the Middle East. The United States vetoed the resolution which prevented it from becoming official; however, outside of the United Nations, the Clinton Administration condemned Israel for the building project.

On March 13, the General Assembly voted again to condemn Israel for building homes in East Jerusalem. The vote was 130-2 condemning Israel. Only Israel and the United States voted against the resolution while 51 nations abstained. The resolution stated that the housing was illegal and a major obstacle to peace. This vote demonstrated the strength of the world's unified opposition against Jerusalem. Outside of the United Nations, President Clinton continued the condemnation of Israel. All this international condemnation of Israel was over the mere building of homes in East Jerusalem!

On March 21, the Security Council again voted to condemn Israel, and once again the United States vetoed the resolution. The United States criticized Israel outside the United Nations for the housing project. On April 25, the General Assembly demanded by a 134-3 vote that Israel stop the housing project in Jerusalem. The resolution also called for international action against Israel. The United States voted against the resolution.

On July 15, the General Assembly again voted by 131-3 for a resolution to condemn Israel for the housing project. This was the strongest resolution yet, as it called for an economic boycott of products made in Jewish settlements in the disputed areas of Israel, including Jerusalem. The United States voted against this resolution.

On March 1, when Arafat arrived in America until mid-April, Israel was constantly under criticism by the Clinton administration for the housing project in Jerusalem. The United States supported Israel in the United Nations, but outside of the UN, President Clinton constantly criticized Israel.

On the very day Arafat landed in America, powerful tornadoes devastated huge sections of the nation. It was one of the worst tornado storms in the nation's history. The states of Texas, Arkansas, Tennessee, Kentucky and Ohio suffered tremendous damage. While Arafat was on this speaking tour, railing against Israel, these storms stalled over Ohio and caused tremendous flooding.

The tornadoes destroyed Arkadelphia, Arkansas, while the flooding destroyed Falmouth, Kentucky. The storms did over one billion dollars in damage. Also, heavy snows fell during March and April in the Northern Plains. These snows melted in April causing the worst flooding of the Red River in a century. The flooding hit the Dakotas hard and caused more than a billion dollars in damage.

The New York Times headlines captured this link between President Clinton meeting with Arafat and condemning Israel, and the destructive tornadoes that devastated Arkansas. On March 4, 1997, the front-page headlines said, *"In Storms Wake Grief and Shock."* Directly touching this article was a picture of President Clinton with Arafat. The heading of the picture said, *"President Clinton Rebukes Israel."* The front page of a national newspaper actually had the destruction caused by the tornadoes and the rebuking of Israel touching each other! The New York Times linked this together so clearly!

On March 11, the Stock Market reached an all time high of 7,085. The Market had been steadily increasing since October 1996. On March 13, the UN General Assembly voted overwhelmingly to condemn Israel, and on this day the Stock Market plunged 160 points. The Market continued to plunge until April 13, when it stabilized and then resumed its upward climb. Between March 13 and April 13, the Market lost 694 points.

On April 7, President Clinton met with Israeli Prime Minister Benjamin Netanyahu to discuss the peace process and the building of homes in East Jerusalem. This meeting coincided with the plunge in the Market. Prime Minister Netanyahu refused to stop the building of the homes. After this meeting, the attacks against Israel over Jerusalem subsided. President Clinton stopped the condemnation of Israel. Very soon after this, the Stock Market stabilized.

March and April 1997, were awesome months for God dealing with America. The combination of Arafat coming to America and Clinton rebuking Israel, all coincided with some of the worst tornadoes and flooding in the last century. It also coincided with the storms in the Dakotas which resulted in the worst flooding ever. Both of these disasters caused billions of dollars in damages. The tornadoes and flooding destroyed entire towns like Arkadelphia, Arkansas; Falmouth, Kentucky; and Grand Forks, North Dakota. The Bible states God judges the nations that divide the land of Israel. In March and April, America pressured Israel for building homes in East Jerusalem and suffered terribly.

As the United Nations condemned Israel over Jerusalem, the Stock Market began to melt down. The very day of the General Assembly's condemnation of Israel over Jerusalem, the Market began a month long slide. The American Market affects the entire world. As the world, through the United Nations came against Israel, the world's largest Stock Market collapsed.

It is interesting to note that Wall Street, the location of the Market, and the United Nations are both located in New York City. God touched the land of America and the Stock Market at the same time the United States touched Jerusalem.

January 1998

On January 21, Israeli Prime Minister Netanyahu met with President Clinton. They discussed the peace plan and Israel surrendering covenant land for peace. In the lead up to the meeting, Netanyahu was under tremendous political pressure at home. Also, Clinton was pressuring Israel. In Israel, there was pressure on Netanyahu not to surrender land. The pressure was so great that politicians in Israel threatened a vote of no confidence of Netanyahu's government, if he gave away the land. This would result in new Israeli elections for a new government.

Clinton met with Netanyahu and coldly received him. Clinton and Secretary of State Albright refused to have lunch with him. Shortly after the meeting ended, a sex scandal involving Clinton became headline news. Clinton became totally involved in the scandal. Clinton was unable to devote any time to Israel. He met with Arafat the next day, but at that time, there was no effort to pressure Israel into surrendering land.

Netanyahu came to the meeting with the possibility that his government might fall. How ironic that literally right after the meeting, it was President Clinton's administration that was in trouble. The President was humiliated and faced legal action against him. On the very day Clinton pressured Israel to give away land; he was humiliated by a sex scandal. Netanyahu returned to Israel as a "conquering hero" because he did not surrender any land.

Because of this scandal, the legal action against the President continued until he appeared before a grand jury on August 17. After his grand jury appearance, the President addressed the nation and admitted he had lied to the grand jury when he testified under oath in January. On September 9, the House of Representatives received the report to determine the possible impeachment and removal of the President from office.

On October 8, 1998, the House of Representatives voted for an impeachment inquiry of President Clinton. On December 11, 1998, the Judiciary Committee of the House of Representatives began deliberations. The purpose was possible articles of impeachment against President Clinton. On December 12 the Committee completed the deliberation and voted to approve four Articles of Impeachment. The Committee then forwarded the articles to the House for an impeachment vote.

What was truly amazing, as the Committee was voting on the four Articles of Impeachment, President Clinton landed in the Palestinian controlled section of Israel! He agreed in October to visit Israel to insure the Wye agreement moved forward. The timing was such that it occurred at the exact time the House issued Articles of Impeachment against him!

Literally, as he landed in Israel, the House of Representatives drew up the four articles of impeachment against him!

On December 11, the headline articles of major newspapers placed the impeachment and Clinton's visit to Israel on the front page. The radio and television news reports linked the stories back to back. The Associated Press reported that the President went to Israel, **"Under an impeachment cloud."** Every type of media tied the Articles of Impeachment and Clinton's Mideast trip together. Everyone following the news could not miss that the House completed the Articles of Impeachment against President Clinton while he was in Israel.

The news sources reported that the President was the first in United States history to visit the Palestinian ruled territory, and that his visit was giving statehood status to the Palestinians. The capital of this state was to be Jerusalem! These same news sources reported that this impeachment of the President was the first in 130 years!

On December 15 President Clinton returned to Washington. Just four days later the House of Representatives voted to accept two of the Articles of Impeachment against the President. The House sent the articles to the Senate for a trial. At every turn of the President's impeachment proceedings, he was pressuring Israel over the covenant land.

September 1998

On September 24, 1998, President Clinton announced a meeting with Yasser Arafat and Israel's Prime Minister Benjamin Netanyahu. The purpose of the meeting was to discuss the stalled peace plan. The President wanted Israel to surrender an additional 13 percent of its land. On this same day the headlines of the national newspapers read that Hurricane Georges was gaining strength and heading toward the Gulf of Mexico. The headlines of the USA Today stated, "Georges gaining strength, Killer storm zeros in on Key West."

On September 27, Secretary of State Madeleine Albright met with Arafat in New York City. Albright was working out final arrangements for Israel to surrender 13 percent of its land. On September 27, Hurricane Georges slammed into the Gulf Coast with 110 mph winds with gusts up to 175 mph. The eye of the storm struck Mississippi and did extensive damage eastward into the Florida panhandle. This hurricane hit the coast and then stalled. The hurricane moved very slowly inland and dumped tremendous amounts of rain causing severe flooding.

On September 28, President Clinton met with both Arafat and Netanyahu in the White House. The meeting was to finalize Israel dividing the land. The three agreed to meet on October 15 and formally announce the agreement. The headlines of the USA Today newspaper stated, "Georges lingers." The article next to it was, "Meeting puts Mideast talks back in motion." The newspapers actually had the hurricane and the Israeli peace talks next to each other on the front page! The New York Times also headlined the hurricane and peace talks together on the front page.

On September 28 Arafat addressed the United Nations and talked about an independent Palestinian state by May 1999. The General Assembly gave Arafat a rousing and sustained ovation when he addressed it. As Arafat was speaking, Hurricane Georges was still smashing the Gulf Coast causing $1 billion in damage! Arafat finished his business in the UN and then left America. Hurricane Georges then dissipated.

October 1998

On October 15, 1998, Yasser Arafat and Benjamin Netanyahu met at Wye Plantation, Maryland, to continue the talks which had ended on September 28. They scheduled the talks for five days, and it centered on Israel giving away 13 percent of the West Bank land. The talks stalled, but President Clinton pressured them to continue until they reached a settlement. They agreed to extend the talks which finally concluded on October 23. In the end, Israel agreed to surrender the land for assurances of peace by Arafat.

On October 17, awesome rains and tornadoes hit eastern Texas. Twenty inches of rain in one day deluged the San Antonio area! The rains caused flash floods and destroyed thousands of homes. Rivers swelled to incredible size. The Guadalupe River, which was normally 150 feet wide, swelled three to five miles wide. The powerful floods nearly swallowed up small towns. The rains and floods continued until October 22 (the end of the Middle East talks) and then subsided. The rains and floods ravaged 25 percent of Texas and did over $1 billion in damage.

On October 21, President Clinton declared this section of Texas a major disaster area, and directed the Federal Emergency Management Agency (FEMA) to assist in the relief for the flood-ravaged families. This was a record flood that hit Texas.

For almost the entire time of the Middle East talks, awesome rains and storms were smashing Texas. The national newspapers once again had the Middle East talks and disaster together on the front page! As the talks ended, the storms and flooding in Texas ended. Once again President Clinton had to declare a section of America a disaster area, at the exact time he was meeting with Arafat to divide Israel!

May 1999

On May 3, 1999, starting at 4:47 P.M. (Central Standard Time), the most powerful tornado storms ever to hit the United States fell on Oklahoma and Kansas. The meteorologists officially measured the winds at 316 MPH making it the fastest ever recorded. The meteorologists nearly classified this tornado as an F-6 on the rating scale. There has never been an F-6 tornado. The storm included many F-4 tornadoes and F-5 tornadoes (F-5 have winds over 260 MPH) which are extremely rare. There were almost 50 confirmed tornadoes with nearly 200 warnings! One F-5 tornado was over a mile wide and traveled for four hours covering 80 miles on the ground. It destroyed everything in its path. This twister was unprecedented in the history of tornadoes. Category F-5 make up less than one percent of all tornadoes. Tornadoes are usually a couple of hundred yards wide at the most, not over a mile; they seldom last for more than 10 - 15 minutes, not for four hours; they stay on the ground for a couple minutes, not four hours.

The damage from this storm was incredible. The headlines of the newspapers stated: "Everything was gone - At least 43 dead in monstrous Plains tornadoes;" "20 hours of terror:" "Stark scene: Miles of devastation;" "Tornadoes shred state." The National Oceanic and Atmospheric Administration stated, "This is an outbreak of historic proportions, no doubt about it." Oklahoma Governor Frank Keating said, "This is the most calamitous storm we've ever seen and probably one of the more calamitous that ever hit the interior of the United States."

The tornadoes destroyed more than 2,000 homes in Oklahoma City alone. Entire small communities disappeared as the winds leveled everything in the towns and destroyed thousands of vehicles. The town of Mulhall, Oklahoma ceased to exist. The storm's destruction totaled billions of dollars. On May 4, the federal government declared large sections of Oklahoma and Kansas as disaster areas.

The storm warnings began at 4:47 PM (CST). In Israel this would haven been 1:00 AM on May 4. May 4 was the date

Yasser Arafat was scheduled to declare a Palestinian state with Jerusalem as its capital. At the request of President Clinton, he agreed to postpone this declaration until December 1999. President Clinton had already stated the Palestinians should have a state and that Jerusalem was negotiable. He even refused to move the United States embassy to Jerusalem.

On May 4 President Clinton declared parts of Oklahoma and Kansas disaster areas. On this very same day the President sent a letter to Arafat. In the letter Clinton, encouraged Arafat's aspirations for his "own land," the President said the Palestinians had a right to "determine their own future on their own land," and the Palestinians deserved "to live free, today, tomorrow and forever."

What an awesome warning to America. Possibly the most powerful tornadoes ever to hit the United States fell the same day (May 4 Israeli time) that Arafat was to proclaim a Palestinian state with Jerusalem as its capital. The very same day Clinton encouraged Arafat about the Palestinian state, he declared parts of America a disaster area from the worst tornadoes in history.

September 1999

Hurricanes

In late August, Hurricane Dennis began to affect the East Coast. This hurricane moved very slowly up the coast drenching the states of Florida, Georgia, and the Carolinas. This was not a powerful hurricane, being a Category 2 with sustained winds of 105 mph. Although this hurricane was not powerful, it had tremendous rainfall.

Hurricane Dennis slowly moved up the coast and then stopped directly east of the Outer Banks of North Carolina. Dennis then acted very strangely. After stalling off North Carolina, the hurricane actually started backwards along the course it came. Then the hurricane reversed itself and came back along the same course. It then stalled again off the Outer Banks and began to drift eastward. Finally, on September 3, after five straight days of lingering off the coast, Dennis struck North Carolina. Dennis' winds diminished quickly and did not cause tremendous damage. However, Dennis dropped tremendous amounts of rain and flooding occurred. On September 1, Secretary of State, Madeleine Albright flew to the Middle East. Albright met with several Arab leaders before meeting with Yasser Arafat and Israeli Prime Minister Ehud Barak on September 3. The purpose of Albright's visit was to restart the Wye agreement which had stalled.

Hurricane Dennis lingered off the coast of North Carolina for nearly a week. The hurricane traveled in a bizarre path. At one point it actually reversed itself, and at another time was heading away from the coast. At nearly the exact time Albright met in Israel to assist in giving away the covenant land, Hurricane Dennis came ashore! This hurricane was literally doing circles in the Atlantic Ocean until the meeting in Israel. On this very day, the hurricane then hit the United States. Remember this hurricane did not do tremendous damage, but it did drop enormous amounts of rain. This would prove to be extremely important just two weeks later when Hurricane Floyd hit.

On September 13, 1999, the Israeli Foreign Minister and one of Arafat's deputies met to work out arrangements for the "Final Status" of Israel giving land away. This meeting was a result of Secretary Albright's trip the week before. On September 13, 1999, Hurricane Floyd strengthened into a very dangerous Category 5 storm with sustained winds of 155 mph.

The forecasters at the National Hurricane Center were astonished how quickly Floyd grew in size and strength in one day. The actual statement was, **"Floyd grew unexpectedly**

into a monster of a storm on Sunday." This was the very day the meeting took place in Israel to surrender the land.

On September 16, Hurricane Floyd slammed into North Carolina. Floyd's winds had diminished to 105 mph which was a Category 2, but the hurricane was huge in size. Hurricane force winds extended 150 miles in front of it. This hurricane caused the greatest evacuation in American history up to this time. As the storm moved up the coast, it caused the evacuation of literally millions of people in front of it.

The awesome destructive force of this storm was the rains. Heavy rains of 20 inches or more fell over the entire eastern part of North Carolina. Hurricane Dennis hit just two weeks before which caused swollen rivers. The destruction of this storm was awesome as it destroyed the entire eastern section of the State, some 18,000 square miles. Twenty-eight counties declared a state of emergency, and a few were nearly totally destroyed.

The destruction closed some 400-500 roads. Farmers estimated the storm killed over 100,000 hogs, 2.47 million chickens and over 500,000 turkeys, along with huge amounts of horses and cattle. The floods knocked out sewerage and water systems. Sewage, chemicals, and dead animals all flowed into the rivers creating an environmental nightmare. The estimated damage to agriculture was $1 billion. The loss to buildings, homes and roads was in the billions. This was the greatest disaster to hit North Carolina since the Civil War.

Thus while the Israelis were meeting with the Palestinians to give away the covenant land, a monster storm ravaged almost the entire East Coast of America.

Stock Market

On September 21, the Dow Jones industrial average fell 225 points for the steepest loss in four months. On September 22, the stock market lost 74 points, and the next day, September 23 the market fell 205 points. The total loss for the three days was 504 points. This was the first time in the history of the stock market it suffered two 200 points losses during the same week! What was amazing about the loss was that it coincided exactly with Arafat visiting President Clinton. They met on September 22, the day between the two 200 point losses on the stock market! Arafat then left Clinton and went to the United Nations. There, he asked the UN to back independence for a Palestinian state. The stock market dropped 524 points for the week that Arafat visited.

October 1999

During the week of October 11, the Israeli government evicted Jewish settlers on 15 West Bank hilltops. The settlers resisted this eviction and the national media reported this confrontation. Remember, President Clinton was the power behind Israel trading land for peace.

On October 16, the New York Times ran a front page article about this confrontation titled, "On the West Bank, a Mellow View of Eviction." What is amazing, also on the front page was an article titled, "Big Sell Off Caps Dow's Worst Week Since October '89." During the week, the market lost 5.7 percent, and it was the worst week since October 1989.

While Israel was forcing the settlers off the covenant land, the stock market was melting down. On October 15, the market lost 266 points! Also on October 15, Hurricane Irene hit North Carolina, and on the morning of the 16th, a powerful 7.1 earthquake rocked the Southwest.

On October 16, the fifth most powerful earthquake to hit America in the 20th Century struck California. The earthquake was 7.1 in magnitude and was located in the desert near a sparsely populated area. The earthquake did little damage but shook three states. The earthquake was so powerful that it tore a 25 mile long gash in the earth. Millions of people in California, Nevada and Arizona felt the power of the quake.

This quake triggered small quakes near the San Andreas Fault which was 120 miles away. Seismologists referred to this as "nerve-rattling conversation" between the two fault lines. Earthquakes as powerful as 4.0 occurred a few miles from the San Andreas fault.

Thus, in a 12 hour span, the stock market closed down 266 points, a hurricane hit the East Coast, and a huge earthquake rocked the West Coast. This all occurred as Jewish settlers were being evicted from the covenant land!

January 2000

On January 3, 2000, President Clinton met with Ehud Barak, the Israeli Prime Minister, and Farouk al-Shara, the Foreign Minister of Syria. They discussed peace between Israel and Syria. This peace plan called for Israel to surrender the Golan Heights. The Golan Heights is critical to Israel's defense. Prior to 1967, Syria controlled the Golan Heights and used this area as an artillery base to shell Israel. The talks were to last two days, January 3 and 4.

On January 4, Israel's Prime Minister agreed to transfer five percent of this territory to the Palestinians. They were to complete the transfer by the end of the week. The hand over of this land came from previous agreements brokered by President Clinton.

By December 31, 1999, the stock market had reached its all time high for this period. On January 4, 2000, the stock market plummeted. Both the Dow and NASDAQ plunged. The Dow fell 359 points for the fourth worst one day decline, and the NASDAQ fell 229 points for the worst drop ever. The combined losses in money for the one day were $600 billion. During the exact time period of the meetings, these stock markets were reeling with huge losses.

When the meetings were completed, the market recovered the losses and went on to register huge gains. The New York Times reflected on the stock market activity for the week with an article titled, "The 3 U.S. Stock Gauges Rally to End a Turbulent Week."

March - April 2000

On March 10, 2000, the NASDAQ reached its all time high of 5048 points. This date proved to be the high water mark for the stock market. The DOW Industrials had already peaked in January 2000. The NASDAQ would soon spiral out of control and lose thousands of points. In a short time, the NASDAQ would lose $4 trillion and never fully recover.

On March 10, 2000, Israel's Prime Minister, Ehud Barak for the first time, agreed to a Palestinian state. After years of negotiations, Israel officially stated on this date it would recognize a Palestinian state. This action by Israel coincided on the very day with the high water mark of the stock market.

In April, President Clinton summoned Israel's Prime Minister Ehud Barak to Washington, DC for a conference regarding the peace process. They met on April 12. President Clinton wanted to get more involved in the peace process. On April 11, 12, and 13, the NASDAQ section of the stock market collapsed. For these three days the market fell over 600 points. The NASDAQ trades in the technical stocks and during the 1990s it had grown $4 trillion dollars in value. For this week, the NASDAQ fell 618 points for the worst week ever.

At the precise time that Israel's Prime Minister was in Washington to meet with President Clinton, the stock market collapsed into the NASDAQ's worst week in history. There was an apparent connection between Barak and Arafat coming to America to discuss the peace process, and huge convulsions in the stock market.

July - August 2000

Starting on July 12, 2000, President Clinton, Israeli Prime Minister Ehud Barak and Palestinian leader Yasser Arafat met at Camp David, Maryland to try and reach an agreement for peace. The talks continued until July 26, when they collapsed. The talks collapsed over Jerusalem.

President Clinton personally was involved in trying to divide Jerusalem into Moslem and Jewish sections. The talks also involved giving away huge sections of land to Palestinian control which the President supported. The Israelis and Palestinians failed to reach an agreement. Arafat made statements that he was declaring a Palestinian state with or without an agreement. Tension became very high after the meeting.

As the meeting was taking place, tremendous forest fires erupted in the West. The fires exploded in intensity at the end of July and then burned out of control during August. By the end of August, some of the worse fires of the century burnt nearly seven million acres. The federal government declared the states of Montana and Wyoming as disaster areas. There was no hope of putting the fires out and only the winter snows and rains could do it.

All available forest fire fighters in America were fighting these fires. The states called for the army and National Guard to help fight the fires. Fire fighters came from all over the world to help. More than 25,000 were battling the fires.

The weather conditions for the fires were the equivalent to The Perfect Storm. Agriculture Secretary Dan Glickman reported the weather patterns over the western section of America were ideal for the fires and were similar to the odd meteorological events that created The Perfect Storm.

There were high temperatures, low humidity, lightning storms with no rain, and high winds. This pattern lasted for months on end. During the month of July, the rains stopped in Texas. On July 28, then Governor George Bush declared the state a disaster area for 195 counties because of the drought and fires. The state also went through the entire month of August without rain. The drought of over 60 days was compared to the one that caused the "Dust Bowl" of 1934. The drought of July-August 2000 was the worst in the state's history.

September - December 2000

On September 28, 2000, which was Rosh Hashana, the Jewish New Year, Ariel Sharon, the famous Israeli General, went to the Temple Mount in Jerusalem. This visit sparked riots. The causes were attributed to the failed Camp David meetings in July 2000. During these meetings, President Clinton pressured Israel to give away large areas of Jewish settlements and sections of East Jerusalem. The sections of Jerusalem included the Temple Mount. The failure of the Camp David meetings destabilized the political situation between the Israelis and Palestinians.

By the end of October 2000, Prime Minister Barak's government had collapsed and Israel was without a government. In the face of the rioting, public support eroded and the Barak government collapsed. Israel had no government!

On December 9, 2000, Barak resigned his position as Prime Minister and called for new elections. The elections were set for February 2001. From the end of October to December 9, Israel was in political chaos.

The United States held its presidential election on November 7. The election resulted in total political chaos as neither candidate won enough electoral votes. The State of

Florida's election results were key in determining the winner of the election.

The election dragged on and on until the Florida election went to the United States Supreme Court. On December 12, 2000, the court made a ruling that resulted in George W. Bush being declared the winner. From November 7, until December 12, the United States government was in disarray. There was no elected government.

President Clinton's action destabilized the Israeli government. Almost during the exact time the Israeli government was in chaos, the United States government was destabilized and in chaos. On December 9, the election was set in Israel. A few days later the United States Supreme Court settled the American election. Both governments were in chaos at nearly the exact time! What happened to the Israeli government, happened at the same time to the American government! The country that was responsible for destabilizing Israel was itself destabilized at the very same time!

The United States Presidential Election was in total chaos. The election was held on November 7. President Clinton invited Arafat to Washington for the purpose of renewing the peace talks. The peace talks had completely broken down after the Camp David failure in July 2000.

Arafat arrived in Washington on November 9, as the United States was in the worst presidential crisis in over 100 years! Arafat met with President Clinton just two days after the election, while the election process was melting down! On November 9, the media headlines displayed the political crisis and also Arafat meeting with Clinton!

June 2001

On June 8 and 9, 2001, one of the greatest rainfalls in the history of the United States happened in eastern Texas. In a 24-hour period, over 28 inches of rain fell in the Houston area. In fact, between June 5 and 11, three feet of rain fell on the area.

The rain was the product of Tropical Storm Allison, whose 10 day history will go down in Weather Bureau records as "weird." Allison formed within one day in the Gulf of Mexico, which was unusual. This storm then headed into Texas, east of Houston and broke up as a storm system. The remnants drifted to the north of Houston and circled around the city before sliding back south to the Gulf. The storm then re-formed into a tropical storm, which began to unleash incredible torrents of rain starting the evening of June 8 and into the next day.

The destruction in Houston alone was catastrophic. The floods destroyed or damaged an estimated 25,000 homes and businesses along with possibly 50,000 automobiles and trucks. The storm closed the city for three days. The federal government declared 28 counties in Texas a disaster area along with 14 parishes in Louisiana. The resulting damage was close to $3 billion in Houston and $4 billion in the state.

This was an incredible storm that did tremendous damage to southeast Texas. The storm then moved into Florida and up the East Coast. The federal government declared disaster areas all the way to Pennsylvania. Meteorologists claim that Allison was the worst tropical storm in history. In the 10 day life of this storm, it unleashed enough rain for the entire United States for a year!

Texas is President Bush's home state. He was vacationing at his ranch in Crawford, Texas at the time of the flooding. He declared the 28 counties in Texas a federal disaster area while he was in Texas.

On June 6, President Bush sent CIA director George Tenet to Israel to try and broker a cease-fire between the Israelis and the Palestinians. This was the Bush administration's first real involvement in the Middle East crisis. Tenet's mission was for Israel to stop building in the settlement areas.

Tenet arrived in the Middle East on June 6. On June 8, the Central Intelligence Agency director hosted talks between senior Israeli and Palestinian security officials, while Assistant Secretary of State William Burns met Palestinian President Yasser Arafat. This was at the same time Allison re-formed as a tropical storm and began dumping tremendous rain. The two events exactly coincided! The nightly news, reported the Houston flooding and the meetings in Israel together! This tropical storm ravaged the United States for the entire time the CIA director was in Israel.

September 11, 2001

On September 11, the greatest attack ever on American soil occurred. The hijacking of four airplanes and the attack on the World Trade Center (WTC) in New York City and the Pentagon left upwards of 3,000 dead. These suicide attacks by Moslem terrorists caused approximately $40 billion in damage and stunned the country.

On this day, America was attacked by terrorists on a scale not imagined. More Americans died on September 11, then on the attack on Pearl Harbor. The attack was a complete surprise and came without any warning.

The attack on the WTC was at the very heart of the United States financial center. The largest stock brokerage firms in the world were located in the WTC along with many international banks. The terrorists aimed the attack directly at the financial heart of the United States. The effect of this attack on the stock market was devastating. The week after the attack was one of the worst ever for the stock market.

Prior to September 11, on August 9, 2001, in Jerusalem a suicide terrorist killed 19 Jews and wounded over 100 people. Later on that day, President Bush made a speech condemning the terrorist attack. After condemning the attack, the President then demanded that Israel abide by the

Madrid Peace Process, the Mitchell Plan, and United Nations Resolutions 242 and 338. An excerpt of the President's speech follows:

"The United States remains committed to implementation in all its elements of the Mitchell Committee Report, which provides a path to return to peace negotiations based on United Nations Security Council Resolutions 242, 338 and the Madrid Conference. To get to Mitchell the parties need to resume effective security cooperation and work together to stop terrorism and violence."

These United Nations resolutions called for Israel to retreat back to the pre-Six-Day War borders. This would require Israel giving up East Jerusalem, the Golan Heights and ending all settlements in the West Bank. The President was totally ignoring God's covenant with Israel. He was telling Israel to retreat to indefensible borders; thus putting Israel in a very dangerous position. The President ended the speech by pressuring Israel to negotiate with the very people who had just committed a horrible terrorist attack.

Looking back to September 2000, Israel had been the subject of dozens of terrorists' attacks and the terrorists had killed hundreds of Jews. The Palestinians engaged in a low grade war against Israel. In the face of the terrorism and war, President Bush wanted Israel to negotiate with the Palestinians and give away the covenant land including East Jerusalem.

Exactly 32 days after the President's August 9 speech, the Moslem terrorists struck America. The United States came under the same type of terror that the Israelis were under. America was engaged in a war against Moslem terrorists just as was Israel. Israel was fighting for its very existence and now America was in the same battle for its existence.

Historically, starting in October 1991, America began to pressure Israel with the Madrid Peace process. This process reached a climax in July 2000 with Israel offering to withdraw from East Jerusalem and most of the West Bank. This offer failed because the Palestinians rejected it. The Palestinians then started the war using intense terrorism against Israel. Israel was politically destabilized, and its economy greatly suffered. The parallel between what happened in Israel since September 2000 and America was eerily the same. These are the parallels:

At the same time the Israeli government was destabilized in late 2000 so was America.

Almost a year to the day that the intense terrorism began against Israel, America was attacked by the same type of terrorists.

Israel was in a low grade war with Moslem terrorists. America also entered into a low grade war with the same terrorists.

Terrorists attacked Israel's capital Jerusalem. Terrorists also attacked America's capital Washington, DC.

Americans had come under the same fear that the Israelis lived under.

Israel's economy suffered because of the terrorism. The American economy fell under the same pressure.

The tourist industry collapsed in Israel because of the terrorism. The tourism industry in America collapsed after the terrorist attacks.

Israel began to win the war against terrorists. America began to win the war against Iraqi terrorists.

Israel's economy recovered from the terrorism. America's economy recovered from the Sept 11 attacks.

The American policy since October 1991 was to pressure Israel to concede covenant land for "peace." This resulted in America suffering in 2001 from terrorism exactly as Israel had suffered. America had touched the "apple of God's eye" and paid an enormous price. God's word says that what a nation does to Israel comes right back upon that nation. What happened to the United States, plainly illustrates this. The pressure from God will only get worse if America continues to force Israel to divide the covenant land.

November 2001

The United Nation's General Assembly meeting set for September 21, was canceled because of the terrorist attack on the WTC, and it was rescheduled for November 10, 2001. On November 10, President Bush addressed the UN and spoke mostly about terrorism. He briefly spoke about the Middle East and stated that there should be two states. There should be an Israel and a Palestine. He called for the borders to be in accordance with Security Council resolutions 242 and 338. The part of the President's speech touching on Israel follows:

"The American government also stands by its commitment to a just peace in the Middle East. We are working toward the day when two states — Israel and Palestine — live peacefully together within secure and recognized borders as called for by the Security Council resolutions.

"We will do all in our power to bring both parties back into negotiations. But peace will only come when all have sworn off forever incitement, violence and terrorism."

On November 11, Yasser Arafat spoke to the United Nations General Assembly. He also spoke about a Palestinian state and blamed Israel for all the fighting since September 2000. Later this day, Secretary of State Colin Powell met with Arafat.

On November 12, 2001, an American Airline jet crashed taking off from JFK Airport killing 265 people. This crash was less then 24 hours after Arafat's speech to the United Nations. The speech was about 15 miles from the crash scene in the very same city! Arafat's activities in the United States, and a national disaster were once again headlines.

April 2002

By April 2002, the Israelis and Palestinians were engaged in serious fighting. This fighting killed hundreds, and there were almost daily terrorist attacks against Israel. Israel quarantined Arafat in his headquarters in the city of Ramallah. On April 28, the United States pressured Israel to lift the siege of Arafat's headquarters.

On this day, a massive tornado storm ravaged the east coast of the United States from Missouri to Maryland. The most powerful tornado ever recorded in Maryland struck on this day. It was a monster F-5 packing winds between 261-318 mph. This was the first time in Maryland's history an F-5 hit the state. The storm came directly over Washington, DC, and the tornado was just south of the city. On May 1, 2002, the President declared Maryland a disaster area.

The headlines for the Washington Post of April 29, 2002 read: "Israel Agrees to Lift Arafat Siege"; and "Deadly Tornado Hits Southern Maryland."

June 2002

On June 24, the President made a major policy speech regarding Israel. He called for two states living side by side. The President declared that the United States was going to take the lead to insure the two states came to pass. He turned this plan over to Secretary of State Colin Powell for implementation.

Throughout the month of June 2002, record forest fires were burning in the West. The worst fire in Colorado's history burnt 138,000 acres. In Arizona two fires merged into a monster that burned 550,000 acres. Only the heroic efforts of fire fighters kept it from burning cities.

Immediately after the President made the two-state policy speeches he traveled to Arizona. He declared Arizona a disaster area and tried to encourage the people and fire fighters. The national newspapers' headlines captured the speech and the fires. The Washington Post's headlines for June 25 read: "President Outlines Vision for Mideast;" and "Everything is Just a Nightmare, Forced to Flee Western Wildfires."

May 2003

On April 30, the United States, Russia, the European Union and the United Nations drafted a Road Map for peace for Israel. This plan called for Israel to surrender parts of the covenant land for peace. On May 4, Secretary of State Colin Powell traveled to Israel and Syria to promote this plan. The Secretary stayed in the Middle East until May 11.

During the entire time of his stay, massive tornado storms were pounding the east coast of the United States. A record total of 412 tornadoes struck causing over $2 billion in damage. This was the worst tornado outbreak since May 1999. When Secretary Powell left Israel to return home, the tornadoes stopped. The Secretary's trip to promote this peace plan bracketed this awesome tornado outbreak.

September 2003

This month witnessed tremendous activity involving Israel. The intifada was vicious in its killing and injuring of thousands of Jews. Israel weighed all options against Arafat including his assassination. The United States condemned Israel for this. On September 12, President Bush also blocked Israel from expelling Arafat from Israel. On this day, Hurricane Isabel reached Category 5 and its course pointed directly at the United States.

On September 16, the United States vetoed a United Nations Security Council resolution against Israel and the hurricane lessened in intensity. King Abdullah of Jordan met with the President to discuss the peace plan. Hurricane Isabel was bearing down on Washington, DC, and caused this meeting to end early! The President left Washington as the storm approached. The hurricane hit on September 19 and caused $4 billion dollars in damage in the Mid-Atlantic States.

August - September 2004

During a six week period a record four hurricanes slammed into Florida. Never in such a short period of time had four major hurricanes hit one state. They did enormous destruction and the combined damages totaled about $40 billion. The hurricanes were named Charlie, Frances, Ivan and Jeanne.

Starting in early August and continuing through September, the United States put enormous pressure on Israel to withdraw from 21 settlements in Gaza and four in Samaria. The Bush administration even made a $1 billion loan guarantee to Israel for relocating Jews from the settlements. In addition, the President wanted Israel to remove security roadblocks, limit settlement construction, and to unfreeze hundreds of millions in Palestinian money. On August 7, he sent the American envoy, Elliot Abrams to pressure Israel in these areas. The key to all this pressure was relocating Jews off the covenant land, primarily Gaza, and providing money to accomplish this.

On August 9, a tropical depression formed in the Caribbean Sea that became Hurricane Charlie. On August 12, Hurricane Charlie was bearing down on the west coast of Florida and forced the evacuation of 1.4 million people. The hurricane intensified rapidly and within hours the destructive winds attained category 4. On August 13, the hurricane slammed into southwest Florida and traveled diagonally across the state. This storm did over $14 billion in damage.

The United States attempted to pressure Jews to evacuate the covenant land and 1.4 million Americans then evacuated their homes. Bush wanted 25 Jewish settlements closed, and he then declared 25 Florida counties disaster areas. The President wanted home construction stopped in the settlements, and this hurricane destroyed 10,000 American homes and damaged 16,000 others.

On September 1, powerful Hurricane Frances was bearing down on the east-central coast of Florida. Frances was tremendous in both size and power. This hurricane was the size of Texas and reached category 4. The approaching hurricane caused the largest evacuation in American history up to this time, as 2.8 million fled their homes. On August 30, Prime Minister Sharon said he would speed up the evacuation of 21 settlements in Gaza. On September 5, Frances smashed into Florida as a category 2 and caused $10 billion in damage.

On September 2, President Bush gave his reelection acceptance speech while at the same time Hurricane Frances had stalled off the coast of Florida. The front page of all the national newspapers had headlines of the President's speech and the hurricane.

On September 12, tens of thousands of Israelis protested the evacuations of the settlements. On September 14, Sharon's cabinet created evacuation guidelines and the Israeli army established a command to oversee the evacuation of the settlers. On this date, President Bush requested an additional $3.1 billion in aid for hurricane damage, bringing the total to $5.1 billion.

On September 15, Hurricane Ivan slammed into Florida's panhandle. Ivan was a powerful category 3 that did over $12 billion in damage not only to Florida but also Alabama, Georgia, South Carolina and other states. Hurricane Ivan caused the evacuation of two million people from its path. Amazingly, this hurricane hit on the Jewish holy day of Rosh Hashanah.

On September 20, Hurricane Jeanne was in the Atlantic Ocean traveling on a course away from the United States. On September 20, Secretary of State Colin Powell gave a speech and said the Israeli pullout from Gaza was just the first step in peacemaking. He went on to say there should not be a long time between the Gaza withdrawal and the final two-state settlement. On September 21, the President spoke to the United Nations General Assembly. During the speech he mentioned Israel and said the following:

> Israel should impose a settlement freeze, dismantle unauthorized outposts, end the daily humiliation of the Palestinian people, and avoid any actions that prejudice final negotiations.

Following the speech the hurricane began turning. It made a complete turn and headed directly toward central Florida. On September 25, Yom Kippur the holiest day for Judaism,

Jeanne roared into central Florida as a category 3 hurricane. Three million fled before this storm, which caused $6.8 billion in damage. On September 28, the President requested $7.1 billion in additional disaster relief for a total of $12.2 billion!

From August 13 through September 25, the United States suffered a record four direct hits from powerful hurricanes. During this very time, President Bush was pressuring to divide the covenant land. America pressured Israel to evacuate Jews off the land and the hurricanes forced nine million Americans to evacuate. The President made a $1 billion loan guarantee to relocate Jews and then it cost the United States $12.2 billion in hurricane related damages. Hurricanes Ivan and Jeanne even hit on Jewish holy days!

January 2005

On November 11, Yasser Arafat died. In January 2005, the Palestinians elected Mahmoud Abbas to replace Arafat. Immediately, President Bush sent congratulations to Abbas and said the road map to peace would go forward. The President's road map meant Israel surrendering covenant land for a Palestinian state. He even invited Abbas to the White House.

Like Arafat before him, Abbas continued to call for the destruction of the State of Israel. On December 30, Zakaria Zbeida, a notorious terrorist who Israel attempted to locate and arrest, hoisted Abbas on his shoulders. On December 31, 2004, Abbas called for Israel to withdraw to the 1949 borders, and claimed Jerusalem as the capital of a Palestinian state. He also declared the right of the millions of Palestinian refugees to return to Israel, which would destroy the nation. And, on January 4, he declared that Israel was the "Zionist enemy." In his victory speech, Abbas said that the election was "a victory for Yasser Arafat and the entire Palestinian people." He added, "The small jihad is over and the big jihad has begun."

Even with all these statements, the President still invited Abbas to the White House and claimed the road map to peace was going forward. The President said:

"The United States stands ready to help the Palestinian people realize their aspirations...We look forward to working with him and the Palestinian people to address these challenges and to advance the cause of Middle East peace consistent with the vision I set forth on June 24, 2002, of two states, Israel and Palestine, living side by side in peace and security."

While the Palestinian elections were taking place and the President was praising Abbas, and even inviting him to the White House, awesome storms were striking the western section of the United States. NASA climatologist William Patzert said the weather in the Western part of the United States was the worst in 119 years, with torrential rains resulting in killer mudslides in California, and cold weather bringing snowfalls of up to 19 feet in Nevada.

The storms were not limited to California. Along the Ohio River, hundreds of Ohio and West Virginia residents evacuated their homes. The river was nearly four feet above flood stage in Ohio and in West Virginia. Meteorologists reported the storms in the Midwest were the worst in 104 years! All this happened when the President merely invited Abbas to the White House.

April 2005

On April 11 and 12, President Bush met with Prime Minister Sharon to discuss the "Road Map to Peace." President Bush said that this meeting with Prime Minister

Sharon was the result of the two-state plan he had initiated on June 24, 2002, and Sharon was now ready to take the necessary steps for peace. The heart of this meeting was the closing of 25 Jewish settlements. Twenty-one settlements were in Gaza, while four were in Samaria. The meeting ended with Sharon agreeing to close all 25 of the settlements.

The President was delighted with Sharon's agreement to close the settlements. He announced, for the first time, they established a timetable to close the settlements. The President's speech in part follows:

"Today, the Prime Minister told me of his decision to take such a step. Israel plans to remove certain military installations and all settlements from Gaza, and certain military installations and settlements from the West Bank. These are historic and courageous actions."

President Bush also requested that Israel not build a 3650 home complex in the Maaleh Adumim section of East Jerusalem. The President said he "opposes any further construction, saying it threatens peace with the Palestinians and violates the 'road map' that calls for a settlement freeze."

During this week the stock market took a huge downturn. This was the worst weekly decline since March 2003. All three sections of the stock market, Dow Industrials, NASDAQ and S&P 500 reached their lows for the year. The mood of investors turned sour that week as the effect of the high oil prices over the last year finally began to hit the stock markets.

At the very time of this meeting over the covenant land of Israel, negative market forces converged and resulted in the big downturn because of the souring mood of investors.

August-September 2005

Hurricane Katrina

"The energy, the near-record low pressure in the storm's core and its huge dimensions added up to an inevitable disaster. That's why they're basically forecasting Armageddon when it goes inland." Bill Read, meteorologist, tracking Hurricane Katrina, August 28, 2005.

The Closing of the 25 Jewish Settlements

After President Bush and Israeli Prime Minister Sharon met in April 2005, Sharon set a timetable to begin the withdrawal from the 25 settlements. Starting in August, the Israelis planned to withdraw from 21 settlements in Gaza and four in Samaria. On August 16, the Israelis began the process. By August 23, the Israeli government completed the withdrawal removing approximately 10,000 Jews from the covenant land.

President Bush and Secretary of State Rice put enormous pressure on the Israeli government to evacuate these 25 settlements. The United States and Israeli governments were negotiating $1.2 billion in aid to help relocate the settlers. The removal of all Jews from Gaza was the first step in President Bush's plan to establish a Palestinian state next to Israel.

In Gaza, 16 of the 21 settlements were collectively known as Gush Katif. The 16 settlements together made a small city with beautiful homes and a population of about 8,000. It was one of the major agriculture producers in Israel, and about 15 percent of all Israeli vegetables were grown there. Gush Katif was famous for its huge greenhouses, some of the largest in the world. There were about 4,000 greenhouses in Gush Katif. This was not a primitive tent type village, but rather a small modern city.

To accomplish the evacuation, the Israeli government sent 40,000 soldiers into Gaza to remove approximately 10,000 residents. The government requested the settlers to leave voluntarily, and forced those that refused out of their homes and off the land. Many of the settlers who refused to leave went on the roofs of their homes and soldiers removed them by force. The army then demolished their homes and destroyed the 21 Gaza settlements. The demolition left only 21 synagogues and the huge vegetable greenhouses standing. It is against Jewish law to destroy a house of worship of any religion, so the Israelis let the synagogues remain.

On August 22, the Israelis removed the last of Jewish settlers from Gaza, while on August 23 they removed the last settlers from Samaria. The removal of the settlers took a mere seven days to complete. President Bush was extremely happy with the Israeli withdrawal from the 25 settlements. He mentioned the Israeli withdrawal in speeches on August 22 and 23. In the speech on August 22, he acknowledged the closing of the settlements caused pain, but called it historic. The President's speech of August 22, in part, follows:

> "This past week, Prime Minister Sharon and the Israeli people took a courageous and painful step by beginning to remove settlements in Gaza and parts of the northern West Bank. The Israeli disengagement is an historic step that reflects the bold leadership of Prime Minister Sharon."

In a speech on August 23, the President again praised Prime Minister Sharon for his "courageous decision to withdraw from Gaza and parts of the West Bank." He felt this was the beginning of the creation of the State of Palestine. The following is an excerpt from the President's speech:

"...I want to congratulate Prime Minister Sharon for having made a very tough decision...The Prime Minister made a courageous decision to withdraw from Gaza...This is step one in the development of a democracy...This is a very hopeful period. Again, I applaud Prime Minister Sharon for making a decision that has really changed the dynamics on the ground, and has really provided hope for the Palestinian people. My vision, my hope is that one day we'll see two states – two democratic states living side by side in peace."

On September 12, Israel handed over the 21 Gaza settlements to the Palestinians. This was the largest evacuation of Jews in modern Israeli history, as never before, were so many Jews forced off their covenant land.

When the Palestinians took control of the settlements, their first objective was to destroy and burn the 21 synagogues. They completely destroyed all the synagogues. Mobs, which were out of control, then looted and burned everything in sight including the huge greenhouses which Israel had left for them.

Hurricane Katrina

On August 23, just as Israel removed the last settler, tropical depression 12 formed over the Bahamas and upgraded to a tropical storm named Katrina. Katrina grew rapidly in power and on August 24 and upgraded to a category one hurricane. On August 25, Katrina hit southern Florida doing about $1 billion in damage. Katrina then weakened over Florida and was downgraded to a tropical storm.

The hurricane then moved into the Gulf of Mexico and again rapidly intensified. By August 29, it was a massive category 5 about 375 miles in diameter. It was heading directly toward New Orleans. The approaching category 5 storm caused 1.5 million to evacuate their homes and flee inland

As Katrina approached New Orleans, the eye veered slightly eastward and missed the city by 50 miles. The storm destroyed entire parishes both east and south of New Orleans and heavily damaged The Port of New Orleans, the fifth largest in the world.

The eye struck the Mississippi coast with a tidal surge of up to 35 feet high. This was the highest tidal surge ever recorded! The storm entirely devastated the 50 mile Mississippi coast. When the eye struck land, the barometric pressure was 27.18. This was the third lowest barometric pressure ever recorded for a hurricane making landfall in the United States. The low pressure is an indication of the storm's power. This was a catastrophic storm in every sense of the word.

The tidal surge reached miles inland destroying all in its path. This surge totally destroyed the small city of Waveland, Mississippi. A 200 mile stretch of the Gulf coast from Louisiana to Florida felt the hurricane's powerful surge. The storm was so powerful that hurricane force winds struck Jackson, Mississippi, 150 miles inland! The winds and rain damaged the entire state of Mississippi.

The direct impact of Katrina initially missed New Orleans, but the next day, August 30, several of the city's levees failed, and water from the surrounding lake poured into the city. Most of the city is below sea level and 80 percent of New Orleans was flooded. In some places, the city was 16 feet under water. This was the greatest disaster of a city in United States history, and the only comparison to it was the destruction of San Francisco in 1906 by a powerful earthquake and fire.

The only comparison to the overall destruction was that which was caused by The Great Hurricane of 1938. The federal government declared a 90,000 square mile area of land, nearly the size of Great Britain, a disaster area. New Orleans ceased to function as a city.

City officials estimated that entire neighborhoods were destroyed, and that 120,000 buildings, or 70 percent of the city's structures, were unsalvageable. Peter Teanen, national Spokesman for the American Red Cross, put the disaster in perspective. He said the following:

> "We are looking now at a disaster above any magnitude that we've seen in the United States. We've been saying that the response is going to be the largest Red Cross response in the history of the organization."

The connection between the United States government pressuring Israel to destroy 25 settlements on the covenant land, and Katrina's destruction, is so obvious. The hurricane destroyed Southern Louisiana and the Gulf Coast of Mississippi merely six days after the completion of the Gaza evacuation of Jews off the covenant land.

Hurricane Katrina was by far the greatest natural disaster ever to occur in the United States as it destroyed an entire major city. Just as the major southern Jewish city in Gaza was destroyed so was a major southern city in the United States.

The New York Times, one of the nation's leading national newspapers, vividly captured the connection between Gaza and Hurricane Katrina. On the Editorial page for August 31, there were two amazingly linked articles. The first titled, "New Orleans in Peril" was about the destruction of New Orleans. The second titled, "The Battle for Israel's Future." was, in part, about the evacuation of Gaza. The articles were actually touching each other!

The following are quotes from the two editorials to show just how the New York Times had Gaza and Katrina linked, so that anyone reading the articles could put this together in their mind:

New Orleans in Peril

"On the day after Hurricane Katrina was declared to be not as bad as originally feared, it became clear that the effects of the storm had been, after all, beyond, devastation. Home owners in Biloxi, Miss., staggered through wrecked neighborhoods looking for their loved ones. In New Orleans, the mayor reported that rescue boats had begun pushing past dead bodies to look for the stranded living. Gas leaks began erupting into flames and looking at the city, now at 80 percent under water, it was hard not to think of last year's tsunami, or even ancient Pompeii."

The Battle for Israel's Future

"Mr. Sharon's withdrawal of Israeli settlers from Gaza completed last week, was a historic shift that should be acknowledged and extended. Now that Mr. Sharon has demonstrated that he is able to carry out a territorial compromise...he needs to extend the principle from Gaza to the crucially important West Bank."

Hurricane Katrina was named as a tropical storm just as Israel forced the last settlers out of their homes. The evacuation forced Israelis from their homes, and two weeks later up to 2.0 million Americans had to evacuate their homes. President Bush promised $1.2 billion in aid for the displaced Jewish settlers. Katrina's destruction might cost $200 billion, and he promised the funds to rebuild.

The evacuation destroyed thousands of Jewish homes and businesses, while Katrina destroyed or damaged up to 500,000 American homes. The evacuated Jews were scattered all over Israel and the evacuees from Katrina were scattered all over the United States. Katrina displaced 1.3 million Americans from their homes. Approximately, 250,000 evacuees were relocated in the President's home state of Texas! Only the Civil War and the Great Depression compared in size to this migration.

Israel sent 40,000 troops to evacuate the settlers while the United States had to send 80,000 soldiers to the destroyed area. Jews went to their roofs to try and delay the eviction, while thousands in New Orleans went to their roofs, to keep from drowning. The Palestinians looted and burned the 25 evacuated settlements just as thugs looted New Orleans and sections of the city burned.

A mere 21 days after the eviction of the last Jew; the President of the United States was publicly humiliated. On September 13, President Bush told the nation that, "Katrina exposed serious problems in our response capability at all levels of government. And to the extent that the federal government didn't fully do its job right, I take responsibility."

The man behind the humiliation of Israel, by forcing Jews from their covenant land, was himself humiliated before the entire world. He had to admit to the failures of the federal government response during the Hurricane Katrina disaster relief.

The Similarities

The following is a list of similarities between the destruction of Gaza and Hurricane Katrina. Remember, there were only seven days between the last Jew's removal off the covenant land and the destruction of New Orleans and surrounding states.

- Prior to removal, the Israeli government called on Jews to evacuate their homes from the 25 settlements. The US government called on residents to evacuate their homes prior to the hurricane.

- On August 17, Israel ordered a mandatory evacuation of the settlements. On September 7, the mayor of New Orleans ordered a mandatory evacuation of the city.
- The evacuation of 12,000 Jews was the largest in Jewish history since 1948. Several million Americans would evacuate from the path of Hurricane Katrina.
- The Israeli government disarmed the settlers, and New Orleans police attempted to disarm its citizens.
- Gaza is located in Israel's southern coastal area. A section of America's southern coast was destroyed.
- The evacuation destroyed thousands of Jewish homes. The hurricane destroyed or damaged over 500,000 American homes.
- The day Katrina hit, Jews were digging up their dead to re-inter them in cemeteries outside Gaza. Katrina's tidal surge uncovered 100s of bodies from Gulf Coast grave yards.
- The Israeli government barred citizens of Gaza from their homes. American citizens in the destroyed areas were barred from their homes.
- Many Jewish people felt abandoned by their government. Many Americans felt abandoned by the United States government's failure to timely respond to Hurricane Katrina.
- The Israelis from the settlements were boarded on buses and taken to locations all over Israel. The people trapped in New Orleans were loaded on buses and taken to shelters all over the United States.
- The President's home state took in 250,000 evacuees and then later Hurricane Rita hit his state.
- Gush Katif was a major agricultural center. The Port of New Orleans is the major agricultural shipping center in the United States and the Midwestern states ship much of their produce through this port.

- President Bush promised $2.2 billion for the reloca-
  tion of the settlers. The early estimates were a cost
  upwards of $200 billion to repair the damage from the
  hurricane.
- On August 23, the President congratulated Prime
  Minister Sharon for dismantling Jewish settlements
  while on August 29, the President declared Louisiana,
  Mississippi and Alabama disasters areas.
- The Israeli government turned the settlements in
  Gaza over to the Palestinians on September 12. On
  September 13, the President was humiliated as he
  publicly took responsibility for the federal government
  failures during Hurricane Katrina relief operations.

Hurricane Rita

While the nation was still reeling from Hurricane Katrina, a
second monstrous storm, Rita, headed into the Gulf of Mexico.
On September 20, Rita brushed Key West, Florida and headed
into the Gulf. Rita exploded to a category 5 on September 21
with 175 mph winds, and headed directly toward Texas.

The people living along the Gulf Coast began to evacuate
and eventually nearly everyone fled Houston. Traffic jams
100 miles long stretched out of Houston as 2.8 million fled
the coast. This would be the greatest evacuation in United
States history.

As Rita headed west, the Hurricane weakened and turned
more northward. The storm dropped to a still powerful category 3 hurricane, packing 125 mph winds. On September 24,
the hurricane came ashore in Texas just west of the Louisiana
border. The eye hit a sparsely populated area of Texas and
devastated the Texas cities of Beaumont and Port Arthur.

The coastal area of western Louisiana was also devastated
and many small cities totally destroyed. The hurricane's tidal
surge reached all the way to New Orleans, and for the second

time in a month the city was again flooded. The total damage inflicted by Hurricane Rita was more than $10 billion.

The Israel Connection

Hurricane Rita also had an Israel connection. The destruction of New Orleans occurred just seven days after the removal of the last Jew from Gaza. On September 12, the Israelis gave control of the 21 settlements in Gaza to the Palestinians. On September 21, Israel completed its pullout from the four settlements in Samaria.

When Israel completed the pullout, the Palestinians poured in and destroyed the settlements, just as in Gaza. The Palestinians overran the settlements and burned everything including all the trees. They then looted everything possible. At the very time Israel transferred the final four settlements to the Palestinians, Hurricane Rita exploded to a category 5 with sustained winds of 175 mph!

On the day Israel surrendered Gaza, New Orleans and huge sections of the Gulf Coast lay in ruins. On the day Israel turned over the Samaria settlements to the Palestinians, a category 5 hurricane bore down on the United States. It seems Katrina was for Gaza while Rita was for Samaria. Within a very short time Rita tore through the oil rigs in the Gulf heading toward some of the major refineries in Texas, and destroyed several small towns along the Texas and Louisiana coasts.

Summary

God's "Perfect Storm Warnings"

The destruction of Houston and East Texas by Tropical Storm Allison was the third time since the Madrid Peace Process began in 1991 that a sitting president's state was the location of a powerful and damaging storm. Presidents George H. W. Bush, William Clinton and George W. Bush were all personally touched by a disaster at the exact time they were forcing Israel to divide the covenant land. God gave each president what appears as a "Perfect Storm Warning."

All three of these storms were ferocious and record-breaking. Both Presidents George W. Bush and William Clinton, declared disaster areas in their own states at the very time they were dealing with Israel. God made the connection between Israel and disasters for them. All three Presidents made disaster declaration at the very time they were involved with touching "the apple of God's eye." It seems God personally warned each President. A clear pattern of warnings now developed.

The Results of Dealing With Yasser Arafat

- September 1, 1993: President Clinton announces he will meet Arafat and Rabin on September 13 in Washington, DC to begin the Oslo Peace Accords. After nearly a week of meandering in the Atlantic Ocean, Hurricane Emily hits North Carolina on this day.
- March 2, 1997: Arafat meets with President Clinton in Washington, DC. The same day awesome tornado storms unleash tremendous damage in Arkansas and flooding in Kentucky and Ohio. Arkansas and Kentucky declared disaster areas.
- January 21, 1998: President Clinton is waiting to meet with Arafat at the White House. At this exact time the President's sex scandal breaks.
- September 27, 1998: Arafat is meeting with the President in Washington. Hurricane Georges hits Alabama and stalls. The Hurricane stalls until Arafat

leaves and then it dissipates. Parts of Alabama declared a disaster area.

- October 17, 1998: Arafat comes to the Wye Plantation meeting. Incredible rains fell on Texas which causes record flooding. FEMA declares parts of Texas a disaster area.
- November 23, 1998: Arafat comes to America. He meets with President Clinton who is raising funds for the Palestinian state. On this day the stock market fell 216 points.
- December 12, 1998: On this day the US House of Representatives votes to impeach President Clinton. At the very time of the impeachment, the President is meeting with Arafat in Gaza over the peace process.
- March 23, 1999: Arafat meets with Clinton in Washington, DC. Market falls 219 points that day. The next day Clinton orders attack on Serbia.
- September 3, 1999: Secretary of State Albright meets with Arafat in Israel. Hurricane Dennis comes ashore on this very day after weeks of changing course in the Atlantic Ocean.
- September 22, 1999: Arafat meets with Clinton in Washington, DC. The day before and after the meeting the market falls more than 200 points each day. This was the first time in history the market lost more than 200 points for two days in a week. The market lost 524 points this week.
- June 16, 2000: Arafat meets with President Clinton. The market falls 265 points on this day.
- July 12-26, 2000: Arafat at the Camp David meetings. Powerful droughts throughout the country. Forest fires explode in West into uncontrolled fires. By the end of August, fire burns 7 million acres.
- November 9, 2000: Arafat meets with President Clinton at the White House to try and salvage the peace

process. This was just two days after the presidential election. The nation was just entering into an election crisis which was the worst in over 100 years.

- November 11, 2001: Arafat speaks at the UN General Assembly and condemns Israel. He later meets with Secretary of State Colin Powell. On this day, Saddam threatens the US with nuclear weapons. Within 24 hours of meeting with Powell, an airplane crashes in NYC killing 265 people. The crash was 15 miles from where Arafat spoke.
- May 1, 2002: Under pressure from the US, Israel releases siege of Arafat's headquarters. Massive tornado storm in eastern US with F-5 tornado very close to White House.

Federal Emergency Management Agency (FEMA)

FEMA is the federal agency that coordinates disaster relief. FEMA also releases federal funds to help disaster victims. This agency keeps a list of its top ten natural disasters ranked by the amount of relief costs. This list is just the funds allotted by FEMA and is not the total cost of damages.

Of the ten disasters, the top nine relate directly to the United States pressuring Israel to divide the covenant land. The funds paid by FEMA for these nine disasters totaled $25.91 billion. The tenth disaster, Hurricane Hugo in 1989, was connected directly to abortion and not listed. The FEMA disasters follow:

Event (With States effected)	**Year**	**FEMA Funding** (Billions)
Hurricane Katrina (AL, LA, MS)	200	$7.20

Northridge Earthquake (CA	1994		$6.96
Hurricane Georges (AL, FL, LA, MS)	1998		$2.25
Hurricane Ivan (AL, FL, GA, MS, others	2004		$1.95
Hurricane Andrew (FL, LA)	1992		$1.81
Hurricane Charley (FL, SC)	2004		$1.56
Hurricane Frances (FL, GA, NC, SC)	2004		$1.43
Hurricane Jeanne (DE, FL, VA)	2004		$1.41
Tropical Storm Allison (FL, LA, MS, TX)	2001		$1.34
		Total	$25.91

(The above list is for the period ending June 2006.)

Billion Dollar Disasters

The National Oceanic and Atmospheric Administration (NOAA) monitor billion dollar disasters. NOAA identified 47 such disasters starting in 1992. Several of these disasters were droughts over a long period of time and thus could not be associated directly with dividing the land of Israel.

Several others connect to abortion and homosexual events and thus are not reported in this book.

America, pressuring Israel over the covenant land, is directly linked to 20 of these disasters and most are identified in this chapter. These 20 totaled $334.8 billion in damages! The billion dollar disasters follow:

September 2005 Hurricane Rita	$5.0 billion
September 2005 Hurricane Katrina	$200.0 billion
September 2004, Hurricane Jeanne	$6.5 billion
September 2004 Hurricane Ivan	$12.0 billion
September 2004 Hurricane Frances	$9.0 billion
August 2004 Hurricane Charlie	$14.0 billion
September 2003 Hurricane Isabel	$5.0 billion
May 2003 Tornado storms	$3.4 billion
July 2002 Western fires	$2.0 billion
March 2002 National drought	$10.0 billion
June 2001 Tropical Storm Allison	$5.0 billion
July 2000 Severe Drought West	$4.2 billion
July 2000 Western Fires	$2.1 billion
September 1999 Hurricane Floyd	$6.5 billion
May 1999 Oklahoma tornadoes	$1.7 billion
October 1998 Texas Flooding	$1.1 billion
September 1998 Hurricane Georges	$6.5 billion
April 1997 North Plains flooding	$4.1 billion
March 1997 Arkansas tornadoes	$1.1 billion
August 1992 Hurricane Andrew	$35.6 billion
Total	$334.8 billion

(The above list is for the period ending June 2006.)

The American Dichotomy

The Madrid Peace Plan and the subsequent two-state policy of Israel and Palestine has placed the United States in a dichotomy over Israel. The dichotomy involves, on one hand, the United States pressuring Israel to divide the land while on the other, supporting and helping Israel in every way.

The official United States policy as first formulated by President Bush, Sr. is that Israel must surrender covenant land for peace. Under George Bush, Jr., this has officially become a two-state policy for Israel and Palestine. This policy is diametrically opposed to God's prophetic plan, and brings America under judgment. Yet, America remains very close and friendly to Israel, and it is Israel's greatest friend in the world. This brings a blessing to America.

This dichotomy is seen in the words of President George Bush, Sr. In October 1991, he initiated the Madrid Peace Process which pressured Israel to surrender sections of the covenant land. Then, on August 11, 1992, the President met with Israel's Prime Minister, Yitzhak Rabin. In a speech during this meeting, President Bush articulated the special relationship that existed between the United States and Israel.

President Bush Library

Bush-Rabin meeting 8/11/92

The President actually stated, in this speech, that there was a special relationship between Israel and America. What the President said is unique among all the countries of the world. The leader of no other country would dare say his nation had a special relationship with Israel. The President claimed this special relationship started in 1948; however, he was just highlighting a special relationship that dates back to the time of President George Washington.

The following are quotes from two of President Bush, Sr's., speeches which plainly demonstrate this dichotomy. The first is from his speech of August 11, 1992, which illustrates the blessing. The second is from his speech of October 30, 1991, initiating the opening of the Madrid Peace process, which illustrates the curse.

The blessing:

"I want to take this opportunity to say a few things about the relationship between the United States and Israel. This is a relationship that goes back more than four decades to Israel's birth in 1948. This is a relationship that's been tested in times of peace and war, one capable not only of weathering differences but of accomplishing great things. This is a relationship based on a shared commitment to democracy and to common values, as well as the solid commitment to Israel's security, including its qualitative military edge. **This is a special relationship. It is one that is built to endure.**"

The curse:

"What we envision is a process of direct negotiations proceeding along two tracks: one between Israel and the Arab States; the other between Israel and the Palestinians. Negotiations are to be conducted on the basis of U.N. Security Council Resolutions 242 and 338."

"Throughout the Middle East, we seek a stable and enduring settlement. We've not defined what this means. Indeed, I make these points with no map showing where the final borders are to be drawn. **Nevertheless, we believe territorial compromise is essential for peace...**"

This same dichotomy is seen in the policy of President George Bush, Jr. This President initiated his roadmap for peace that calls for dividing Israel into two states. He has stated this plan many times since he introduced this policy in June 2002. Yet, when the Iranian President Mahmoud Ahmadinejad threatened to destroy Israel with nuclear weapons, President Bush rushed to Israel's defense.

In a speech on March 20, 2006, President Bush said Israel is an ally, and the United States will use military might to defend Israel from Iran. There is no other country in the world that so boldly declared its allegiance with Israel. What other country would come to Israel's aid should it be attacked? A section of the President's March 20, speech follows:

But now that I'm on Iran ... the threat from Iran is, of course, their stated objective to destroy our strong ally Israel. That's a threat, a serious threat. It's a threat to world peace; it's a threat, in essence, to a strong alliance. I made it clear, I'll make it clear again, that we will use military might to protect our ally, Israel

Even the United States government is divided over Jerusalem. Congress passed The Jerusalem Embassy Act of 1995, a law recognizing Jerusalem as the capital of Israel. This act also called for the relocation of the American Embassy from Tel Aviv to Jerusalem by 1999. Yet, Presidents William Clinton and George Bush Jr. have thwarted this law and failed to relocate the American Embassy. Very few nations recognize Jerusalem as Israel's capital America being one of them. This further shows this special relationship between the United States and Israel.

The American people, for the most part, respect and want good relations with Israel. President George Washington's benevolent attitude toward the Jewish people is still the same position of most Americans. Huge numbers of American Christians support Israel and the Jewish people. In America, the Jews are not subject to European type anti-Semitism, but they live in peace. America still is a great blessing to the Jewish people and the nation of Israel.

This dichotomy also creates an enigma. As the United States government continues to interfere with God's prophetic plan, how long can the benevolence towards Israel and the Jewish people hold back total judgment? Hurricane Katrina is an example of how close total judgment might be.

Only in America! Thousands of Christians gather in Washington DC for Israel. 7/19/06

PART TWO

Israel Future

Chapter Ten

The Day of the LORD

"For yourselves know perfectly that the day of the Lord so cometh as a thief in the night. (4) But ye, brethren, are not in darkness, that that day should overtake you as a thief."

1 Thessalonians 5:2, 4.

The Bible does not conclude with the rebirth of the nation of Israel, but it goes into great detail about what happens after the nation is reborn. The Bible shows that the nations of the world reject reborn Israel. The wars that Israel suffered since its rebirth together with the rejection of the nation by nearly all religious, political and economic organizations, perfectly fit Bible prophecy.

The wars involving Israel in 1948, 1956, 1967 and 1973 are minor compared to the future battles described in the Bible. The continuing warfare against God's covenant people does not persist forever. These wars come to an abrupt end. The end comes when God supernaturally saves Israel at the

Second Coming of the Lord Jesus. God's intervention occurs during what the Bible calls the Day of the Lord.

The phrase, Day of the Lord, is one of the major prophetic themes of the Bible. For example, a major portion of the Book of Revelation deals with the Day of the Lord. The prophets Isaiah, Ezekiel, Joel, Obadiah, Zephaniah, Zechariah and others all describe in great detail the events taking place during the Day of the Lord. By looking at these prophets, a clear picture develops of the events leading up to and including the Day of the Lord.

The world's political and religious rejection of Israel eventually results in a worldwide military attack on the nation. The Bible describes at least three future wars which go beyond anything the world has witnessed before. Each war becomes progressively greater and greater until the last, known as Armageddon, involves all the nations of the world. This last battle occurs during the Day of the Lord.

The wars involving Israel are greater in magnitude than World War II. These future wars are cataclysmic. The wars result in the annihilation of huge armies together with the destruction of entire nations. The destruction is so extensive that these lands become uninhabitable. The Bible says the last war kills one-third of mankind! With today's world population of six billion, that would equal two billion people! Imagine a world war that kills two billion people!

There is a progression to these wars. The first war involves the Arab nations immediately surrounding Israel. It appears from the Bible's description of this war that these nations are destroyed with weapons of mass destruction. The second war involves additional nations, including the rest of the Islamic countries. God uses natural disasters, with supernatural timing, to destroy this huge army invading Israel. The final war includes the nations of the world attacking Israel with a massive army of hundreds of millions. Jesus Christ, at His Second Coming, supernaturally ends this war.

What is the Day of the Lord?

The Day of the Lord is an expression referring to a long period of time which begins with God's judgment on the world for both rejecting Him and the everlasting covenant with Abraham. It is the time when God interferes directly in the affairs of man. This is God's last attempt to reach man before the Second Coming of the Lord Jesus.

Israel and Jerusalem play a key role in the Day of the Lord. The Day of the Lord focuses on the awesome Second Coming of the Lord Jesus. It includes His 1000 year reign from Jerusalem as King Messiah. This reign is also known as the Kingdom Age.

The judgment part of the approaching Day of the Lord involves two phases. The first phase involves incredible wars. The wars are compressed into a short time period around seven to ten years. These wars lead to a total world war which culminates in the battle of Armageddon. The prophet Zechariah goes into detail about this war which begins in the Day of the Lord. This final war centers around Jerusalem and all the nations of the world are involved.

"Behold, the day of the LORD cometh, and thy spoil shall be divided in the midst of thee. For I will gather all nations against Jerusalem to battle..."
Zechariah 14:1, 2.

The second phase involves natural disasters which affect the entire world. These disasters include earthquakes, fires, famines and pestilence. The earthquakes during this period are so massive they level all the cities of the world. The judgment part of the Day of the Lord is short but a very intense period of time.

> "Behold, the day of the LORD cometh, cruel both with wrath and fierce anger, to lay the land desolate: and he shall destroy the sinners thereof out of it. (10) For the stars of heaven and the constellations thereof shall not give their light: the sun shall be darkened in his going forth, and the moon shall not cause her light to shine."
>
> Isaiah 13:9, 10.

In the future, these wars and natural disasters are all happening simultaneously in this short time period. Even today, the breathtaking timing of natural disasters that struck America serves as a warning of things to come. These disasters coincided with the United States pressuring Israel to divide the covenant land. All this foreshadows the events happening culminating in the Day of the Lord. The judgment phase of the Day of the Lord climaxes with both the greatest war and greatest earthquake in history.

The war:
> "For they are the spirits of devils, working miracles, which go forth unto the kings of the earth and of the whole world, to gather them to the battle of that great day of God Almighty...(16) And he gathered them together into a place called in the Hebrew tongue Armageddon."
>
> Revelation 16:14, 16.

The earthquake:
> "And the seventh angel poured out his vial into the air; and there came a great voice out of the temple of heaven, from the throne, saying, It is done.

(18) And there were voices, and thunders, and lightnings; and there was a great earthquake, such as was not since men were upon the earth, so mighty an earthquake, and so great."

Revelation 16:17, 18.

The Day of the Lord is the time God holds people while on earth accountable for rejecting Him and following false gods and religions. It is a time when God deals with the pride and rebellion of man. Mankind for the most part lives separate from God. God exposes man's heart to show how evil it is through all the wars and killing on a scale never seen before. God lets man's evil heart have its way for a brief time, and then brings judgment on these actions. Through it all, God always has the way of salvation for man open to Him.

As the Day of the Lord approaches, many turn to Jesus Christ and repent as they see there is no hope outside of trusting God. God uses this time to bring man to his senses. Everything that can be shaken will be shaken, and only that which is of God stands in the future.

"The lofty looks of man shall be humbled, and the haughtiness of men shall be bowed down, and the LORD alone shall be exalted in that day. (12) For the day of the LORD of hosts shall be upon every one that is proud and lofty, and upon every one that is lifted up; and he shall be brought low"

Isaiah 2:11, 12.

It appears that the world-wide war phase involving the Day of the Lord, as described by the ancient prophets, is now coming together with rapid speed. Nation after nation is armed with weapons of mass destruction. The United States, Russia, China and Israel all have huge arsenals of these fearful weapons. Both India and Pakistan have developed nuclear weapons and threaten to use them against each other.

Terrorist nations such as Iran and Syria have biological and chemical weapons and Iran is working around the clock to develop nuclear weapons. The Iranian government has publicly stated that when it possesses these weapons it will use them against Israel.

Think of nuclear weapons in the hands of the tyrants in the Middle East! How long before one of these nations builds such a weapon? Could the world be on the verge of the Day of the Lord? Let us look at what the Bible describes as the Day of the Lord and the events which are now transpiring.

Key Indicators The Day of the Lord is at Hand

There are certain general indicators in the Bible which must be in place for the Day of Lord to occur. Remember, the Day of the Lord includes the Second Coming of the Lord Jesus Christ. These indicators are now falling into place.

Some of these indicators are: the rebirth of Israel. Jewish people return to Israel from a worldwide dispersion. Jerusalem once again is the capital. Israel is a great military power. The nations of the world reject Israel. Israel is the target of horrific wars. Russia is a major military power. Russia aligns with Iran and other Islamic nations. Asia is able to field an army of two hundred million. A one world system of government will be in place.

In addition to the general indicators, the Bible gives specific key indicators that the Day of Lord is near. The first key indicator is the total destruction of Iraq. The ancient name for Iraq was Babylon. The Babylonian Empire of 2600 years ago was located in what today is Iraq. The prophet Isaiah zeros in on Iraq, as the one of the key indicators to watch.

Isaiah writes that as the Day of the Lord nears, God brings a nation from the "end of heaven" to completely destroy the area of ancient Babylon. This particular nation possesses fierce weapons which can totally destroy Iraq to the degree it is uninhabitable.

The geographical center of the Bible is Israel. So the expression "end of heaven" means as far away as possible from Israel. It appears from the way Isaiah describes this nation, it did not exist in Isaiah's day. This nation does exist just prior to the Day of the Lord.

At the time just prior to the Day of the Lord, the entire world is upset with Iraq. It is the focus of world attention, but one unnamed nation, that is as far away from Israel as possible, destroys the land that encompasses ancient Babylon. Isaiah writes that God is directing the actions of this nation to destroy the area of land that the Bible describes as Babylon.

"The burden of Babylon, which Isaiah the son of Amoz did see... (4) The noise of a multitude in the mountains, like as of a great people; a tumultuous noise of the kingdoms of nations gathered together: the LORD of hosts mustereth the host of the battle.

(5) They come from a far country, from the end of heaven, even the LORD, and the weapons of his indignation, to destroy the whole land."

Isaiah 13:1, 4, 5.

Babylon is destroyed like Sodom and Gomorrah and it becomes uninhabitable. These Scriptures about Babylon were never completely fulfilled. God never judged ancient Babylon with awesome devastation. The city of Babylon and the empire fell in 539 BC to the Persians; however Babylon remained a great city. This total destruction, as described in the Bible, occurs far in the future from 539 BC. The destruction takes place just prior to the Day of the Lord.

"And Babylon, the glory of kingdoms, the beauty of the Chaldees' excellency, shall be as when God overthrew Sodom and Gomorrah.

(20) It shall never be inhabited, neither shall it be dwelt in from generation to generation: neither shall the Arabian pitch tent there; neither shall the shepherds make their fold there."

Isaiah 13: 19, 20.

The prophet Isaiah, writing in 700 BC, reports the complete destruction of Babylon is the key indicator. The total destruction of Babylon by a nation from the "end of heaven" is the sign for all to see that the Day of the Lord is at hand. Let us look at this verse.

"Howl ye; for the day of the LORD is at hand; it shall come as a destruction from the Almighty."

Isaiah 13:6.

America fits perfectly into this Biblical scenario because it is a nation from "the end of heaven" and possesses fearful weapons which could completely destroy Iraq; thus, it is possible for the soon fulfillment of Isaiah 13. It is very possible that America is the very nation that Isaiah described!

In 1991, America entered into a war with Iraq. Then in 2003, the United States for a second time engaged Iraq in war. A nation from the "end of heaven" with awesome weapons of indignation came to "Babylon." It appears that the two wars with Iraq are leading to a third which could result in the destruction of the entire nation. This destruction is so horrific that everyone has to flee and the land becomes uninhabitable.

This complete and utter destruction has not occurred; however the circumstances for this possibility are now in place. It appears that Iraq degenerates into total chaos that requires complete destruction. Maybe the nation becomes a center for terrorists who use weapons of mass destruction.

Watch for the total destruction of Iraq and then know the Day of the Lord is at hand. At this point, the world has run out of time with the holy God of Israel. The terrible Day of the Lord is about to begin. The awesome Second Coming of Jesus Christ is near.

"Howl ye; for the day of the LORD is at hand; it shall come as a destruction from the Almighty. (7) Therefore shall all hands be faint, and every man's heart shall melt:

(9) Behold, the day of the LORD cometh, cruel both with wrath and fierce anger, to lay the land desolate: and he shall destroy the sinners thereof out of it. (11) And I will punish the world for their evil, and the wicked for their iniquity; and I will cause the arrogancy of the proud to cease, and will lay low the haughtiness of the terrible."

Isaiah 13:6, 7, 9, 11.

The First War

"For it is the day of the Lord's vengeance, and the year of recompenses for the controversy of Zion."

Isaiah 34:8.

As the Day of the Lord nears, the Bible describes three different battles. Each battle gets progressively larger in scope. The first battle involves the destruction of Iraq, mentioned above, and the nations bordering Israel. The second battle is lead by Russia with the rest of the Islamic nations, and the third is the battle of Armageddon which involves Asia with an army of 200 million.

The destruction of Iraq is the opening salvo of the wars, but along with Iraq other nations are destroyed. It appears the people facing judgment with Iraqis are the Palestinians, Jordanians, Egyptians, Syrians and possibly Saudi Arabians. God judges these nations when they attempt to annihilate Israel.

With the weapons of mass destruction that the nations have acquired, this war could eclipse all previous wars in horror. A major war in the Middle East would soon destabilize the entire world, as even the hint of a disruption of the oil flow would send the world economy crashing. Let us look at what the prophets say about the nations involved in this coming first war.

Palestinians - Philistines, House of Esau

On September 28, 2000, the final battle over Jerusalem may have begun. The conflict over the Temple Mount which started on this day has not really subsided. The major trigger point is Jerusalem and the Temple Mount. Any disturbance on the Temple Mount or destruction of the Al-Aksa Mosque or the Dome of the Rock could instantaneously ignite an all out Moslem assault against Israel. Jerusalem is the flash point for a war of no return.

The Bible speaks directly to the current Israeli - Palestinian conflict. The Palestinians have fought Israel at every turn since 1920. Many Palestinians participated in the attacks on Israel in 1948 and 1967. They formed terrorist groups and attacked Israel non-stop. In January 2006, the Palestinians elected the terrorist group Hamas to head their government.

The Bible states that as the Day of the Lord nears, the Jews drive the Palestinians completely from the land of Israel. The complete removal of the Palestinians is another key sign of the approaching the Day of the Lord.

It is very easy to follow the explosive situation between the Palestinians and Israelis to an all out war and the elimination of the Palestinians from the covenant land. The prophet Obadiah, writing in 600 BC, speaks to us today about this situation. The prophet ties this conflict with the coming Day of the Lord.

> "For the day of the LORD is near upon all the heathen: as thou hast done (to Israel), it shall be done unto thee: thy reward shall return upon thine own head.
>
> (18) And the house of Jacob shall be a fire, and the house of Joseph a flame, and the house of Esau for stubble, and they shall kindle in them, and devour them; and there shall not be any remaining of the house of Esau; for the LORD hath spoken it.
>
> (19) And they of the south shall possess the mount of Esau; and they of the plain the Philistines: and they shall possess the fields of Ephraim, and the fields of Samaria: and Benjamin shall possess Gilead."
>
> Obadiah 1:15, 18, 19.

The prophet Obadiah states that as the Day of the Lord draws near a horrific war erupts between the Jews, "House of Jacob," and the Palestinians, "House of Esau." This war results in all the Palestinians being driven from the covenant land. The prophet states that Israel will possess the Plain of the Philistines, which is Gaza. Ephraim and Samaria located in the West Bank, are brought under Israeli control, along with Gilead. Gilead is the East Bank of the Jordan River.

Hamas means strength and bravery, and this Palestinian terrorist organization refers to itself as the Islamic Resistance Movement. Hamas formed in the 1980s, and on August 18, 1988, Hamas officially declared its covenant. This covenant outlined the objectives and methods of Hamas. In the Preamble, Hamas declared, "Israel will exist and will continue to exist until Islam will obliterate it, just as it obliterated others before it"

Hamas does not recognize the right of Israel to exist as a nation. Article Eleven contains this doctrine:

> "The Islamic Resistance Movement believes that the land of Palestine is an Islamic Waqf consecrated for future Moslem generations until Judgment Day. It, or any part of it, should not be squandered: it, or any part of it, should not be given up"

The Hamas Covenant leaves no room for negotiations with Israel. Hamas calls for the total destruction of Israel. It calls for no negotiations with Israel but continual Jihad until Israel is destroyed. Let's look at Article Thirteen:

> "There is no solution for the Palestinian question except through Jihad. Initiatives, proposals and international conferences are all a waste of time and vain endeavors. The Palestinian people know better than to consent to having their future, rights and fate toyed with."

With Hamas now in control of the Palestinians, it is just a matter of time before an all out war erupts. The circumstances for this happening, and leading to the Day of the Lord, are certainly plausible as even now the battle rages every day in Israel. This fighting in Israel cannot go on forever.

The combinations of the Israeli - Palestinian conflict along with the United States involvement in Iraq are powerful signs that the Day of the Lord is drawing very near.

Syria and Lebanon

Syria is Israel's longtime worst enemy. Israel fought Syria in 1948, 1967 and 1973. Syria is the base for several terrorist organizations such as Hamas. Syria also controls Lebanon and uses this country as a front to attack Israel. Under the control of Syria many terrorist groups, such as Hezbollah, have attacked Israel, even up to July 2006 when fighting once again erupted. The word hezbullah means "the party of god."

The relationship between Hezbullah and Syria is complicated. Syria controls Lebanon, but Hezbullah is religiously aligned with Iran. Hezbullah was first formed in Iran during the revolution started by Ayatollah Khomeini and transplanted to Lebanon. Both Syria and Iran supply Hezbullah with weapons to attack Israel. These weapons include thousands of missiles which can reach deep into Israel.

Hezbullah is a terrorist organization that formed in 1982 to fight against Israel. In 1983, it was responsible for the explosion that killed 281 United States Marines. This terrorist group now controls most of Lebanon's southern border with Israel. It has evolved beyond a military organization to now reaching political power in Lebanon along with providing social services. Hezbullah is well entrenched in Lebanon.

It also has grown into an international organization with agents all over the world including the United States. Hezbullah uses illegal tactics to raise tens-of-millions of dollars in the United States. Hezbullah is extremely well organized, supplied and trained by both Iran and Syria. This is a formidable fighting force.

Hezbullah's two main goals are to conquer the world through the spread of Islam and the destruction of both Israel and the United States. The destruction of Israel is the main driving force behind Hezbullah. The mere existence of Israel is viewed by Hezbullah as proof Israel is a terrorist state! Hezbullah views Israel as organized terrorism supported by the United States, and therefore will use terrorism against Israel. The following is a quote from a June 20, 1997, broadcast from Manar TV, Beirut, stating Hezbullah's views and concepts:

> "... Hizbullah views the Zionist Jews' occupation of Palestine, displacing its people and establishing the entity of Israel on its usurped land as the living materialization of the most hideous kinds of aggression and organized terrorism that is supported by the USA, the sponsor of international terrorism, and some other states that claim to be democratic and protecting human rights whilst they support Israel that was founded on invasion, killing and bloodshed, besides its daily violations of human rights in Lebanon and Palestine."

The Israeli borders with both Syria and Lebanon are now a flash point for a horrifying war. During the Six-Day War in 1967, Syria lost the Golan Heights and wants it back while Hezbullah wants the total annihilation of Israel. An all out war between Israel and the Palestinians would certainly bring Syria and Hezbullah right into this conflict. As with Hamas, there cannot be a negotiated peace with Hezbullah. Hezbullah completely rejects Israel. It waits for the opportunity to destroy Israel. Thus an all out war cannot be too far into the future.

The prophet Isaiah speaks of a war that crushes Syria but also weakens Israel. This first war totally destroys Damascus and the nation of Syria ceases to exist. The destruction of Damascus is so great the city is never rebuilt. This war begins a chain reaction to the battle of Armageddon. When

Israel totally destroys Syria, this is another key indicator that the Day of the Lord is very near.

"The burden of Damascus. Behold, Damascus is taken away from being a city, and it shall be a ruinous heap.

(3) The fortress also shall cease from Ephraim, and the kingdom from Damascus, and the remnant of Syria: they shall be as the glory of the children of Israel, saith the LORD of hosts.

(4) And in that day it shall come to pass, that the glory of Jacob shall be made thin, and the fatness of his flesh shall wax lean."

Isaiah 17:1, 3, 4.

During this war, the fortress (military power) ceases from Ephraim (a name for Israel). Syria also ceases from being a nation. Israel becomes thin, or loses a large percentage of its population. Israel is presently a mighty military power and this means the war is horrific to the point of totally destroying Syria, and yet greatly weakening Israel.

The destruction of Damascus is also tied to the start of the final battle involving all the nations of the world, or as it is called the battle of Armageddon. The destruction of Syria is the signal that the Day of the Lord is extremely close, and the battle of Armageddon is very near.

"Woe to the multitude of many people, which make a noise like the noise of the seas; and to the rushing of nations, that make a rushing like the rushing of mighty waters!

(13) The nations shall rush like the rushing of many waters: but God shall rebuke them, and they shall flee far off, and shall be chased as the chaff of the mountains before the wind, and like a rolling thing before the whirlwind.

(14) And behold at eveningtide trouble; and before the morning he is not. This is the portion of them that spoil us, and the lot of them that rob us."

Isaiah 17:12-14.

Iran and the Mahdi

Iran's final confrontation with Israel is found in the second battle; however, it does have an important place in the first battle. Iran is an extremely important player in the wars leading to the Day of Lord; therefore, it needs special attention.

On August 3, 2005, Mahmoud Ahmadinejad became the president of the Islamic Republic of Iran. His election set in motion powerful forces in the Middle East rushing toward a climax in a cataclysmic war with Israel. With both Ahmadinejad rising to power, and a few months later Hamas, the die was cast for a huge confrontation with Israel.

It is very important to understand Ahmadinejad's theology to realize the depth of his hatred for Israel and the confrontation course he is on with the United States. He follows Shiite Islam and fanatically believes in the coming of the Mahdi. The Mahdi is central to his beliefs and motivates his agenda. As time goes on the term Mahdi will become more and more common. Let us examine the Islamic Mahdi.

The Mahdi is Arabic for "rightly-guided one." He is a special ruler in rank just below the Prophet Muhammad. The Mahdi is the restorer of Islam and justice who will rule just before the end of the world. He is a military figure who leads the Islamic armies in conquering the entire world. Under the generalship of the Mahdi, the entire world becomes Islamic. Those who fail to submit to Islam must die. This is the Islamic theology of the Mahdi.

The background of the Mahdi is very unusual. Ahmadinejad believes that the Mahdi is the 12th Imam, Mohammed ibn Hasan, who was a direct descendant of

Muhammad. Ibn Hasan lived in the ninth century and when he was five years old he fell into a well. He went into a state of concealment until the end of time when he emerges as the Mahdi. Ahmadinejad believes this is the end of time and the Mahdi is soon to be revealed.

Ahmadinejad is then a mahdaviat, which means "the belief in and efforts to prepare for the Mahdi." This is evident when he spoke before the United Nations in September 2005. During his speech, he offered a prayer for the hastening of the Mahdi to bring "justice and peace." This prayer follows:

"O mighty Lord, I pray to you to hasten the emergence of your last repository, the Promised One, that perfect and pure human being, the one that will fill this world with justice and peace."

Because Ahmadinejad is a mahdaviat, he has no fear of war with the United States or Israel. To him, a war with Israel might immediately reveal his Mahdi and begin the Islamic world conquest. Not since the days of Adolph Hitler's Aryanism has the world seen someone with this religiously driven concept of world conquest.

Iran is building both nuclear weapons and long range missiles to deliver these weapons of mass destruction. There is no doubt, if Iran develops these weapons, they will be used against Israel and possibly the United States. Iran is on a course for the Islamic world conquest, and Israel is viewed as an obstacle in the way.

According to the Bible, Persia (Iran) is destroyed during the second battle. During this battle, Persia is aligned with Russia and is part of the huge land army that invades Israel. The fact that Iran is part of the second battle means it survived the first battle. It appears that during the first war, Iran's weapons of mass destruction along with its long range capability to attack Israel are eliminated. Iran survives only to be destroyed in the second war.

With Iran, Hezbullah and Hamas united against Israel, the picture has become very clear that terrible wars are on the horizon. This first war is not far into the future, but is staring right now at Israel and the United States. Iran wants this war and is providing the means to start it. The LORD God of Israel is going to finish it.

Egypt

The fighting draws Egypt into this first battle. The future of Egypt is very bleak as this war totally destroys the nation. It appears that the fighting raging between the Israelis and Palestinians spills over to Egypt. Egypt attacks Israel to its own doom.

The destruction of Egypt is so complete that the survivors flee into the nations of the world. The Nile River stops flowing. Prophet after prophet describes the terrible destruction coming to Egypt. These prophecies about the destruction of Egypt have never been fulfilled. They await fulfillment when the Day of the Lord is near.

> "Egypt shall be a desolation, and Edom shall be a desolate wilderness, for the violence against the children of Judah, because they have shed innocent blood in their land."
>
> Joel 3:19.

> "And the land of Egypt shall be desolate and waste; and they shall know that I am the LORD: because he hath said, The river is mine, and I have made it.
>
> (10) Behold, therefore I am against thee, and against thy rivers, and I will make the land of Egypt utterly waste and desolate, from the tower of Syene

even unto the border of Ethiopia. (11) No foot of man shall pass through it, nor foot of beast shall pass through it, neither shall it be inhabited forty years.

(12) And I will make the land of Egypt desolate in the midst of the countries that are desolate, and her cities among the cities that are laid waste shall be desolate forty years: and I will scatter the Egyptians among the nations, and will disperse them through the countries."

Ezekiel 29:9-12.

Jordan - Saudi Arabia

In the Bible, the modern nation of Jordan is made up of three small nations. These nations are Ammon, Moab and Edom. Ammon is the northern section of Jordan. Moab is the central section, while Edom is the southern. The prophet Zephaniah speaks about the Day of Lord and the total destruction of Ammon and Moab. This destruction has never happened and waits future fulfillment.

Jordan faces the same dire fate as the other nations. Jordan ceases to exist because of its confrontations with Israel. These three nations which make up modern Jordan have a long history in the Bible of warring against Israel. Jordan was the first nation to attack Israel in 1948. In fact, King Abdullah of Jordan led the attack. Jordan attacked Israel in 1967 and was defeated.

Jordan has been at peace with Israel for several years, and it is one of the few Moslem nations which recognize Israel. Jordan's population is about 60 percent Palestinian. It appears the conflict with the Palestinians drags Jordan into the battle, and the war destroys this nation. This destruction is a prelude to the Day of the Lord.

The prophet Zephaniah mentions the total destruction of Moab and Ammon with the Day of the Lord. He does not mention Edom.

> "The great day of the LORD is near, it is near, and hasteth greatly, even the voice of the day of the LORD: the mighty man shall cry there bitterly."
>
> Zephaniah 1:14.

The destruction is so great that it turns parts of Jordan into Sodom and Gomorrah.

> "I have heard the reproach of Moab, and the revilings of the children of Ammon, whereby they have reproached my people, and magnified themselves against their border.
>
> (9) Therefore as I live, saith the LORD of hosts, the God of Israel, Surely Moab shall be as Sodom, and the children of Ammon as Gomorrah, even the breeding of nettles, and saltpits, and a perpetual desolation: the residue of my people shall spoil them, and the remnant of my people shall possess them."
>
> Zephaniah 2:8, 9.

The prophet Isaiah describes the awesome judgment on Edom. Edom is also referred to as Idumea. The region of Idumea would include southern Jordan but would also extend to the northwest corner of Saudi Arabia. The fact that Idumea includes part of modern day Saudi Arabia is very important.

Isaiah says that during the Day of the Lord, this area is going to burn with pitch or oil! The very nation known for oil is going to be on fire with oil! The oil producing region of Saudi Arabia is near the Persian Gulf and not near Israel. But, the Bible is clear in the future that sections of Saudi Arabia near Israel are on fire because of burning oil.

Isaiah calls the time of judgment on Idumea as the year of God's recompense for what this nation did to Israel. God's judgment falls directly on Jordan and Saudi Arabia. The judgment is on the land.

"For it is the day of the Lord's vengeance, and the year of recompenses for the controversy of Zion."
Isaiah 34:8.

"For my sword shall be bathed in heaven: behold, it shall come down upon Idumea, and upon the people of my curse, to judgment."
Isaiah 34:5.

This area burns so intensely that no one can pass through it.

"And the streams thereof shall be turned into pitch, and the dust thereof into brimstone, and the land thereof shall become burning pitch.
(10) It shall not be quenched night nor day; the smoke thereof shall go up for ever: from generation to generation it shall lie waste; none shall pass through it for ever and ever."
Isaiah 34:9, 10.

Thus the Bible shows that the hostility against Israel by the Palestinians erupts into an awesome war with the destruction of entire nations. The conflict draws in Egypt, Syria, Jordan and Lebanon. It appears that weapons of mass destruction are used and entire nations cease to exist. The combined population of Egypt, Syria, Iraq, Jordan and Lebanon is approximately 120 million.

How long can the tensions with Israel continue? How long before a war erupts and quickly turns into the use of weapons of mass destruction? The Moslem hatred for Israel is so strong it seems they would risk annihilation in an attempt to destroy God's covenant nation. These nations fail and face total destruction.

Ring of Fire Around Israel

This first war results in an impassible ring of destroyed countries to the south and east of Israel. The nations of Egypt, Jordan, Iraq and part of Saudi Arabia are totally destroyed. According to the Bible, they become like Sodom and Gomorrah. This means a total wasteland that becomes not only uninhabitable, but also impassible.

This area of land becomes completely impassable because of the use of nuclear, chemical or biological weapons. The soil of the destroyed nations is so poisoned that it is impossible to pass through. The area of Idumea is on fire, much like Kuwait was after the 1991 Gulf War. The approaches to Israel from the south and east are blocked. This ring of fire results in the north being the only avenue left to attack Israel.

In the two wars that follow, the only avenue to Israel will be through Lebanon and part of Syria. The Mediterranean Sea blocks a land invasion from the west. This blockage results in huge numbers of soldiers compressed into a very narrow area of land focused in the Mountains of Israel. It is as if the huge armies are funneled into a gigantic killing field, as they rush to take Jerusalem. These armies are destroyed during the second battle and also Armageddon.

God has set the nation of Israel like a big trap and Jerusalem is the bait. As the nations reject the everlasting covenant and attack Israel, they are destroyed. In these wars God's posture is defensive. If the nations do not attack, God does not destroy them. The nations are destroyed as they attempt to invade the covenant land, and not before. Israel then becomes an anvil for God's judgment of the nations.

DAY OF THE LORD
RING OF FIRE AROUND ISRAEL

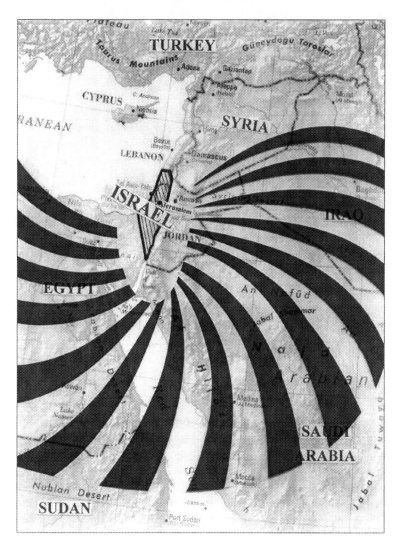

This dreadful confrontation between Israel and the surrounding nations is the key sign of the approaching Day of the Lord. These signs cannot be missed. All the alarms, bells, whistles and warnings are going forth that the awesome Day of the Lord is near. Only unbelief prevents a person from seeing these signs.

The Second War

"And thou shalt come up against my people of Israel, as a cloud to cover the land; it shall be in the latter days"

Ezekiel 38:16

The prophet Ezekiel writing 2600 years ago speaks directly to us today. He describes a huge battle that takes place after the nation of Israel is reborn. This war is the second of the three. Ezekiel, with great detail, foretells of the rebirth of Israel in chapters 36 and 37. In chapter 40-48, the prophet then describes the rule of the Lord Jesus from His magnificent temple in Jerusalem.

Between the rebirth of Israel and kingdom age, Ezekiel, in chapters 38 and 39, describes a horrific battle. The war is often referred to as the battle of Gog and Magog. This is the second battle connected to the approaching Day of the Lord.

Ezekiel lists a confederacy of nations united in this attack against Israel. Russia leads these nations which include Turkey, Iran, Libya, Ethiopia, parts of Eastern Europe and many other un-named nations. Immediately, when looking at this list something appears strange. The prophet fails to mention the nations directly bordering Israel! These countries are Egypt, Iraq, Jordan, Lebanon, "Palestine" and Syria. The reason these nations are not mentioned is because they were all destroyed in the first battle.

Ezekiel sets the time frame of this battle as taking place after Jews return to Israel from a world-wide dispersion. He identifies this period the "latter years." Jewish people have come from nearly all the nations of the world to recreate Israel. Jews were scattered into all the nations for nearly 2,000 years, but In Ezekiel 38 they are home again.

"...in the latter years thou shalt come into the land that is brought back from the sword, and is gathered out of many people, against the mountains of Israel, which have been always waste: but it is brought forth out of the nations, and they shall dwell safely all of them."
Ezekiel 38:8.

As in the first battle, this one also involves many other Islamic nations. This second war increases in scope and destruction. The destruction of the countries of the first war may be one reason for this second battle. The time period between the first and this war is unknown.

Russia: The Land of Magog

The prophet Ezekiel identifies the chief antagonist against Israel in this coming battle. He identifies Russia as leading this confederacy to destroy Israel. Russia has a long history of hating and persecuting Jewish people. With the pogroms starting in 1881, untold numbers of Jews died at the hands of the Russians. Russian Jews were the first to return to Israel in the 1880's. They left Russia because of persecution.

It is ironic that the Russian hatred for Jews drove them to Israel, and then God, in the future, destroys Russia in a devastating war with Israel! All the centuries of Russian hatred for Jews culminates in this battle, which results in Russia's destruction. What irony this is! This is divine retribution for all the Russian persecution of Jews. Let's take a close look at Ezekiel's prophecy.

"And the word of the LORD came unto me, saying, (2) Son of man, set thy face against Gog, the land of Magog, the chief prince of Meshech and Tubal, and prophesy against him, (3) And say, Thus saith the Lord GOD; Behold, I am against thee, O Gog, the chief prince of Meshech and Tubal"

Ezekiel 38:1.

Gog is a title, such as chief prince or president. The nation is the land of Magog, Meshech and Tubal. This war is often referred to as the battle of Gog and Magog. The three names Magog, Meshech Tubal identify the modern nation of Russia.

Magog was the name of a people at the time of Ezekiel. The First Century Jewish historian Flavius Josephus identified the Magogites. In his book, *Antiquities of the Jews*, Josephus writes, "Magog founded those that were from him named Magogites, but who are by the Greeks called Scythians."

The ancient Greek historian Herodotus wrote of the Scythians. He identified them as controlling the land between the Danube to the Don River and from the Black Sea north for several hundred miles. Today this area is located in the nation of Russia.

Russia is the nation identified as modern Magog. The names Meshech and Tubal sound very similar to the Russian cities of Moscow and Tubalsk. Ezekiel also identified Magog as coming from the north parts. Moscow is directly north of Jerusalem, *"And thou shalt come from thy place out of the north parts"* (v. 15).

Thus both the geographical location and history identify Russia as leading this second war against Israel. Russia has a substantial Moslem population which fits right in with a major attack on Israel. The combination of historical Russian hatred of Jews and its Moslem population could prove to be the catalyst for attacking Israel.

Ezekiel then identifies the confederation of nations that form and attack Israel. Persia is modern day Iran. Persia changed its name to Iran in 1935. Iran has publicly declared it wants the complete destruction of Israel. Russia is Iran's main supplier of weapons. Iran and Russia become a perfect match for the attack on Israel.

The Bible refers to Ethiopia as the land south of Egypt. Today this would include the nations of the **Sudan**, Ethiopia and Somalia. The Sudan and Somalia are both Islamic nations. The Sudan is identified as a terrorist state and hates Israel. Ethiopia has a large Moslem population of about 30 percent. Sudan and Somalia are a natural fit with Russia in the confederated attack.

In the Bible, Libya is all the land west of Egypt. This would include the nations of Libya, Tunisia and Algeria and Morocco. All these nations are Islamic and could easily fit into this confederation against Israel. Libya is a terrorist nation, and its leader Colonel Muammar Gaddafi is legendary in his terrorism and hatred of Israel. Russia is Libya's major supplier of weapons. Algeria is in the midst of a civil war that started in 1995 and has killed over 100,000. Moslem fundamentalists are trying to take over the country, and such a take over would make Algeria ready for war with Israel.

Ezekiel identifies Togarmah as a country north of Israel. This is Turkey, which is nearly 100 percent Moslem. Turkey is a part of NATO and has a military treaty with Israel. For this battle to happen, Turkey must line up with Russia. Turkey is key to this confederation, showing that the battle is very near. When Turkey aligns with Russia, know the day of this battle is drawing near.

The identity of Gomer is not as clear as the other nations. It is possible that Gomer is Germany or some East European countries. Gomer's exact location is not known. Russia is going to be a guard, or weapons supplier to these nations. Russia is one of the world's largest suppliers of weapons and already arms most of these nations with weapons. The confederation of nations follows:

> "Persia, Ethiopia, and Libya with them; all of them with shield and helmet: (6) Gomer, and all his bands; the house of Togarmah of the north quarters, and all his bands: and many people with thee. (7) Be thou prepared, and prepare for thyself, thou, and all thy company that are assembled unto thee, and be thou a guard unto them."
>
> Ezekiel 38:5.

The United States currently prevents this battle from taking place. For this battle to happen, the United States has to be weakened or eliminated from the Middle East. NATO has to be weakened by Turkey joining an alliance with Russia. Russia becomes the dominant force at this time and not America. For this war to happen, something disastrous needs to have happened in the future to the United States.

The Russian army is massive and well equipped. Since the collapse of the Soviet Union, Russia has fallen in many areas into a third world status. The Russian army is still huge, and well equipped. With the right leadership and motivation, the Russian army could be formidable. The Russian bear is far from being dead.

> "I will bring thee forth, and all thine army, horses and horsemen, all of them clothed with all sorts of armour, even a great company with bucklers and shields, all of them handling swords"
>
> Ezekiel 38:4.

The confederation led by Russia is enormous. The army will cover the land like a cloud. Many other nations join Russia. Perhaps all the remaining Islamic nations not mentioned by the prophet Ezekiel join in this attack.

> "Thou shalt ascend and come like a storm, thou shalt be like a cloud to cover the land, thou, and all thy bands, and many people with thee. (15) And thou shalt come from thy place out of the north parts, thou, and many people with thee, all of them riding upon horses, a great company, and a mighty arm"
>
> Ezekiel 38:9.

It seems after the destruction of Iraq and Egypt, that Israel enters into a short period of peace. It is during this time that the confederation comes against Israel. God emphasizes for the second time, that the army led by Russia, is coming against Israel in the "latter days." This is an awesome army that covers the land like a cloud. God is allowing this army to come against Israel so that the entire world can see His mighty power.

> "Therefore, son of man, prophesy and say unto Gog, Thus saith the Lord GOD; In that day when my people of Israel dwelleth safely, shalt thou not know it".
>
> And thou shalt come from thy place out of the north parts, thou, and many people with thee, all of them riding upon horses, a great company, and a mighty army"
>
> Ezek 38:14, 15.

When God destroys Russia and its Islamic allies, there is no doubt that it was accomplished by the hand of the holy God of Israel. The nation of Israel is unable to defend itself against this army. God defends His everlasting covenant with Abraham, Isaac and Jacob. He defends His people Israel.

"And thou shalt come up against my people of Israel, as a cloud to cover the land; it shall be in the latter days, and I will bring thee against my land, that the heathen may know me, when I shall be sanctified in thee, O Gog, before their eyes."

Ezekiel 38:16.

God reacts with intense anger to this attack. All the centuries of these nations rejecting God will climax in this cataclysmic confrontation between this huge army and the living God. God uses natural disasters, with supernatural timing, to destroy this army.

"And it shall come to pass at the same time when Gog shall come against the land of Israel, saith the Lord GOD, that my fury shall come up in my face"
(19) For in my jealousy and in the fire of my wrath have I spoken, Surely in that day there shall be a great shaking in the land of Israel; (22) And I will plead against him with pestilence and with blood; and I will rain upon him, and upon his bands, and upon the many people that are with him, an overflowing rain, and great hailstones, fire, and brimstone."

Ezekiel 38:18, 19, 22.

The Mountains of Israel

"But ye, O mountains of Israel, ye shall shoot forth your branches, and yield your fruit to my people of Israel; for they are at hand to come."

Ezekiel 36:8.

Ezekiel in chapter 36 records a tremendous prophecy regarding the Mountains of Israel. This prophecy is specifically about these Mountains. The mountains run through the center of Israel. They run north-south like a spine down the middle of Israel. They start about 50 miles north of Jerusalem and run about 30 miles south. The city of Jerusalem sits on the Mountains of Israel.

> "Also, thou son of man, prophesy unto the mountains of Israel, and say, Ye mountains of Israel, hear the word of the LORD"
>
> Ezekiel 36:1.

Ezekiel sets the background for this prophecy by describing the desolation of the Mountains of Israel. This desolation was the result of God judging the nation for rebellion against Him. This judgment includes the land made barren and cities destroyed. The Jews also were scattered throughout all the nations. The Jews were driven from the land and non-Jews then populated the mountains. With the background that the nation was destroyed and the mountains desolate, this sets the stage for Ezekiel's prophecy.

> "Therefore, ye mountains of Israel, hear the word of the Lord GOD; Thus saith the Lord GOD to the mountains, and to the hills, to the rivers, and to the valleys, to the desolate wastes, and to the cities that are forsaken, which became a prey and derision to the residue of the heathen that are round about"
>
> Ezekiel 36:4.

> "And I scattered them among the heathen, and they were dispersed through the countries: according to their way and according to their doings I judged them."
>
> Ezekiel 36:19.

The prophet then issues a prophecy regarding the Mountains of Israel that the God of Israel would one day bring the people back. The desolation and destruction was not permanent. God would bless these mountains with both abundant rain and crops. The people would return and rebuild the cities.

> "But ye, O mountains of Israel, ye shall shoot forth your branches, and yield your fruit to my people of Israel; for they are at hand to come. (9) For, behold, I am for you, and I will turn unto you, and ye shall be tilled and sown: (10) And I will multiply men upon you, all the house of Israel, even all of it: and the cities shall be inhabited, and the wastes shall be builded"
>
> Ezekiel 36:8-10.

God's prophetic word hovers over the Mountains of Israel. The prophet declared God would bless these mountains when He brought the Jewish people back from the nations. The people would rebuild the cities and farm the land.

The ring of fire creates a funnel pointed at the Mountains of Israel. The invading army led by Russia, swarms over the Mountains of Israel. God does not judge this army hundreds of miles away, but when the army crosses into the covenant land and starts overrunning the Mountains of Israel, this invading army hits headlong into God's prophetic word. At this point, the holy God of Israel sends awesome judgment. The invasion is stopped in it tracks and the army destroyed. This awesome destruction takes place directly on the Mountains of Israel.

> "And I will turn thee back, and leave but the sixth part of thee, and will cause thee to come up from the north parts, and will bring thee upon the mountains of Israel:
>
> Thou shalt fall upon the mountains of Israel, thou, and all thy bands, and the people that is with thee: I will give thee unto the ravenous birds of every sort, and to the beasts of the field to be devoured."
>
> Ezekiel 39:2, 4.

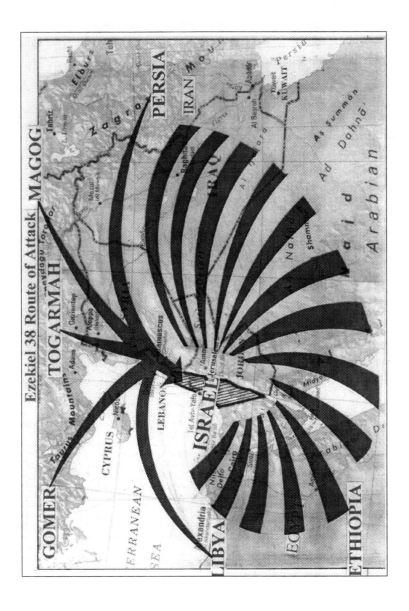

The judgments God sends include, a massive earthquake that shakes the entire earth, pestilence, great hailstones, fire and brimstone. The armies turn against each other and begin killing one another. All this judgment results in the destruction of the entire army. God then judges the nations involved in this attack. Russia meets its doom on the Mountains of Israel, as God applies Obadiah 1:15 to the Russians. God destroys perhaps the greatest Jew-hating nation as it attempts to destroy Israel:

> "And I will call for a sword against him throughout all my mountains, saith the Lord GOD: every man's sword shall be against his brother. (22) And I will plead against him with pestilence and with blood; and I will rain upon him, and upon his bands, and upon the many people that are with him, an overflowing rain, and great hailstones, fire, and brimstone."
>
> Ezekiel 38:21, 22.

The defeat of Russia and the last of the Islamic armies opens the eyes of Israel to their God. Although they do not recognize the Lord Jesus as their Messiah as yet, this starts Jewish people turning to God and His Messiah. They are in awe of what God did. For 2,000 years Israel wandered from nation to nation. Now, the times of the Gentiles, which the Lord Jesus spoke about, draws to a close. God once again is dealing directly with His people Israel.

This battle opens the spiritual eyes of many people throughout the world. It breaks the hold of Islam. Muslims that survive realize that the God of Israel is the true God. The destruction of this army causes many to turn to God through the Lord Jesus.

"Thus will I magnify myself, and sanctify myself; and I will be known in the eyes of many nations, and they shall know that I am the LORD."

Ezekiel 38:23.

"So will I make my holy name known in the midst of my people Israel; and I will not let them pollute my holy name any more: and the heathen shall know that I am the LORD, the Holy One in Israel."

Ezekiel 39:7.

The two outstanding events that lead to the Day of the Lord, massive wars and incredible natural disasters coincide at this time. The prelude to what is coming upon the earth can be seen in the timing of the major disasters hitting the United States when pressuring Israel over the covenant land!

The Third War - Armageddon

"And he gathered them together into a place called in the Hebrew tongue Armageddon."

Revelation 16:16.

Armageddon is one word in the Bible almost everyone has heard. This is the final battle between evil and God. Armageddon is not a battle between good nations and evil nations. It is the battle where God Himself directly intervenes and destroys the largest army in history. This battle ends man's corrupt rule over the nations. Armageddon is the third and final attempt to destroy Israel and take Jerusalem.

Armageddon means Mount Megiddo which is about 70 miles north of Jerusalem. Mt. Megiddo is at the southern edge of the Esdraelon Valley, this valley is also called the Plain of Megiddo. This is a huge valley that runs from southeast to the northwest, right at Mt. Megiddo. This valley is the center of the final battle. The Mountains of Israel start at the southern edge of this valley.

Jerusalem is the objective of the final war. After the defeat of Russia and its confederation, the remaining nations converge on Israel. God uses Jerusalem as a lure and the people in rebellion against Him come literally by the hundreds of million. The prophet Zechariah shows this final battle, before the Second Coming of the Lord Jesus, is over Jerusalem.

> "Behold, the day of the LORD cometh, and thy spoil shall be divided in the midst of thee. (2) For I will gather all nations against Jerusalem to battle…"
> Zechariah 14:1, 2.

All of man's rebellion against God culminates at this battle over Jerusalem. During the previous battles, there is no indication from Scriptures that the armies overrun Jerusalem. In this final battle an army of two hundred million invades the Middle East. This huge army comes from Asia. All of Asia is at this battle along with the other nations of the world. Asia marches to Israel with a unified army. The Apostle John in the Book of Revelation states this army numbers two hundred million.

> "And the four angels were loosed, which were prepared for an hour, and a day, and a month, and a year, for to slay the third part of men. (16) And the number of the army of the horsemen were two hundred thousand thousand (Two Hundred million): and I heard the number of them."
> Revelation 9:15, 16.

The Euphrates River is the traditional dividing line between the Middle East and Asia. This army is going to cross the

Euphrates River and pour into the Middle East. On the way to Euphrates River this army is going to spread into other nations and kills a third of mankind. The Bible says the unified kings of the East or Asia lead this army.

"And the sixth angel poured out his vial upon the great river Euphrates; and the water thereof was dried up, that the way of the kings of the east might be prepared. (14) ...to gather them to the battle of that great day of God Almighty. (16) And he gathered them together into a place called in the Hebrew tongue Armageddon.

Revelation 16:12, 14, 16.

Like the previous battle of Magog, this army meets its doom on the Mountains of Israel. The ring of fire is still around Israel and the only way to attack is from the north. This massive army fills the Valley of Megiddo and then reaches all the way to Jerusalem. Remember, Jerusalem is located in the Mountains of Israel. This army is about to destroy Israel and Jerusalem, and God stops it when it reaches Jerusalem.

The Lord Jesus Christ's direct intervention stops this army. This attempted destruction of Jerusalem triggers His awesome Second Coming. He personally destroys the armies gathered for Armageddon and defends His covenant land and people. This is not a battle between the nations of the world. It is a battle where God directly intervenes through Jesus Christ.

According to the prophet Zechariah, the Lord Jesus stands in Jerusalem on the Mount of Olives. There is an enormous earthquake which splits this mountain. He is in His full glory. It is the presence of Jesus Christ in His glory which destroys this invading army. The radiating glory of Jesus Christ at His Second Coming totally annihilates Israel's enemies. God's glory affects human flesh like a neutron bomb. The prophet describes the destruction of this army.

> "And this shall be the plague wherewith the LORD will smite all the people that have fought against Jerusalem; Their flesh shall consume away while they stand upon their feet, and their eyes shall consume away in their holes, and their tongue shall consume away in their mouth."
>
> Zechariah 14:12.

The Day of the Lord has arrived, Israel now realizes that Jesus of Nazareth was the Messiah of Israel. They see Him standing on the Mount of Olives and understand He is their Messiah. The entire nation of Israel turns to Him, and then goes into deep mourning with true repentance. Israel is finally reunited with the Lord Jesus.

> "And I will pour upon the house of David, and upon the inhabitants of Jerusalem, the spirit of grace and of supplications: and they shall look upon me whom they have pierced, and they shall mourn for him, as one mourneth for his only son, and shall be in bitterness for him, as one that is in bitterness for his firstborn. (11) In that day shall there be a great mourning in Jerusalem…"
>
> Zechariah 12:10, 11.

The Day of the Lord then continues through the building of a magnificent the temple which the Lord Jesus reigns in for 1000 years. The nation of Israel has a wonderful future awaiting it. After coming under the kingship of Jesus Christ, Israel enters the kingdom age. God fulfills all prophecies in the Old Testament about Israel being blessed during this time.

God is not finished with Israel, but the Day is soon coming when Israel is blessed above all nations. This takes place during the Day of the Lord. For a detailed study of the events that follow the Second Coming of Jesus Christ, please see my book *Only Jesus of Nazareth Can Sit on the Throne of David.*

The Future of America

For the fulfillment of Bible prophecy about the war of Gog-Magog and Armageddon, something has to have happened to the United States' world power and influence. American military power and NATO would block any attempt by Russia to form a coalition and invade Israel. For this to happen, America can no longer be a world power. There has to be a tremendous shift of power away from America to Russia.

For the countries of Asia to unite in a massive army, something has to happen to American power in Asia. At the present time, the United States is blocking this from happening. For all of Asia to be united, America has to cease as a world power in Asia. Taiwan will have to be reunited with China and North Korea has to overcome the South.

According to Bible prophecy, the future for the United States does not appear to be good. God has warned America over and over again with warning judgments. The American policy has destabilized Israel, God's covenant nation. The American government has done much to trigger God's judgment. It appears that God is going to remove America from being a world power because of national sin and rebellion against Him.

If the events we are witnessing are the start of the approach to the Day of the Lord, then America's time as a super power is very short. God in His mercy has warned and warned of the coming judgment, but the Church has failed to recognize the warnings and lead the nation in repentance before God. It appears that worldliness and false doctrines neutralize the church and America falls under the judgment of God. America's interference with God's prophetic plan for Israel brings this judgment.

Although America ceases to exist as a world power, repentance could preserve the nation from total destruction. The integrity of the United States is in the hands of the true church. God is about to end the religious game many Americans are playing.

> "For the day of the LORD is near upon all the heathen: as thou hast done (to Israel), it shall be done unto thee: thy reward shall return upon thine own head."
> Obadiah 1:15.

CHAPTER ELEVEN

The Clouds of Heaven

"Jesus saith unto him, Thou hast said: nevertheless I say unto you, Hereafter shall ye see the Son of man sitting on the right hand of power, **and coming in the Clouds of Heaven**."

Matthew 26:64.

The heart of the Day of the Lord is the Second Coming of Jesus Christ. All current world events are lining up and pointing to His Second Coming. The wars described in the Bible are awesome, but they pale in comparison to the coming of Jesus Christ. He returns during the Day of the Lord to save Israel from total destruction. When the Lord Jesus returns, it is not to Washington or London or Mecca, but it is to Jerusalem.

The prophet Zechariah describes the Second Coming. He sees the Lord Jesus standing in Jerusalem on the Mount of Olives. A tremendous earthquake which shakes the entire world coincides with His coming. Jesus Christ then destroys the forces of evil gathered around Jerusalem.

"Behold, the day of the LORD cometh... (2) For I will gather all nations against Jerusalem to battle... (3) Then shall the LORD go forth, and fight against those nations, as when he fought in the day of battle. (4) And his feet shall stand in that day upon the mount of Olives, which is before Jerusalem on the east, and the mount of Olives shall cleave in the midst thereof..."

Zechariah" 14:1-4.

The Lord Jesus comes directly from heaven to set up His universal, everlasting Kingdom. No world organization elects Him, nor is He appointed. He will not head any political organization like the United Nations. It is God's supernatural power that establishes His kingdom on the earth. The Bible describes His coming as flaming fire in great glory.

"And to you who are troubled rest with us, when the Lord Jesus shall be revealed from heaven with his mighty angels...in flaming fire..."

2 Thessalonians 1:7, 8.

When Jesus Christ returns to defend Jerusalem, a massive number of believers accompany Him. Zechariah describes the effect of the incredible earthquake, and then he states that the Lord Jesus is returning with all His saints. These saints are not on earth at Jesus' Second Coming, but this huge throng accompanies Him from heaven. In the Day of the Lord, Jesus Christ returns with a vast array of people. Zechariah identifies them as saints.

"...And the LORD my God shall come, and all the saints with thee."

Zechariah 14:5.

Throughout the Bible, it describes a massive number of believers returning with the Lord Jesus Christ. The usual phrase describing this throng is the "Clouds of Heaven." The New Testament uses the phrase "The Clouds of Heaven" several times, but it actually originated in the Old Testament.

The prophet Daniel first uses this phrase, and he identifies what exactly are the Clouds of Heaven. Daniel gives a rare glimpse into heaven, in the Old Testament. The prophet actually sees events taking place before the very throne of God. He refers to the holy God of Israel as the Ancient of Days. He sees God on His throne, and the prophet uses fire to describe everything about God's appearance including the surroundings of His throne.

Daniel saw something else around the throne which was a countless number of believers. The prophet recorded the number of believers as thousand times thousands and ten thousand times ten thousand. This huge number is beyond calculation.

The Clouds of Heaven then, are the innumerable number of believers who are in heaven with the Lord Jesus, and return with Him. These are the saints that Zechariah stated are coming with Jesus Christ. The following verses show God's throne and this huge number of believers around it:

> "...the Ancient of days did sit, whose garment was white as snow, and the hair of his head like the pure wool: his throne was like the fiery flame, and his wheels as burning fire. (10) A fiery stream issued and came forth from before him: thousand thousands ministered unto him, and ten thousand times ten thousand stood before him..."
>
> Daniel 7:9, 10.

The Clouds of Heaven are this enormous number of believers who surround the throne of God. It appears the Bible uses the term "Clouds of Heaven" because this huge throng of believers, from a distance, appears as a massive cloud. From other Scriptures, the Bible reveals that the believers are dressed in pure white.

The Lord leads this massive white cloud, the Clouds of Heaven. They return with Him and are present when He establishes His kingdom on earth. The following verses from Daniel 7 show the Son of Man, the Lord Jesus, returning with the Clouds of Heaven to set up His kingdom on earth.

"I saw in the night visions, and, behold, one like the Son of man came with the Clouds of Heaven, and came to the Ancient of days, and they brought him near before him."

(14) And there was given him dominion, and glory, and a kingdom, that all people, nations, and languages, should serve him: his dominion is an everlasting dominion, which shall not pass away, and his kingdom that which shall not be destroyed."

Daniel 7:13, 14.

At His trial, when the Lord Jesus was questioned by the high priest concerning His claim of being the Son of God, He answered by joining two Scriptures together. He used Daniel 7:13 and Psalm 110:1 and referred them to His Second Coming. The Lord Jesus stated He was returning with the Clouds of Heaven. The high priest fully understood Jesus was quoting the prophet Daniel and the meaning of this verse. He used this statement to condemn Jesus to death for blasphemy, because this phrase related to the coming of Israel's King Messiah.

"Jesus saith unto him, Thou hast said: nevertheless I say unto you, Hereafter shall ye see the Son of man sitting on the right hand of power, **and coming in the Clouds of Heaven**."

Matthew 26:64.

Thus the "Clouds of Heaven" is obviously a very important term because the prophet Daniel used it, and the Lord Jesus quoted it to the high priest.

The Blessed Hope:
The Coming of Jesus Christ
With The Clouds of Heaven

"Looking for that blessed hope, and the glorious appearing of the great God and our Saviour Jesus Christ"

Titus 2:13.

With this foundation, let's now look at the New Testament, and the coming of the Lord Jesus with the Clouds of Heaven. When Jesus' disciples asked what the sign of His coming was, He listed several events. These events include both awesome wars and natural disasters. Then, when all is fulfilled, the people of earth would see Him coming with power and great glory. And, when He returns in great glory, the Clouds of Heaven are with Him. Jesus directly linked His coming with the Clouds of Heaven.

All the gospel writers link the Second Coming with the Clouds of Heaven. The verses from the gospels follow:

"And then shall appear the sign of the Son of man in heaven: and then shall all the tribes of the earth mourn, **and they shall see the Son of man coming**

in the Clouds of Heaven with power and great glory."

> Matthew 24:30.

"And then shall they see the Son of man coming **in the clouds** with great power and glory."

> Mark 13:26

"And then shall they see the Son of man coming **in a cloud** with power and great glory."

> Luke 21:27.

The Apostle John also makes the link between the Second Coming and the Lord returning with the Clouds of Heaven. John, in the Book of Revelation, sees the Lord's return with the clouds, and all the people of the earth mourning.

"Behold, he cometh **with clouds**; and every eye shall see him, and they also which pierced him: and all kindreds of the earth shall wail because of him. Even so, Amen."

> Revelation 1:7.

The Apostle John, in the book of Revelation, identifies the Clouds of Heaven as the Church. These are the true believers in the Lord Jesus who are in heaven and then return with Him. This is not just the dead in Christ, but it is the entire Church. It is the Lord's completed Church that returns with Him.

"And saviours shall come up on mount Zion to judge the mount of Esau; and the kingdom shall be the LORD'S."

> Obadiah 1:21.

John describes a scene in heaven where the entire Church is at the marriage supper of the Lamb. There are an innumerable number of people with Jesus. A number, just like Daniel witnessed, that were before the throne of God. There can be no doubt that this event is taking place in heaven.

> "And after these things I heard a great voice of much people **in heaven**, saying, Alleluia; Salvation, and glory, and honour, and power, unto the Lord our God: (6) And I heard as it were the voice of a great multitude, and as the voice of many waters, and as the voice of mighty thunderings, saying, Alleluia: for the Lord God omnipotent reigneth."
>
> Revelation 19:1.

After John identifies the location, he goes on to describe what is taking place. He identifies what is occurring in heaven as the marriage supper of the Lamb. The Lamb is a title for Jesus Christ, and His bride is the Church. This is the Church in heaven with Jesus.

> "Let us be glad and rejoice, and give honour to him: for the marriage of the Lamb is come, and his wife hath made herself ready. (8) And to her was granted that she should be arrayed in fine linen, clean and white: for the fine linen is the righteousness of saints.
>
> (9) And he saith unto me, Write, Blessed are they which are called unto the marriage supper of the Lamb..."
>
> Revelation 19:7.

After the marriage supper is finished, the Lord Jesus has work to do on earth. John sees heaven open, and Lord returning to earth. He is returning as a mighty man of war. He then executes the fierceness of God's wrath over the nations in rebellion against Him. He finally judges the nations at the battle of Armageddon.

> "And out of his mouth goeth a sharp sword, that with it he should smite the nations: and he shall rule them with a rod of iron: and he treadeth the winepress of the fierceness and wrath of Almighty God."
>
> Revelation 19:15.

When the Lord Jesus returns, His feet are going to stand on the Mount of Olives. Then, He destroys the armies surrounding Jerusalem as the prophet Zechariah stated. Jesus' return in Revelation 19 with His feet standing on the Mount of Olives in Zechariah 14, tie directly together. The Old Testament clearly maps this out, and the events of Revelation in the New Testament directly tie in.

John sees more than just the Lord Jesus returning. He sees the Church returning with Him. He refers to the Church not as the Clouds of Heaven, but "the armies in heaven." This army returns with Him clothed in pure white linen. This "army in heaven" that John writes about are the Clouds of Heaven which Daniel saw in his vision. This is the Clouds of Heaven which the Lord Jesus told the high priest He was returning with. He is coming back with His bride, the Church.

The Clouds of Heaven then, is the glorious Church returning with the Savior. The Church is in heaven and then returns with the Lord Jesus to defend Jerusalem. What a sight to witness, the Son of God returning in His power and glory with the Clouds of Heaven!

> "And **the armies which were in heaven** followed him upon white horses, clothed in fine linen, white and clean."
>
> Revelation 19:14.

God is setting an incredible backdrop to the Second Coming of Jesus Christ. The sky is totally darkened through either natural events, or manmade actions. It is so dark that even the sun's light is blocked. There is total darkness. With this background suddenly there is an explosion of light as the glory of Jesus Christ lights the sky. Directly behind Him are the Clouds of Heaven dressed in pure white.

Imagine being on earth and seeing this happening. The entire sky filled from one end to the other with this massive white cloud, and at the head is the Lord Jesus in flaming fire, manifesting His glory! What Daniel actually witnessed was the Church returning with King Messiah, the Lord Jesus! The verses to show this follow:

> "Immediately after the tribulation of those days shall the sun be darkened, and the moon shall not give her light... (30)...And then shall appear the sign of the Son of man in heaven...and they shall see the Son of man coming in the clouds of heaven with power and great glory."
>
> Matthew 24:29, 30.

The Church returns with the Lord Jesus at His Second Coming. Since the Church is in heaven enjoying the marriage supper of the Lamb, how and when did it get there? At Jesus' command, He summons the Church to heaven. This event occurs before He returns to save Israel at the battle of Armageddon.

It happens, as the Apostle Paul says, in the twinkling of an eye. Not everyone is going to die. But, those that are alive at the Lord's summons for the believing Church, are immediately changed. They receive eternal life and an incorruptible body. God raises from the dead the people who believed in Jesus, and He then joins them with those who are still alive.

"Behold, I show you a mystery; We shall not all sleep, but we shall all be changed, (52) In a moment, in the twinkling of an eye, at the last trump: for the trumpet shall sound, and the dead shall be raised incorruptible, and we shall be changed.

1 Corinthians 15:51, 52.

This will happen when the Lord Jesus comes for His bride the Church. He will descend from heaven with a tremendous shout and the blast of the trumpet. The dead in Christ shall arise first, and then the believers which are alive at this time shall receive a resurrected body. God takes the entire Church to heaven, and they shall forever more be with the Lord Jesus. The Church goes with Him to the marriage supper of the Lamb.

"For this we say unto you by the word of the Lord, that we which are alive and remain unto the coming of the Lord shall not prevent them which are asleep.

(16) For the Lord himself shall descend from heaven with a shout, with the voice of the archangel, and with the trump of God: and the dead in Christ shall rise first: (17) Then we which are alive and remain shall be caught up together with them in the clouds, to meet the Lord in the air: and so shall we ever be with the Lord. (18) Wherefore comfort one another with these words."

1 Thessalonians 4:15-17.

The idea of the Lord's coming for the Church is so powerful that the Bible tells us to comfort one another with this in our times of sorrow over the loss of a loved one. The loss is only temporary, as there will be a uniting with the loved ones when the Lord comes for the believers. This is truly the blessed hope, the coming of the Lord for the Church and being with Him forever.

"Looking for that blessed hope, and the glorious appearing of the great God and our Saviour Jesus Christ."

Titus 2:13.

Looking for the coming of the Lord Jesus, is the blessed hope. It is not just a hope, but it is a blessed hope. Immediately following the Church's gathering with the Lord is the marriage supper of the Lamb. And, it is a blessing to be called to the marriage supper of the Lamb.

There is a double blessing for those who are waiting for the Lord's return. There is the blessed hope, and then the blessing of anticipating the marriage supper of the Lamb. All believers should be living with the blessed hope and the excitement of the marriage supper.

If these two hopes are not motivating a believer, there is something radically wrong with that person's faith. Living with the blessed hope is one of the true signs of a believer. Jesus is only returning for those who are waiting for Him.

"So Christ was once offered to bear the sins of many; and unto them that look for him shall he appear the Second time without sin unto salvation."

Hebrews 9:28.

The Second Coming for the Church is not just a doctrine, but it is to be a living reality in a believer's life. If this reality is not in a person's heart, it is a sign something is drastically wrong. Sin and the love of the world kill the blessed hope. Wrong doctrine about the blessed hope also deadens the reality of the Lord's coming for the Church and the marriage supper of the Lamb.

The two comings of the Lord, first for His Church, and then to defend Israel, can be viewed as the two comings identified in the Old Testament. The Bible in the Old Testament does not say directly that King Messiah is coming twice. But, when you study the Old Testament the teaching of the two comings are there.

In one coming, King Messiah is lowly on a donkey, while in the other, He is coming in power and great glory with the "Clouds of Heaven." These two comings can appear irreconcilable until you realize there are actually two distinct appearances. With the understanding of two comings, the Scriptures fit together beautifully. The following Scriptures show the two comings:

"Rejoice greatly, O daughter of Zion; shout, O daughter of Jerusalem: behold, thy King cometh unto thee: he is just, and having salvation; lowly, and riding upon an ass (donkey), and upon a colt the foal of an ass."

Zechariah 9:9.

"I saw in the night visions, and, behold, one like the Son of man came with the Clouds of Heaven, and came to the Ancient of days, and they brought him near before him."

Daniel 7:13.

The same pattern in Scriptures holds true for the last of the two comings, and it is called "the Lord's Second Coming." This coming is in two stages or phases. During the first stage, He comes for the Church, followed by the marriage supper of the Lamb in heaven. The second stage begins at the completion of the marriage supper, when the Jesus Christ returns with the Clouds of Heaven to Jerusalem. The Lord's feet will then stand on the Mount of Olives. Jesus Christ meets His Church in the air at the first stage. His feet stand on the Mount of Olives during the second stage. The verses to show this follow:

> "Then we which are alive and remain shall be caught up together with them in the clouds, to meet the Lord in the air: and so shall we ever be with the Lord."
>
> 1 Thessalonians 4:17.

> "And his feet shall stand in that day upon the mount of Olives, which is before Jerusalem on the east, and the mount of Olives shall cleave in the midst thereof toward the east and toward the west...(5)... and the LORD my God shall come, and all the saints with thee."
>
> Zechariah 14:4, 5.

The Coming of the Lord Draweth Nigh

> "And every man that hath this hope in him purifieth himself, even as he is pure."
>
> 1 John 3:3.

The reality of the blessed hope has an awesome effect on the believer. It is not just the doctrine of the blessed hope, but it is the living reality that affects lives. This reality causes tremendous spiritual growth.

In Paul's letter to Titus, the Bible lists eight effects the blessed hope has on a believer's heart. When a person lives with the anticipation of the Second Coming, the results include: victory over ungodliness and worldly lusts; to be sober minded; righteousness; godly living; victory over iniquity; purifying; and a zealousness for good works. Maybe the weakness of many Christians is because they lack the blessed hope in their heart. The Bibles verses to show the effect of the blessed hope follow:

> "For the grace of God that bringeth salvation hath appeared to all men, (12) Teaching us that, denying ungodliness and worldly lusts, we should live soberly, righteously, and godly, in this present world;
>
> (13) Looking for that blessed hope, and the glorious appearing of the great God and our Saviour Jesus Christ;
>
> (14) Who gave himself for us, that he might redeem us from all iniquity, and purify unto himself a peculiar people, zealous of good works."
>
> Titus 2:11-14.

The blessed hope is spiritual life to a believer, and without it, worldliness sets in and chokes the word of God in a person's life. Notice in Titus 2:11-14 the blessed hope is in the very middle of this admonition to live godly. This verse was placed there to show how important the blessed hope is to our spiritual life. False doctrines that do not teach the reality of the blessed hope rob spiritual power from believers. These types of teachings create weak believers because of the false teaching about the Lord's Second Coming.

The Bible even draws a connection between the blessed hope and being zealous of good works. If one believes in the blessed hope this should motivate that person to work for God and not relax in this world. This is not a time for coasting, rather it is the time to live holy and do great things in the name of the Lord Jesus. If one is not zealous for the Lord Jesus, that is sign something is wrong with that person's faith.

Who gave himself for us, that he might redeem us from all iniquity, and purify unto himself a peculiar people, zealous of good works."

Titus 2:14.

The Bible tells us we are to wait for the return of the Lord Jesus. We are to wait with patience for His return. Just as a farmer plants his crops and patiently waits until the crops mature, so we are to wait for the coming of the Lord.

The Bible also tells us to establish our hearts about His coming. When a person establishes the blessed hope in his heart, holiness naturally flows. The Bible leaves no doubt that we are to focus on the blessed hope and live every day as if the Lord could return for His Church. We are to live with patience looking for His coming for the Church. The Scriptures to show this follow:

"Be patient therefore, brethren, unto the coming of the Lord. Behold, the husbandman waiteth for the precious fruit of the earth, and hath long patience for it, until he receive the early and latter rain. (8) Be ye also patient; stablish your hearts: for the coming of the Lord draweth nigh."

James 5:7, 8.

"To the end he may stablish your hearts unblame- able in holiness before God, even our Father, at the coming of our Lord Jesus Christ with all his saints."

1 Thessalonians 3:13.

The blessed hope is an anchor for our soul. This is the hope which God has set before us. He requires that we keep the blessed hope with full assurance until He returns, or until we pass away. This hope steadies us during the storms of life.

We are to lay hold of this hope and let no one or anything take it from us. The Bible verses to show this follow:

"And we desire that every one of you do show the same diligence to the full assurance of hope unto the end:
(18) That by two immutable things, in which it was impossible for God to lie, we might have a strong consolation, who have fled for refuge to lay hold upon the hope set before us: (19) Which hope we have as an anchor of the soul, both sure and stedfast, and which entereth into that within the veil"

Hebrews 6:11, 18, 19.

The Bible places nothing in the way of the Lord's coming for His Church. There is no event which is required to take place before He descends from heaven with a shout for His bride. We are to be aware of world events in the light of Bible prophecy, but our anticipation should be for the blessed hope. Focusing on world events rather than the blessed hope can hinder one's faith and often create fear. No matter what happens in the world, we are to stay focused on the Lord Jesus' Second Coming. This is the anchor for your soul in the time of trouble.

"And to wait for his Son from heaven, whom he raised from the dead, even Jesus, which delivered us from the wrath to come."

1 Thessalonians 1:10.

Faithful or Evil Servant

Jesus gave a parable identifying who is God's faithful servant and who is an evil servant. The key to these two servants is how they are prepared for the Second Coming.

The faithful servant is living by the blessed hope. He is watching and waiting for the Second Coming of Jesus Christ. And, not only does God call this servant faithful, but He also calls him wise. Living with the blessed hope, makes a person both faithful and wise.

Living ones life anticipating the return of the Lord Jesus, is not a hard or difficult task. A person can easily be a faithful servant by living in the blessed hope.

> "Watch therefore: for ye know not what hour your Lord doth come. (45) Who then is a faithful and wise servant... (46) Blessed is that servant, whom his lord when he cometh shall find so doing."
>
> Matthew 24:42, 45, 46.

Jesus then identified the evil servant. The evil servant said the Second Coming of the Lord Jesus was delayed. He then lived without the blessed hope and failed to focus His life on God, but on this world. He even hated the faithful servant who was living in the blessed hope.

When Jesus Christ returns, He casts this evil servant from His presence. God sends the evil servant to hell with the hypocrites. Someone who claims to believe in Jesus Christ and lives without the blessed hope, is a hypocrite. Living in the blessed hope is one of the hallmarks of a Christian. Just tampering with the Second Coming, by saying it is delayed until sometime in the future, and becoming aggressive against those who live in the blessed hope, makes one a hypocrite as the following verses show:

> "But and if that evil servant shall say in his heart, My lord delayeth his coming; (49) And shall begin to smite his fellowservants, and to eat and drink with the drunken;

> (50) The lord of that servant shall come in a day when he looketh not for him… (51) And shall cut him asunder, and appoint him his portion with the hypocrites: there shall be weeping and gnashing of teeth."
>
> Matthew 24:48-51.

Thus, we are to wait for the Lord Jesus with patience. The waiting should intensify the anticipation for His Second Coming and not weaken it. As we wait for His return, God works in us to fulfill all eight characteristics. Remember, those characteristics are: victory over ungodliness and worldly lusts; to be sober minded; righteousness; godly living; victory over iniquity; purifying; and a zealousness for good works.

If you have not been living with the blessed hope in your life, now is the time to confess this to God. And, ask Him to place the reality of the Second Coming of the Lord Jesus in your heart. Now is the time to ask God to make the gathering of the believers at the marriage supper of the Lamb real to you (For how to obtain the reality of the blessed hope, see Addendum E.)

> "I have fought a good fight, I have finished my course, I have kept the faith: (8) Henceforth there is laid up for me a crown of righteousness, which the Lord, the righteous judge, shall give me at that day: and not to me only, but unto all them also that love his appearing."
>
> 2 Timothy 4:7.

CHAPTER TWELVE

Until The Times of The Gentiles Be Fulfilled

"... and Jerusalem shall be trodden down of the Gentiles, until the times of the Gentiles be fulfilled."

Luke 21:24.

*A*merica has a tremendous track record in supporting God's plan for the Jewish people. God raised up America as a world power at the exact time He was restoring His people back to the covenant land. America played a major part in this restoration.

The United States blessed the Jews. When the tyrants of Europe were slaughtering them, the people of America opened their arms and took them in. Millions escaped and came to America. The Church was the main force behind America's support for the Jewish people and then later the nation of Israel.

President George Washington's vision for the Jewish people was for America to resemble the Messianic Kingdom. In a sense it has. He set the example and laid the foundation for America to bless the Jewish people. President Abraham Lincoln followed his example and personally protected the Jews, when, unfortunately, they were targeted for discrimination during the Civil War. There were some rough spots in American history for the Jewish people, but overall America has greatly blessed the Jew.

The American Church in the late 1800s seized the spiritual opportunity to support the Jew and focus on the restoration of Israel. The Church lined up with God's everlasting covenant for the land of Israel. Throughout America, believers were praying for the Jewish people and the restoration of Israel. Just six years after the Blackstone Memorial, the modern Zionist movement was born.

God continued to answer the prayers and intercession of the Church. Just 26 years after the Memorial, the Muslim Turks lost control of the Covenant land. Modern Israel was reborn in 1948, and God's prophetic plan was once again moving. The American Church was the primary spiritual force behind this.

During the late 1800s and into the 1900s, the Church also focused on the Second Coming. The Church was highly motivated by the blessed hope of Christ's Second Coming. The nation was alive with the blessed hope. These two dynamics, praying for the nation of Israel and focusing on Christ's Second Coming, generated a tremendous response from God. Focusing on the Lord Jesus' Seconding Coming saved the American Church from destruction. The great power generated by preaching the Lord's return carried down through the decades to today.

In the 1800s, the European Church failed to focus on Christ's coming and it grew steadily "worldly" and cold. Worldly means to focus on things other than God and His word. For generation after generation, the European Church grew colder and colder and further and further away from the Bible and God until today, the Church in Europe is almost nonexistent. The Church in Europe is dead. There are more Muslims in Europe today, than true believers in Jesus Christ. The Church has little impact on Europe and now Islam is filling this void. The Europeans had the opportunity, as did the American Church, but they failed to seize the moment and now suffer greatly.

Europe has a long history of hating the Jewish people. The European Church failed to stand with the Jews when Tsarist Russia was persecuting them. Millions of Russian Jews left "Christian" Europe and traveled thousands of miles to America. The European Church failed miserably. The combination of failing to preach the Lord Jesus' Second Coming, and standing with God's covenant people, left Europe spiritually bankrupt.

America took a different road than the Europeans. The great evangelists, preachers and seminaries of America continued to proclaim the Second Coming. The Church continued to stand with the Jewish people and later the restored nation of Israel. The Church in America remained vibrant and alive while the European Church died a slow death.

The American Church still enjoys great blessings from the revivals that swept America from the late 1800s into the early 1900s; however, powerful forces are eating away at the strength of the American Church. False doctrines such as preterism, dominion and replacement theology, which affect a person's view of Israel and the Second Coming, are drawing away large numbers of Christians.

The Church focusing on wealth and materialism is also draining power from the believers. There are huge numbers of people completely focused on material gain and not the Second Coming of the Lord Jesus. This focus on materialism is called the "prosperity message." Christians are to focus on Christ's Second Coming and not material wealth. Focusing on wealth starts the process to lead a person directly away from Christ. Each succeeding generation departs further from the blessed hope.

> "And take heed to yourselves, lest at any time your hearts be overcharged with surfeiting (eating), and drunkenness, and cares of this life, and so that day (of the Lord) come upon you unawares."
>
> Luke 21:34.

In general, there is lack of preaching and teaching about the awesome Second Coming of the Lord Jesus Christ. The combination of all these factors has resulted in huge numbers of believers becoming dead to God's prophetic move and His prophetic plan in the hour we live. In fact, they are heading down the same road as the Europeans. False doctrine is deadly to the Church.

God has not hid His prophetic plan. It is on page after page in the Bible. God is not hiding the coming Day of the Lord. It is visible to all who focus on the Second Coming and understand God's covenant nation Israel.

The entire Christian Church, and the American Church in particular, has to choose which road to travel. God's road is to focus on the Second Coming of Jesus Christ and His prophetic plan for Israel. Any other road leads directly to spiritual decay. God has set His plumb line. The true road is getting back to focusing on the Second Coming and lining up with God's prophetic plan for Israel. The Church in America did 120 years ago, and shook the world.

As the Day of the Lord approaches, the integrity of the United States depends upon the believers. America has already interfered with God's prophetic plan, and suffered greatly for this. God has clearly warned America of the coming judgment. Entire nations will disappear during the Day of the Lord and the United States could be one.

The coming wars indicate America will not be a great power. But maybe, just maybe, if the Church repents and rises up, God will spare America from total destruction. Then the nation might survive to the Second Coming and enter Jesus' Kingdom reign.

America has a great spiritual heritage. Let us not lose it over materialism and false doctrine. As with our predecessors, let us once again, as a Church, focus on the Second Coming and stand with the Jewish people. On God's prophetic time-table, we are now on the other side of the rebirth of Israel. The "times of the Gentiles" are drawing to a close. God's prophetic clock is accelerating. If the "times of the Gentiles" are drawing to a close, then how much sooner is the awesome coming of Jesus Christ for His Church!

The Wise Shall Understand.

"… but the wicked shall do wickedly: and none of the wicked shall understand; but the wise shall understand."

Daniel 12:10.

The context of the above Bible verse is the Day of the Lord. The prophet Daniel stated as the Day of the Lord approached, none of the unbelievers would recognize the time was drawing near, but those who were wise in God's word would understand the events of the hour.

In the above verse, the prophet Daniel uses the word *understand* twice. The Hebrew word understand means, "to be separate or distinguish mentally." In our modern expression, it means to put two and two together. The word wise means to act circumspectly and therefore intelligently.

289

As the Day of the Lord nears the people anchored in the Bible and correct doctrine can see it approaching. They are able to think things through, put two and two together, and clearly see God's prophetic plan. They act intelligently and align their life according to God's prophetic plan. The wicked, those in rebellion against God, are unable to put two and two together, and see the reality of God's prophetic plan. Almost daily, this plan is played out on the front pages of the newspapers.

The wicked are opposed to God's prophetic plan and do not live in the blessed hope. They face eternal judgment from the holy God of Israel. The true Church lines up with God's prophetic plan as outlined in the Bible. The true Church blesses the Jewish people. The true Church is the faithful and wise servant, living in the blessed hope, patiently waiting for the coming of the Lord Jesus and the marriage supper of the Lamb.

In the hour we live in, the difference between both the faithful and evil servants is clearly manifested for all to see. Are you a faithful and wise servant? Are you living in the blessed hope? Will you be one in the Clouds of Heaven?

"... Hereafter shall ye see the Son of man sitting on the right hand of power, and coming in the clouds of heaven."

Matthew 26:64.

Addendum A

The Major Text of George Washington's 1789 Letter to the Hebrew Congregation of Savannah, Georgia.

*G*entlemen:-I thank you with great sincerity for your congratulations on my appointment to the office which I have the honor to hold by the unanimous choice of my fellow citizens, and especially the expressions you are pleased to use in testifying the confidence that is reposed in me by your congregation

I rejoice that a spirit of liberality and philanthropy is much more prevalent than it formerly was among the enlightened nations of the earth, and that your brethren will benefit thereby in proportion as it shall become still more extensive; happily the people of the United States have in many instances exhibited examples worthy of imitation, the salutary influence of which will doubtless extend much farther if gratefully enjoying those blessings of peace which (under the favor of heaven) have been attained by fortitude in war, they shall conduct themselves with reverence to the Deity and charity toward their fellow- creatures.

May the same wonder-working Deity, who long since delivered the Hebrews from their Egyptian oppressors, planted them in a promised land, whose providential agency has lately been conspicuous in establishing these United States as an independent nation, still continue to water them with the dews of heaven and make the inhabitants of every denomination participate in the temporal and spiritual blessings of that people whose God is Jehovah

Addendum B

The Full Text of George Washington's 1790 Letter to the Hebrew Congregation of Newport, Rhode Island.

While I received with much satisfaction your address replete with expressions of esteem, I rejoice in the opportunity of assuring you that I shall always retain grateful remembrance of the cordial welcome I experienced on my visit to Newport from all classes of citizens

The reflection on the days of difficulty and danger which are past is rendered the more sweet from a consciousness that they are succeeded by days of uncommon prosperity and security

If we have wisdom to make the best use of the advantages with which we are now favored, we cannot fail, under the just administration of a good government, to become a great and happy people.

The Citizens of the United States of America have a right to applaud themselves for giving to Mankind examples of an enlarged and liberal policy: a policy worthy of imitation. All possess alike liberty of conscience and immunities of citizenship. It is now no more that toleration is spoken of, as if it was by the indulgence of one class of people that another enjoyed the exercise of their inherent natural rights. For happily the Government of the United States, which gives to bigotry no sanction, to persecution no assistance, requires only that they who live under its protection, should demean themselves as good citizens

May the Children of the Stock of Abraham, who dwell in this land, continue to merit and enjoy the good will of the other Inhabitants; while every one shall sit under his own vine and fig tree, and there shall be none to make him afraid.

May the father of all mercies scatter light and not darkness in our paths, and make us all in our several vocations useful here, and in his own due time and way everlastingly happy."

Addendum C

Jewish Messenger, **April 26, 1861: Editorial by Samuel Mayer Isaacs titled: Stand By The Flag.**

It is almost a work of supererogation for us to call upon our readers to be loyal to the Union, which protects them. It is needless for us to say anything to induce them to proclaim their devotion to the land in which they live. But we desire our voice, too, to be heard at this time, joining in the hearty and spontaneous shout ascending from the whole American people, to stand by the stars and stripes!

Already we hear of many of our young friends taking up arms in defense of their country, pledging themselves to assist in maintaining inviolate its integrity, and ready to respond, if need be, with their lives, to the call of the constituted authorities, in the cause of law and order.

The time is past for forbearance and temporizing. We are now to act, and sure we are, that those whom these words may reach, will not be backward in realizing the duty that is incumbent upon them—to rally as one man for the Union and the Constitution. The Union—which binds together, by so many sacred ties, millions of free men—which extends its hearty invitation to the oppressed of all nations, to come and be sheltered beneath its protecting wings—shall it be severed, destroyed, or even impaired? Shall those, whom we once called our brethren, be permitted to overthrow the fabric reared by the noble patriots of the revolution, and cemented with their blood?

And the Constitution—guaranteeing to all, the free exercise of their religious opinions—extending to all, liberty, justice, and equality—the pride of Americans, the admiration of the world—shall that Constitution be subverted, and anarchy usurp the place of a sound, safe and stable government, deriving its authority from the consent of the American People?

The voice of millions yet unborn, cried out, 'Forbid it, Heaven!' The voice of the American people declares in tones not to be misunderstood: `It shall not be!'

Then stand by the Flag! What death can be as glorious as that of the patriot, surrendering his life in defense of his country—pouring forth his blood on the battlefield—to live forever in the hearts of a grateful people. Whether native or foreign born, Gentile or Israelite, stand by it, and you are doing your duty, and acting well your part on the side of liberty and justice!

We know full well that our young men, who have left their homes to respond to the call of their country, will, on their return, render a good account of themselves. We have no fears for their bravery and patriotism. Our prayers are with them. G-d speed them on the work which they have volunteered to perform!

And if they fall—if, fighting in defense of that flag, they meet a glorious and honorable death, their last moments will be cheered by the consciousness that they have done their duty, and grateful America will not forget her sons, who have yielded up their spirit in her behalf

And as for us, who do not accompany them on their noble journey, our duty too, is plain. We are to pray to Heaven that He may restore them soon again to our midst, after having assisted in vindicating the honor and integrity of the flag they have sworn to defend; and we are to pledge ourselves to assume for them, should they fall in their country's cause, the obligation of supporting those whom their departure leaves unprotected. Such is our duty. Let them, and all of us, renew our solemn oath that, whatever may betide, we will be true to the Union and the Constitution, and Stand By The Flag.

Addendum D

The Blackstone Memorial, March 1891:
Presented to the president of the United States
in favor of the restoration of Palestine to the Jews.

*W*hat shall be done for the Russian Jews? It is both unwise and useless to undertake to dictate to Russia concerning her internal affairs. The Jews have lived as foreigners in her dominions for centuries and she fully believes that they are a burden upon her resources and prejudicial to the wellfare of her peasant population, and will not allow them to remain. She is determined that they must go. Hence, like the Sephardim of Spain, these Ashkenazim must emigrate. But where shall 2,000,000 of such poor people go? Europe is crowded and has no room for more peasant population. Shall they come to America? This will be a tremendous expense, and require years.

Why not give Palestine back to them again? According to God's distribution of nations it is their home, an inalienable possession from which they were expelled by force. Under their cultivation it was a remarkably fruitful land sustaining millions of Israelites who industrially tilled its hillsides and valleys. They were agriculturists and producers as well as a nation of great commercial importance — the center of civilization and religion.

Why shall not the powers which under the treaty of Berlin, in 1878, gave Bulgaria to the Bulgarians and Servia to the Servians now give Palestine back to the Jews? These provinces, as well as Roumania, Montenegro and Greece, were wrested from the Turks and given to their natural owners. Does not Palestine as rightfully belong to the Jews? It is said that rains are increasing and there are evidences that the land is recovering its ancient fertility. If they could have autonomy in government the Jews of the world would rally to transport and establish their suffering brethren in their time-honored- habitation. For over seventeen centuries they have patiently waited for such an opportunity. They have not become agriculturists elsewhere because they believed they were mere sojourners in the various nations, and were yet to return to Palestine and till their own land. Whatever vested rights, by possession may have accrued to Turkey can be easily compensated, possibly by the Jews assuming an equitable portion of the national debt. We believe this is an appropriate time for all nations and especially the Christian nations of Europe to show kindness to Israel. A million of exiles, by their terrible suffering, are piteously appealing to our sympathy, justice, and humanity Let us now restore to them the land of which they were so cruelly despoiled by our Roman ancestors.

To this end we respectfully petition His Excellency Benjamin Harrison, President of the United States, and the Honorable James G. Blaine, Secretary of State, to use their good offices and influence with the Governments of their Imperial Majesties-

Alexander III, Czar of Russia; Victoria, Queen of Great Britain and Empress of India; William II, Emperor of Germany; Francis Joseph, Emperor of Austr-Hungary; Abdul

Hamid II, Sultan of Turkey; His Royal Majesty, Humbert, King of Italy; Her Royal Majesty Marie Christiana, Queen Regent of Spain; and the Government of the Republic of France and with the Governments of Belgium, Holland, Denmark, Sweden, Portugal, Roumainia, Servia, Bulgaria and Greece. To secure the holding at an early date, of an international conference to consider the condition of the Israelites and their claims to Palestine as their ancient home, and to promote, in all other just and proper ways, the alleviation of their suffering condition.

Addendum E

Assurance of The Blessed Hope

*W*hen a person lives in the blessed hope, it gives him the assurance of eternal life with the Lord Jesus. It also gives one the assurance of returning with the Lord Jesus Christ as one in the Clouds of Heaven.

According to the Bible, this assurance is obtained by realizing that God loves you, and He wants you to have eternal life with Him. God personally cares about you and desires that you have eternal life with Him.

> "For God so loved the world, that he gave his only begotten Son, that whosoever believeth in him should not perish, but have everlasting life."
>
> John 3:16.

The way of believing in Jesus Christ as your Savior is to repent of sin and to trusting Him completely as your Lord and Savior. When you trust Jesus Christ in your heart, as your Savior all your sin is forgiven by God, as Jesus paid the penalty on the cross for you. Without repentance of sin and the confession of Jesus Christ as Lord and Savior, it is impossible to have eternal life with God

> "That if thou shalt confess with thy mouth the Lord Jesus, and shalt believe in thine heart that God hath raised him from the dead, thou shalt be saved. (10) For with the heart man believeth unto righteousness; and with the mouth confession is made unto salvation."
>
> Romans 10:9.10.

When you confess Jesus as your Lord and Savior, you are now to live with the expectation of His Second Coming in your heart. This is the blessed hope; the expectation of the Second Coming of the Lord Jesus and being with Him forever. With the confession of Jesus Christ and living with the expectation of His Second Coming, this is the evidence you will be with the Lord Jesus when He returns with the Clouds of Heaven.

> "Looking for that blessed hope, and the glorious appearing of the great God and our Saviour Jesus Christ;"
>
> Titus 2:13

The Lord Jesus has paid the penalty for your sin by His shed blood on the cross. God has provided His way for you to have eternal life with Him. Right now, you can turn to God by prayer through faith in Jesus Christ as your Lord and Savior. Please do not put this off, because now is the Day of salvation.

Bibliography

Books

Allen, Everett S. *A Wind to Shake the World*, Little, Brown and Company, Boston, 1976.

Arno Press, *Call to America to Build Zion*, New York Times Co, New York, 1977.

Baldwin, Neil, *Henry Ford and The Jews*, Public Affairs, New York, NY, 2001

Baron, H.S., *Haym Salomon*, Bloch Publishing Co. New York, 1929.

Birmingham, Stephen, *America Sephardic Elites the Grandees*, Harper and Row, New York, 1971.

Birnbaum, Pierre, *The Anti-Semitic Moment*, Hill & Wang, New York, 1998.

Burns, Cherie, *The Great Hurricane of 1938*, Atlantic Monthly Press, New York, 2005.

Currie, William E., *God's Little Errand Boy*, AMF anniversary booklet *100 Years of Blessing*, http://www.amfi.org/contact.htm

Diamond, Sander A., The *Nazi Movement in the United States 1924-1941*, Disc-Us Books, www.disc-us.com, 2001.

Elsner, James B., *Hurricanes of the North Atlantic*, Oxford University Press, New York, 1999.

Federal Writer's Project, New *England Hurricane a Factual Pictorial Record*, Hale, Cushman & Flint, Boston, 1938.

Gordon, Bernard L. *Hurricane in Southern New England*, The Book Shop, Watch Hill, RI, 1976.

Goudsouzian, Aram, *The Hurricane of 1938*, Commonwealth Editions, Beverly, MA, 2004.

Higham, Charles, *American Swastika*, Doubleday & Co, Garden City, NY, 1985.

Hitler, Adolph, *Mein Kampf*, Reynal & Hitchcock, New York, 1941.

Jenkins, Philip, *Hoods and Shirts*, The University of North Carolina Press, Chapel Hill, NC, 1997.

Junger, Sebastian, *The Perfect Storm*, Harper Collins Press, New York, 1997.

Karp, Abraham, *From the Ends of the Earth - Judaic Treasures of the Library of Congress*, Library of Congress, Washington, DC., 1991. (This was a tremendous source of information. I highly recommend this book.)

Knight, Jr., Vick, *Send For Haym Salomon*, Borden Publishing Company, Alhambra, CA, 1976.

Longshore, David, *Encyclopedia of Hurricanes, Typhoons, and Cyclones*, Checkmark Books, New York, 2000.

Marcus, Jacob Rader, *Early American Jewry New York New England and Canada*, Vol. 1, The Jewish Publication Society of America, New York, 1951.

Marcus, Jacob Rader, *Early American Jewry Pennsylvania and the South*, Vol. 2, The Jewish Publication Society of America, New York, 1953.

McTernan, John and Koenig, Bill, *Israel: The Blessing or The Curse*, Hearthstone Publishing, Oklahoma City, OK, 2001.

Miller, Marvin D., *Wunderlich's Salute*, Malamud-Rose Press, Smithtown, NY, 1983.

Minsinger, William E., *The 1938 Hurricane- an Historical and Pictorial Summary*, GreenHills Books, Vermont, 1988.

Obenzinger, Hilton, *In the Shadow of "God's Sun-dial,"* Stanford University, http://www.stanford.edu/group/SHR/5-1/text/obenzinger.html

Perry, Margaret B., *The 1938 Hurricane As We Remember It*, Quogue Historical Society, Quogue, NY, 1995.

Providence Journal Co, *The Great Hurricane and Tidal Wave, Rhode Island*, Providence Journal Co. (No author, location or date of publishing, but this book by far had the best photographs of the awesome destruction of the hurricane.)

Russell, Charles Edward, *Haym Salomon and the Revolution*, Cosmopolitan Book Corp, New York, 1930.

Sachar, Howard M., *A History of Jews in America*, 1992, Vintage Books, New York, 1992.

Scotti, R.A., *Sudden Sea*, Little Brown and Company, Boston, 2003.

Magazines, Journals and Miscellaneous

Adolph Hitler Street, Yaphank, NY: New York State, County of Suffolk, Town of Brookhaven, map number 129, abstract 1238, filed January 5, 1937.

Ahern, John L. *Flood and Hurricane*, New England Power Association, Boston, MA, 1938.

AMF International, *The Blackstone Memorial*, P.O. Box 5470, Lansing, IL 60438-5470, http://www.amfi.org/blackmem.htm

Colton, F. Barrows, *The Geography of a Hurricane*, The National Geographic Magazine, Vol. LXXV, Number 4, National Geographic Society, Washington DC, April 1939.

Department of the Navy, Naval Historical Center, *War Plans and Preparations and Their Impact on U.S. Naval Operations in the Spanish-American War,* http://www.history.navy.mil/wars/spanam.htm#anchorn3

The Jewish Messenger, Volume 8, Number 25, 12/28/1861, article titled: A Day of Prayer.

Keppler, Joseph, *Cartoons and Comments*, Volume 10, No. 247, Puck Magazine, Keppler & Schwarzmann, New York, November 30, 1881.

Life Magazine, *Fascism in America,* Time Inc, New York, Volume 6, Number 19, March 6, 1939, Page 57.

Mazelev, Julia, *Pogroms: late 19th, Beginning of 20th Century*, http://econc10.bu.edu/economic_systems/nationalidentity/fsu/russia/pogroms-naional_ident

Puck Magazine, Volume 10, Number 247, November 30, 1881, New York,

Sarna, Jonathan D., *The Jewish Week*, Faith and Freedom in the New World, http://www.thejewishweek.com/bottom/specialcontent.php3?artid

United States Sea Power 1865-On, Department of the Navy, Naval Historical Center, Washington, DC 20374, http://www.history.navy.mil/wars/spanam.htm

The Virtual Library, The American-Israeli Cooperative Enterprise, Americans React to Damascus Blood Libel, http://www.jewishvirtuallibrary.org

Francis Salvador, Jewish Virtual Library, http://www.jewish-virtuallibray.org

Video

Allen, Everett S. *A Wind to Shake the World – The Story of the 1938 Hurricane*, Produced and directed by M. L. Baron, 1988

Federal Works Agency, *The Shock Troops of Disaster – The Story of the New England Hurricane of September 21, 1938,* The Works Projects Administration, The Federal Work Agency.

George Bush Presidential Library, President Bush Speaks at the Madrid Peace Conference, October 30, 1991.

Footnotes

Chapter One

Quote from Czech Premier Jan Syrovy: New York Times, October 1, 1938, front page article titled, *Peace Aid Pledged.*

Quote from Neville Chamberlain: New York Times, October 1, 1938, front page article titled, *Peace With Honor Says Chamberlain.*

Chamberlain's return to Great Britain: New York Times, October 1, 1938, front page article titled, *Peace With Honor Says Chamberlain.*

British-German anti war pact: New York Times, October 1, 1938, front page article titled, *Britain and German Agree.*

President Roosevelt's second appeal: New York Times, September 28, 1938, page nine, article titled, *Text of President Roosevelt's Plea.*

Herman Goering's speech on September 10, 1938: Radio Days-Munich Crisis, page two, http://otr.com/munich.html

Weather related background to hurricane: Monthly Weather Review, August 1939, Volume 67, Number 8, Article titled; *The Meteorological History of the New England Hurricane of September 21, 1938*, By Charles H. Pierce.

Seismograph record of the hurricane: The National Geographic Magazine, April 1939, page 533, article titled: *The Geography of a Hurricane*, by F. Barrows Colton.

Destruction caused by the hurricane: *The Long Island Express – the Great Hurricane of 1938*, , http://www2.sunysuffolk.edu/mandias/38hurricane/

Lowest Barometric pressure at Bellport, NY, *The Long Island Express – the Great Hurricane of 1938*, http://www2.sunysuffolk.edu/mandias/38hurricane/

Information about Henry Ford: http://history.hanover.edu/hhr/99/hhr99_2.html, *Power, Ignorance, and Anti-Semitism: Henry Ford and His War on the Jews*, by Jonathan R. Logsdon. (This is a tremendous source of information about Henry Ford and his crusade against the Jews.)

Henry Ford and the Jews cause war: NY Times, October 29, 1922, article titled: *Ford, Denying Hate*, Lays War to Jews.

Bund Declarations of Principles: Free America – Fight Jews, Deutscher Weckruf und Beobachter, Volume 4, Number 11, page 1,2, September 8, 1938. (This was the official publication of the Bund.)

Bund Amendment to Constitution: Ibid

Background information about Bund: Brooklyn Daily Eagle, *U.S. Citizens Drilled By Bund in 28 Camps*, March 26, 1938, Front page article; Longwood High School, http://www.longwood.k12.ny.us/history/index.htm

Adolph Hitler Street, Yaphank, NY: New York State, County of Suffolk, Town of Brookhaven, map number 129, abstract 1238, filed January 5, 1937.

Nazi Rallies at Camp Siegfried:

40,000: NY Times, *40,000 at Nazi Camp Fete*, 8/15,1938, page 13;

30,000: Mid-Island Mail, *30,000 at Camp Siegfried Sunday*,
   http:www.longwood.k12.ny.us/history/yaphank/
   bund14.htm
12,000: http:www.longwood.k12.ny.us/history/yaphank/
   bund6.htm
5,000: http:www.longwood.k12.ny.us/history/yaphank/
   bund3.htm
5,000: http:www.longwood.k12.ny.us/history/yaphank/
   bund2.htm

Chapter Three

Quote of George Washington opening this chapter: *From the Ends of the Earth-Judaic Treasures of the Library of Congress*, Chapter To Bigotry No Sanction, page 236, Library of Congress, 1991.

Background information on Jews in early America: *A History of Jews in America*, Howard M Sachar, pages 9-37,

Peter Stuyvesant quote: *The Jewish Week*, Faith and Freedom in the New World, Jonathan D. Sarna, http://www.thejewishweek.com

Francis Salvador information: *Jewish Virtual Library*, Francis Salvador, http://www.jewishvirtuallibray.org.

Background information about Jews in the American Revolution: *A History of Jews in America*, pages, 21-28, Howard M. Sachar.

The Little Jew Broker: *The Grandees*, Stephen Birmingham, pages 132-142 and *Haym Salomon*, H.S. Baron

George Washington's Letters: *From the Ends of the Earth-Judaic Treasures of the Library of Congress*, pages 231-239.

President Van Buren's quote: The Virtual Library, The American-Israeli Cooperative Enterprise, Americans React to Damascus Blood Libel, www.jewishvirtuallibrary.org

Samuel Mayer Isaacs quote 12/28/1860: *The Jewish Messenger*, Volume 8, Number 25, 12/28/1861, New York, article titled: A Day of Prayer.

Samuel Mayer Isaacs quote 4/28/1861: The Jewish Messenger, 4/28/1861, editorial titled: Stand by the Flag.

Civil War Background: *A History of the Jews in America*, pages 72-76.

Joseph Seligman: Jewish Heroes and Heroines in America, Florida Atlantic University Library, A Judaica Collection, http://www.fau.edu/library/brody/33.htm

President Lincoln's note revoking General Order 11: *Jewish Virtual Library*, General Grant's Infamy, http//www.jewishvirtuallibrary.org/jsource/anti-semitism/grant.html

Statements by Rabbi Wise: Ibid

Additional background about General Grant and General Order 11: A History of The Jews in America, pages 78-80.

Eulogy of President Lincoln: *From the Ends of the Earth – Judaic Treasures of the Library of Congress*, page 271.

Quotes from the London Jewish Chronicle: The Jewish Messenger, March 7, 1862, article titled: The American Israelites.

Chapter Four

Background information about Russian treatment of Jews: *A history of the Jews in America*, pages 116-140.

May Laws: *The May Laws, 1882*, http://www.jewishgates.com/file?.asp_id=101

Background of Pogroms: Mazelev, Julia, *Pogroms: late 19th, Beginning of 20th Century*, http://econc10.bu.edu/economic_systems/nationalidentity/fsu/russia/pogroms-naional_ident

Mary Antin quote: A History of the Jews in America, page 119.

Puck Magazine Quote: *Puck Magazine*, November 30, 1881, Cartoon and Comments.

Background information about William Blackstone: Currie, William E., *God's Little Errand Boy,*

Blackstone Memorial: AMF International, The Blackstone Memorial, http://www.amfi.org/blackmem.htm

Chapter Five

US Navy 1880-1900: *United States Sea Power 1865-On,* http://www.history.navy.mil/wars/spanam.htm

Congress began debating navy in 1881: Department of the Navy, Naval Historical Center, *War Plans and Preparations and Their Impact on U.S. Naval Operations in the Spanish-American War,* http://www.history.navy. mil/wars/spanam.htm#anchorn3

Treaty of Portsmouth: Treaty of Portsmouth September 5, 1905, http://www.portsmouthpeacetreaty.com/treaty/text. cfm.

President Roosevelt Nobel Peace prize: Letter to Congressman James A. Gallvan, dated August 22, 1918, http://www. theodoreroosevelt.org/life/nobelportsmouth.htm#money

Chapter Seven

William Blackstone father of Zionism: Hilton Obenzinger, *In the Shadow of "God's Sun-dial,"* http://www.stanford. edu/group/SHR/5-1/text/obenzinger.html

Quote of Justice Brandeis regarding William Blackstone: A Collection of Addresses and Statements by Louis D. Brandeis, World Zionist Organization, http://www.hags-hamma.org.il/en/resources/view.asp?id=1642

The Balfour Declaration: Balfour Declaration 1917, The Avalon Project at Yale Law School, http://www.yale.edu/ lawweb/avalon/mideast/balfour.htm

Chapter Nine

President Bush's UN speech 11/10/2002: *President Bush Speaks to United Nations,* Remarks by the President To

United Nations General Assembly, U.N. Headquarters, New York, NY, The White House website,: http://www. whitehouse.gov/news/releases/2001/11/20011110-3.html
President Bush's speech 6/24/2002: *President Bush Calls for New Palestinian Leadership,* The White House website: http://www.whitehouse.gov/news/releases/2002/06/200206 24-3.html

November 1991

Opening of Madrid peace talks: *USA Today,* October 31, 1991, front page article titled "Delegates Bring Optimism to Table."

The land of Israel key issue: *USA Today,* November 1, 1997, front page article titled "One-on-One Peace Talks Next."

Storm developments and results: *New York Times,* November 1, 1997, article titled "Nameless Storm Swamps the Shoreline"; *USA Today,* November 1, 1997, front page article titled "East Coast Hit Hard by Rare Storm" and article titled "Bob the Sequel a Smash (Maine to Florida under siege)."

President Bush's home smashed by the storm: *New York Times,* November 1, 1997, article titled "Stormy Waves Heavily Damage Bush Vacation Compound in Southern Maine."

The book, *The Perfect Storm,* by Sebastian Junger, 1997, HarperCollins Publisher. The power of the storm pages 118, 119.

Rare condition create the Perfect Storm: Associated Press, June 29, 2000, article titled "Perfect Storm Recalled."

August 1992

Hurricane Andrew and Madrid peace plan together: *USA Today,* August 24, 1992, front page articles titled "1

Million Flee Andrew; Monster Storm Targets Fla.," and "Mideast Peace Talks to Resume on Positive Note."

Damage done by Andrew: *USA Today,* September 14, 1992, article titled "Tale of the Hurricanes"; *USA Today,* September 18, 1992, article titled "Andrew 3rd-Worst Storm."

September 1993

Hurricane Emily and dividing the land of Israel: *New York Times,* September 1, 1993, front page articles (these articles touched each other) titled "Israel and PLO Ready To Declare Joint Recognition," and "Hurricane Hits the Outer Banks, As Thousands Seek Safety Inland."

January 1994

President Clinton and Assad meet in Geneva: *Harrisburg Patriot-News,* January 17, 1994, front page article titled "Clinton: Syria Set for Peace."

Earthquake in L.A.: *Los Angeles Times,* January 18, 1994, front page article titled "33 Die, Many Hurt in 6.6 Quake." (For more details of this earthquake, see chapter one, January 1994 heading.)

March 1997

Arafat arrives in America and meets with Clinton: *New York Times,* March 3, 1997, article titled "Welcoming Arafat, Clinton Rebukes Israel."

Arafat on speaking tour: *New York Times,* March 6, 1997, article titled "Arafat Lobbies U.S. Against Israel's Housing Plan."

Security Counsel's resolution of March 6, 1997: *New York Times,* March 7, 1997, article titled "U.S. Vetoes U.N. Criticism of Israel's Construction Plan."

General Assembly resolution of March 13, 1997: *New York Times*, March 14, 1997, article titled "Israel's Plan of Jerusalem Is Condemned by Assembly."

Security Counsel's resolution of March 21, 1997: *New York Times*, March 22, 1997, U.S. Again Vetoes a Move by U.N. Condemning Israel."

General Assembly resolution of April 25, 1997: *New York Times*, April 25, 1997, article titled "Israel Warned to Halt Housing for Jews."

General Assembly resolution of July 15, 1997: *New York Times*, July 16, 1997, article titled "U.N. Renews Censure of New Israeli Housing in East Jerusalem."

Stock market reaches all-time high: *USA Today*, March 12, 1997, article titled "Dow Achieves Record Despite Rate Fears."

Stock market falls 160 Points: *USA Today*, March 14, 1997, article titled "Dow Plunges 160 Points on Rate Fears."

Stock market stabilizes and begins rebound: *USA Today*, April 15, 1997, article titled "Stock Market Summary."

Prime Minister Netanyahu meets with Clinton: *New York Times*, April 8, 1997, article titled "Netanyahu Holds White House Talks."

January 1998

Clinton meets with Netanyahu: *New York Times*, January 22, 1998, article titled "U.S. and Israel Talk Mainly of More Talks"; *USA Today*, January 22, 1998, article titled "A Mideast Battle for Good Press."

Clinton meets with Arafat: *USA Today*, January 23, 1998, article titled "Arafat Calls Talks Encouraging."

Clinton's sex scandal breaks during meeting with Netanyahu: *New York Times*, January 22, 1998. Front page article titled "Subpoenas Sent as Clinton Denies Reports of an Affair with Aide at White House."

Clinton coldly treats Netanyahu and Netanyahu returns as a hero: *New York Times,* January 30, 1998, article titled "Analysis: In Clinton Crisis, Netanyahu Gains, Arafat Loses."

House votes to begin impeachment of president: Associated Press, October 8, 1998, article titled, "House Approves Impeachment Inquiry"

Judicial Committee votes on December 11 for three articles of impeachment: *USA Today,* December 11, 1998, front page article titled "Panel Sets Stage for Historic Vote on Impeachment"

Clinton on route to Israel while the fourth article of impeachment is being voted: Associated Press News Service, December 12, 1998, article titled "Clinton Heads for Israel," and article titled "Fourth Impeachment Article Debated"

Clinton is the first president to visit Palestinian-controlled area: *USA Today,* December 12, 1998, front page article titled "Clinton Fights for Mideast Agreement"

Clinton's visit gives status to a Palestinian state: *USA Today,* December 12, 1998, front page article titled "Peace Hits Snag Despite Vote"

On December 19 Clinton impeached by the House of Representatives: *Harrisburg Patriot-News,* December 20, 1998, titled "Impeached"

September 1998

Clinton to meet with Netanyahu and Arafat: *New York Times,* September 25, 1998, article titled "Clinton to See Netanyahu and Arafat Next Week"

Hurricane gains strength: *USA Today,* September 25, 1998, front page article titled "Georges Gaining Strength: Killer Storm Zeros in on Key West"

Secretary of State Albright meets with Arafat in NYC: *New York Times,* September 28, 1998, article titled "US Is Hoping to Announce Details on Israel-Palestine Talks"

Hurricane Georges slams into Gulf Coast: *New York Times,* September 28, 1998, front page article titled "Recharged Hurricane Batters Gulf Coast With 110 m.p.h. Winds"

Hurricane Lingers on Gulf Coast: *USA Today,* September 29, 1998, front page article titled "Georges Lingers"

President Clinton meets with Arafat and Netanyahu in White House: *USA Today,* September 29, 1998, front page article titled "Meeting Puts Mideast Talks Back in Motion"

Hurricane and Mideast peace talks together: *New York Times,* September 29, 1998, front pages articles titled "U.S., Israel and Arafat Inch Toward Pact" and "Floods Trap Hundreds"

Arafat speaks at United Nations: *New York Times,* September 29, 1998, article titled "Arafat, at U.N., Urges Backing for Statehood"

Hurricane causes $1 billion in damage: *USA Today,* September 30, 1998, article titled "Hurricane Racks Up $1 Billion in Damage"

October 1998

Netanyahu and Arafat met in United States: *Harrisburg Patriot News,* October 15, 1998, front page article titled "Time Is Running Out in Mideast"

Israel to give away 13 percent of the land: *New York Times,* October 24, 1998, front page article titled "Arafat and Netanyahu in Pact on Next Steps Toward Peace; Modest Deal to Rebuild Trust"

Powerful storms hit Texas: *Harrisburg Patriot News,* October 18, 1998, article titled "4 Killed as Storms, Floods, Tornado Ravage Parts of Texas"

Extent of the flooding and damage: *New York Times,* October 20, 1998, article titled "Record Flooding Kills at Least

14 in Central Texas," and *USA Today,* October 22, 1998, article titled "Hope Dwindles in Flooded Texas"

Texas declared a disaster area by president: News release, October 21, 1998 from FEMA. Release was titled "President Declares Major Disaster for Texas: Twenty Counties Designated for Aid to Flood Victims"

This disaster and Mideast talks together on front page of newspaper: *New York Times,* October 20, 1998, articles titled "Clinton Keeps Up Hope of Mideast Talks" and "Knee-deep in the San Jacinto"

November 1998

Stock Market reached all time high on November 23, 1998: Associated Press News Service, December 10, 1998, article titled "Stocks Fall for Third Straight Session"

Clinton and Arafat met on November 30 to raise money for Palestinians: *Baltimore Sun,* December 1, 1998, front page article titled "Nations Pledge $3 Billion in Aid to Palestinians"

Stock market drops 216 points on November 30: *Baltimore Sun,* December 1, 1998, front page article titled "Expected Correction Cools Off Wall St." (The articles about Arafat and the stock market were next to each other on the front

page) European stock markets crash: Associated Press News Service, December 2, 1998, article titled "UK Stocks Hammered"

May 1999

Clinton and the Palestinian State: Associated Press, May 4, 1999, article titled "Clinton Encourages Arafat."

Power and wind speed of the tornadoes: *USA Today,* May 11, 1999, article titled "318-mph storm wind fastest ever"; *USA Today,* may 5, 1999, article titled "Disasters declared in two states"; *Harrisburg Patriot-News,* May 5, 1999, article titled "20 hours of terror."

September 1999

Hurricane Dennis: *Harrisburg Patriot-News,* September 4, 1999, front page article titled "Enough already N.C. tires of Dennis." Middle East meetings regarding Israel: *Harrisburg Patriot-News,* September 4, 1999, front page article titled "Talks yield reworking of Wye pact."

Hurricane Floyd: *Harrisburg Patriot-News,* September 19, 1999, article titled "Floodwaters devastating N. Carolina."

Floyd Strengthens: Associated Press, September 13, 1999, article titled "Floyd Strengthens, Near Bahamas."

Middle East talks open: Associated Press, September 13, 1999, article titled "Israel, Palestinians To Open Talks."

Arafat meets with Clinton: Associated Press, September 22, 1999, article titled "Clinton Hosts Arafat at White House."

Stock market crash sets record: Reuters, September 23, 1999, article titled "Dow, Nasdaq Take Late-Day Tumble"

October 1999

Eviction of Israeli settlers: *New York Times,* October 16, 1999, front page article titled "On the West Bank, a Mellow View of Eviction."

Stock market crash: *New York Times,* October 16, 1999, front page article titled "Big Selloff Caps Dow's Worst Week Since October '89."

Earthquake: *Los Angeles Times,* October 17, 1999, front page article titled "7.0 Earthquake in Mojave Desert Rocks Southland."

Hurricane Irene: *USA Today,* October 18, 1999, article titled "Battered North Carolina suffers third hurricane in two months."

January 2000

Meetings: *New York Times,* January 4, 2000, front page article titled "Israel and Syria Return to Search for a Major Accord."

Stock market crash: *USA Today,* January 5, 2000, front page article titled "Market sell-off was overdue."

Turbulent stock week: *New York Times,* January 8, 2000, article titled "The 3 Main U.S. Stock Gauges Rally to End a Turbulent Week."

March-April 2000

Barak meets with Clinton: Associated Press, April 12, 2000, article titled "Israel OKs US Involvement in Talks."

Stock market collapse: *New York Times,* April 15, 2000, front page article titled "Stock Market in Step Drop as Worried Investors Flee; NASDAQ Has Its Worst Week"

July–August 2000

Camp David meetings: Reuters, November 21, 2000, article titled "Jerusalem Sovereignty Debated in Public Amid Talks"; Associated Press, dated July 20, 2000, article titled "Jerusalem at Heart of Mideast Talks."

Forest fires: Associated Press, August 3, 2000, article titled "Fire Season Storms Into West"; Reuters, August 27, 2000, article titled "U.S. Wildfires Converge in 'Perfect Storm.'"

Drought: Associated Press, July 28, 2000, article titled "Bush Declares Texas Disaster Areas."

September–December 2000

Fighting erupts at Temple Mount: *New York Times,* September 30, 2000, front page, article titled "Battle at Jerusalem Holy Site Leaves 4 Dead and 200 Hurt.""

Collapse of Barak's government: *Washington Post,* December 10, 2000, front page, article titled "Israeli Prime Minister Says He Will Resign."

Presidential election: *New York Times,* November 10, 2000, front page, article titled "Gore Campaign Vows Court Fight Over Vote with Florida's Outcome Still Up in the Air."

Arafat meets with Clinton: *New York Times,* November 10, 2000, article titled "Arafat-Clinton Talks in Washington Yield No Progress."

Elections set in Israel: *New York Times,* December 11, 2000, front page, article titled "Opening Campaign Netanyahu Invokes Will of the Nation."

Election resolved: *New York Times,* December 11, 2000, front page, article titled "Bush-Gore Is Now in the Hands of the Supreme Court."

June 2001:

Tropical Storm Allison great rainfall: *Houston Chronicle,* June 10, 2001, article titled "Allison rivals Claudette's 79 record." *Houston Chronicle,* June 14, 2001, article titled "Mayor: Storm city's biggest disaster ever."

President Bush declares five states disaster areas: Associated Press, June 23, 2001, article titled "Bush Releases $500M in Storm Aid."

Forming of Allison: *Houston Chronicle,* June 6, 2001, article titled "Tropical surprise US involvement in mediation in cease fire: Reuters, June 8, 2001, article titled "US

Steps Up Middle East Peace Drive Amid Violence." Associated Press, June 9, 2001 Article titled "US Steps Up Mideast Efforts." Jerusalem Post, June 14, 2001, article titled "Settlers: Tenet plan amounts to our abandonment." article titled "US Steps Up Mideast Peace Efforts." *Jerusalem Post,* June 14, 2001, article

September 11, 2001

President Bush's speech on August 9, 2001: CNN, August 9, 2001, article titled "Bush condemns Jerusalem suicide bombing."

Tourist industry hurt: Cybercast News Service, *cnsnews. com*, dated October 15, 2001, article titled "Travel and Tourism Hurt by Fear of Flying."

U.S. to recognize a Palestinian state: *New York Times*, October 2, 2001, article titled "Before Attacks, US Was Ready to Say It Backed Palestinian State." *Washington Post*, October 2, 2001, article titled "US Was Set to Support Palestinian Statehood."

November 2001

The president's speech before the U.N.: *New York Times*, November 11, 2001, front-page article titled "All Must Join Fight Against Terror, Bush Tells UN."

Secretary of state meets with Arafat: *New York Times*, November 12, 2001, article titled "Arafat Thankful for Bush Remark about 'Palestine.'"

Powell says use of Palestine correct: Associated Press, November 11, 2001, article titled "Powell: Use of 'Palestine' Deliberate."

Rumsfield worried about nuke threat: News Max, *newsmax. com*, November 11, 2001, article titled "Rumsfield: 'Seriously Worried' about bin Laden Nuke Threat."

Jet crash from JFK: *New York Times*, November 13, 2001, front-page article titled "Jet with 260 Crashes in Queens; 6 to 9 Missing as 12 Homes Burn; US Doubts Link To Terrorism."

April 2002

Pressure from Bush on Israel and tornadoes: The Washington Post, April 29, 2002, front page articles titled, "Israel

Agrees to Lift Arafat Siege," and "Deadly Tornado Hits Southern Maryland."

June2002

President's two state speech: The Washington Post, June 25, 2002, front page articles titled, "President Outlines Vision for Mideast," and "Everything is Just a Nightmare-Forced to Flee Western Wildfires, Thousands Uncertain and Afraid."

May 2003

Record week for tornadoes: Associated Press, May 11, 2003, articled titled, "Week's Barrage of Tornadoes Sets a Record.

Powell's trip to Mideast: Pittsburgh Post-Gazette, May 12, 2003, front page article titled, "Powell's Mideast blitz fails to make headway," and "Picking Up The Pieces (Story about tornado outbreak."

September 2003

US blocks Arafat expulsion: The Associated Press, September 12, 2003, article titled, "Powell: U.S. Opposes Expulsion of Arafat."

Hurricane headed for DC: The Associated Press, September 18, 2003, article titled, D.C. prepares for direct hit."

Hurricane's damage: The Patriot-News, September 20, 2003, front page article titled, "A Trail of Misery- Property damage could surpass $4 billion."

August-September 2004

Bush pressured Israel to evacuate parts of covenant land and hurricanes: Koenig's Eye View, August 23, 2004, Bush Administration Applies Major Pressure on Israel to Leave Covenant Land: While Hurricane Charlie and other News

Intensifies." hhttp://www.watch.org/resources/newsletter/koeing-sr-charley.html

Evacuation of Gaza and hurricanes: The Miami Herald, 8/13/04, front page article titled; Nearly 1 million in path of storm told to leave." The Associated Press; 8/30/04, article titled: Gaza Settlement Evacuation Plan Sped Up." AP, 9/10/04, article titled: Sharon Says Gaza Pullout Still Planned." AP, 9/12/04, Thousands Protest Gaza Evacuation plan." Jerusalem Post, 9/13/04, article titled: Compensation to Gaza setters $1b." The Washington Post, 9/13/04, front page article titled: Settlers are inciting civil war, Sharon says." AP, 9/14/04, article titled: Bush Wants $3.1 Billion for Hurricane Aid." AP, 9/20/04, Powell Seeks Israel's Assurance on Gaza." AP, 9/21/04, article titled: Sharon Faces Critics, Vows Gaza Pullout." AP, 9/25/04, article titled: Three Million told to Flee Jeanne in Fla." AP, 9/28/04, article titled: Bush Seeks $7.1B More for Hurricane Relief

Cost of Hurricanes

January 2005

Abbas' statements about Israel: Jewish World Review, 1/7/05, article titled: The 'Zionist enemy' and her supporters is in denial yet again." www.jewishworldreview.com/0105/krauthammer-abbas

Abbas invited to White House while devastating in West: USA Today 1/11/05, front page articles titled: "Bush offers to meet Abbas" and "California rocked by storm." The Associated Press, 1/10/05, article titled: "Bush invites Abbas to White House"

Storms in West: Live Science, 4/8/05, article titled: Christmas Storm in Midwest Ranked Worst in 104 Years.""

April 2005

Bush and Sharon meet: The White House website, 4/11/05, article titled: "President and Prime Minister Sharon Discuss Economy, Middle East"

Stock Market down turn: Fox News, 4/15/05 "Dow Down Almost 200 Pts on IBM, Data Disappointments"

August-September 2005

Facts about the closing of the 25 settlements: Jerusalem Post, 11/16/05, article titled: "US, Israel resume talks on aid"; NY Times, 8/16/05, front page article titled: "Israeli Troops Press Settlers to Quite Gaza"; Harrisburg Patriot News, 8/12005, front page article titled: "Eviction Day" NY Times, 8/18/05, front page article titled: "Tearfully but Forcefully, Israel Removes Gaza Settlers": NY Times, 8/20/05, front page article titled: Israeli Troops and Police Clear All But 5 Gaza Settlements": NY Times, 8/23/05, front page article titled: Israel Completes Pullout Ahead of Schedule, Without Serious Violence"; MSNBC.com, 9/11/05, article titled: Departure marks first time Palestinian have control over defined territory www.msnbc.msm.com/id/9279728; WorldNetDaily, 9/14/05, article titled, "Jews sickened by Palestinian desecration," www.worldnetdail.com/news/printer-friendly.asp?article-id=46310

President Bush's speeches: 8/23/05, White House Website, speech titled: President Honors Veterans of Foreign Wars at National Convention, www.whitehouse.gov/news/releases/2005/08

8/24/05, White House Website, Question and answers, www.whitehouse.gov/news/releases/2005/08

Facts about Hurricane Katrina: Wikipedia encyclopedia, History of storm, article titled: Hurricane Katrina; NY Times, 8/29/05, front page article titled: "Residents Flee as Strom Storm Nears Gulf Coast" NY Times, 8/30/05, front page article titled: Hurricane Slams Into Gulf Coast

Dozens are Dead"; NY Times, 9/1/05, front page article titled: Bush Sees Long Recovery For New Orleans; 30,000 Troops in Largest U.S. Relief Effort."; NY Times, 12/11/05, editorial, "Death of an American City"; Washington Post, 1/13/06, article titled, "2 Million Displaced by Storms"

President Bush takes responsibility for Katrina response: White House Website, 9/13.05, speech titled: "President Welcomes President Talabani of Iraq to the White House" www.whitehouse.gov/news/releases/2005/09

Katrina exodus: USA Today, 9/29/05, article titled: "Katrina exodus reaches all states"

Hurricane Rita:

Israeli Pullout of Samaria: Israelinsider website, 9/21/05, article titled: After IDF completes pullout from in Samaria, Palestinians flood in." and Ynetnews.com, 9/22/05, article titled, "Hundreds of Palestinians loot Homesh."

Facts about the hurricane: NY Times, 9/22/05, front page article titled: "Gulf Hurricane of Top Strength Menaces Texas" and Harrisburg Patriot-News, 9/22/05, front page article titled: "One million flee a growing monster"

American Dichotomy:

The American dichotomy:

President Bush's speech of 8/11/92:

http://bushlibrary.tamu.edu/research/papers/1992/92081100.html

Moving the embassy to Jerusalem:

http://www.jewishvirtuallibrary.org/jsource/US-Israel/Jerusalem_Relocation_Act.html

President Bush's speech of 3/20/2006:

http://www.whitehouse.gov/news/releases/2006/03/20060320-7.html

Chapter Ten

The Hamas Covenant, The Avalon Project at Yale Law school, http://www.yale.edu/lawweb/avalon/mideast/hamas.htm

Flavius Josephus, Magog: *Antiquities of the Jews*, Chapter Six (How Every Nation Was Nominated From Their First Inhabitants), http://www.earlychristianwritings. com/text/josephus/ant-1.htm

Scythians: The Scythians, http://www.silk-road.com/artl/ scythian.shtml

Background on Hezbullah

Background on Ahmadinejad and the Mahdi: Scott Petterson, Christian Science Monitor, *Waiting for the rapture in Iran,* http://www.csmonitor.com/2005/1221/p01s04-wome. html